THE PROVIDENTIAL ORDER
OF THE WORLD

THE PROVIDENTIAL ORDER
OF THE WORLD

BY

ALEXANDER BALMAIN BRUCE, D.D.

PROFESSOR OF
APOLOGETICS AND NEW TESTAMENT EXEGESIS IN THE
FREE CHURCH COLLEGE, GLASGOW

Eugene, Oregon

Wipf and Stock Publishers
199 West 8th Avenue, Suite 3
Eugene, Oregon 97401

The Providential Order of the World
the Gifford Lectures, 1897
By Bruce, A.B.
ISBN: 1-59244-599-3
Publication date 3/17/2004
Previously published by Hodder and Stoughton, 1899

PREFATORY NOTE

THESE Lectures appear here substantially as they were delivered in the Bute Hall of Glasgow University, on the Sunday afternoons of January, February, and March, 1897, with the exception that some passages were omitted to keep each Lecture within the usual time limit. Lecture VIII, being broken up into two parts, occupied two Sundays, and hence Lecture IX, on *Providence in the Individual Life*, had to be omitted.

A. B. BRUCE.

CONTENTS

LECTURE I
THE SUBJECT INTRODUCED 1

LECTURE II
MAN'S PLACE IN THE UNIVERSE 22

LECTURE III
THEISTIC INFERENCES FROM MAN'S PLACE IN THE UNIVERSE 45

LECTURE IV
NON-MORAL DEITY, OR THE GODS OF MODERN PESSIMISM   71

LECTURE V
THE WORTH OF LIFE 99

LECTURE VI
THE WORTH OF MAN 128

LECTURE VII
THE POWER MAKING FOR RIGHTEOUSNESS 155

LECTURE VIII

THE POWER WORKING IN AND FOR HUMANITY.

    PART I. HISTORIC DAWNS 183

    PART II. HISTORIC DAYS 205

LECTURE IX

PROVIDENCE IN THE INDIVIDUAL LIFE 231

LECTURE X

PROVIDENTIAL METHODS: ELECTION 256

LECTURE XI

PROVIDENTIAL METHODS: SOLIDARITY 280

LECTURE XII

PROVIDENTIAL METHODS: PROGRESS BY SACRIFICE . . 311

INDEX 339

THE PROVIDENTIAL ORDER
OF THE WORLD

LECTURE I

THE SUBJECT INTRODUCED

I FEEL deeply, and I now desire sincerely to acknowledge, the honour conferred upon me by the appointment to be Gifford Lecturer in this University for this and the next session. I am aware, however, that the best way of showing my appreciation of the privilege is to make a serious endeavour to discharge the duties of the office so as to give some measure of satisfaction to the appointing body. This, God helping me, I will try to do. I enter on my task with diffidence; yet not without hope, certainly with the desire, to treat the subject I am to deal with in harmony with the views of the Founder, as set forth plainly in his Deed of Trust.

Four things in the statement by which Lord Gifford explains his aim seem to me specially noteworthy.

1. His earnest belief in the supreme value of the knowledge of God. 'Whom truly to know'—these are his words—'is life everlasting.'

2. His desire that every sincere thinker, be his theological position what it may, may have his chance of saying what he thinks on this supreme theme. He believes in the value of absolutely free discussion, and thinks it may be for the advantage of the faith in God that an Agnostic, or even an Atheist, should tell the

world unreservedly the grounds on which he is constrained to occupy a position of dissent or suspended judgment.

3. His wish that the discussions carried on under this foundation should be of a generally useful character; not merely academic, in respect of the audience in view and the mode of treatment, but 'popular,' aiming, that is, at the benefit of the many, and handling topics in a manner level with the comprehension of men who bring to the study ordinary intelligence and an honest interest in religion.

4. The fourth and last noteworthy feature in Lord Gifford's will is the stipulation that theistic inquiries under the Foundation shall be carried on on a scientific method. The sphere of study is thereby restricted to what is called 'Natural Theology,' as opposed to 'Revealed Theology.' 'I wish it considered,' says the Testator, 'just as astronomy or chemistry is.' The Gifford Lecturer is directed to give his attention to the observation and interpretation of any facts which in his judgment justify theistic inferences.

I do not feel hampered by these restrictions; on the contrary, I find myself in entire harmony with their general spirit. I need not say that I am in full accord with the Founder as to the value he attaches to the knowledge of God. But it is not so much a matter of course that a theologian by profession should sympathise with the desire for free unfettered inquiry in this region of thought. Nevertheless I do. I am convinced it is a gain to faith in God when the conflicting thoughts of men on this high theme are fully revealed.

It is a great, vital question, whether there be a God, and I should wish very much to know why an intellectually honest, morally earnest man doubts or denies the truth of the affirmative answer. The reasons of unbelief might in some cases be more instructive than the reasons offered by many, who have never doubted, for their faith. To state explicitly reasons of unbelief may even help the unbeliever himself to faith. The *nay* may lead on to a *yea*, and to a yea all the more emphatic because of the foregoing nay. Nothing, shrewdly remarked Richard Baxter, is so firmly believed as that which has once been doubted. I do not know that the world would have been favoured with those posthumous *Thoughts on Religion* from the pen of Mr. Romanes, had he not previously written the *Candid Examination of Theism*. Had the sceptical thoughts and processes of anti-theistic reasoning that haunted the mind of *Physicus* not found expression in that vigorous onslaught on the theistic creed, the author might have lived and died neither a believer nor an unbeliever, but weakly and miserably halting between two opinions. Such is the law in individual experience, and somewhat similar is the fact among men collectively. When unbelief is free in a community, faith is sincere and strong. On the other hand, it is hard to say who really believes when disbelief is interdicted under heavy penalties. Prudence takes the place of conviction, and make-believe becomes the order of the day. It would not be reasonable to expect the Church to grant as much liberty as the Founder of this Lectureship allows. That might mean requiring the Church to become a debating society instead of a community of faith. But there can be little doubt that she would gain something from the exercise within her borders of a freedom in discussing topics relating to the character and providence of God similar to that so splendidly exemplified in the book of Job. It would help to keep within her pale the good men to whom Lord Gifford refers as preferring to be without.

One cannot but recognise the wisdom of the requirement that these lectures shall be popular, not merely academic. This need not mean superficiality, but it ought to mean the choice of a theme, and of a method of handling it, which shall make what is spoken of general utility. Religion is the affair of every man, and if one can by a well-weighed plain statement on an important aspect of that wide subject remove doubts, clear up difficulties, and help towards a firmer grasp of truth by the hand of faith among the large number of people who are more or less conversant with the conflicting currents of opinion, it is well worth while to attempt the task.

It is quite possible to do this compatibly with full compliance with the requirement that *scientific method* shall be adhered to. If indeed that requirement meant that one must prove the Being of God as you prove a proposition in Euclid, it would be a prescription of the impossible. The thing cannot be done, and, if it could, it would not be worth doing. A faith in God that could be forced on a man by absolutely demonstrative reasoning would not be of much value to anybody. But that, I take it, is not the meaning of the term scientific in the present connection. It means rather that what we say about God is to rest on observation of the world we live in — of nature, of man, of human history — and to consist of such statements as may be verifiable by such observation. It excludes nothing which belongs to the world in any department, therefore nothing which belongs to the religious history of humanity, therefore not the Hebrew and Christian sacred literatures which occupy a prominent place in that history. It excludes the use of these literatures as authorities, but not as *witnesses*. If our subject should lead us to discuss the relative history of religious thought, the thoughts of Hebrew prophets and of Jesus Christ will relevantly come in, and legitimately count for what they are worth. If on a comparison it should turn out that they are worth more than thoughts to be found elsewhere, that will certainly tend to give them authority, but it will be authority of a kind with which no scientific man will be disposed to quarrel ; and, I may add, with which religious people will do well to make themselves familiar. Authority resting upon — I use the words of Lord Gifford — 'any supposed special, exceptional, or so-called miraculous revelation' may be legitimate in its own place. But the authority which rests on the power, say, of the teaching of Christ, to commend itself to our minds more than anything we have met with elsewhere in the religious literature of mankind, is after all that which carries most weight. The author of the Epistle to the Hebrews was content to say in behalf of Christianity: It is *better* than Leviticalism. If without straining or special pleading I should find myself able to say of the teaching of Christ concerning God: It is the best I know, I should feel that I had every reason to be well satisfied.

Theism is a wide field. To say anything effectively, in a comparatively short course of lectures, one must select a special aspect. In view of all that the Founder aimed at, I think I shall not do amiss if I choose as my theme a topic for which the most convenient and familiar title is *The Providential Order of the World*. Without attempting formal definition, I may say that the kind of thoughts I have in view are such as these: That God cares for man individually and collectively; that His nature is such, and that He sustains such a relation to man, as makes that care natural and credible; that His care covers all human interests, but especially the higher, ethical interests — righteousness, goodness — in the individual and in society; that He is a moral Governor, and a benignant Father, a Power making for righteousness, and a Power overcoming evil with good; that He ruleth over all things with a view to a kingdom of the good.

This is a subject of universal interest. Every man that cometh to God 'must believe that He is, and that He is a rewarder of them that seek Him.' Especially must he believe the latter of these two propositions. Believing that God is does not of itself amount to much. The great matter is not *that* God is, but *what*

God is. The word 'God' may mean much or it may mean almost nothing. Under some ways of conceiving God, to ascertain that He is, is of as little importance for life as would be the discovery of the long-sought-for North Pole for the practical purposes of commerce. The number of men who deny the being of God in every shape and form is comparatively few. Even the Materialist finds a kind of a God in the ultimate atoms of matter conceived of as eternally existing. The fiery mist out of which the world has been evolved is his Infinite and Absolute Being. By the distinguished author of the *Synthetic Philosophy* God is confessed as the unknowable, ultimate ground of all that exists, the ultimate force by which the evolutionary process is propelled. But in the very act of confessing God as the Unknowable, Mr. Spencer, while admitting *that* God is, denies that you can know anything of *what* He is. What is the worth for life of this unknowable God, of whom, or which, you can affirm nothing except that by an intellectual necessity you are compelled to recognise its existence? Such a God has an interest only for theoretic thought; for all practical purposes He may simply be ignored. Other philosophers offer us a God, of whom, at least, a little is supposed to be knowable beyond the bare fact that He is. Spinoza confessed an ultimate substance out of which all being has flowed in two parallel streams, possessing the distinctive attributes of matter and mind, extension and thought. God, said Spinoza, is at once a *res externa* and a *res cogitans*. This is a slight contribution to the knowledge of *what* God is. But it does not carry us far. What of the relation of the ultimate substance to man and to morality? Does God care for man, have moral distinctions any meaning for Him? Spinoza answers frankly: God cares no more for man than for beast, all beings are alike to Him; God cares nothing for moral distinctions. He made the fool and the knave, as well as the wise man and the saint, and for Him both are equally legitimate constituent parts of the universe. It takes them all to make a world. More recent philosophers, such as Schopenhauer and Hartmann, may seem to improve upon Spinoza when they offer us for a God a will acting blindly and thoughtlessly in the world, or a Great Unconscious One possessing both will and intellect, and using them both with marvellous power and skill, yet without being aware of what He is doing. Will seems to take us into the moral region and to give promise of a God for whom right and wrong have meaning. But the will of these philosophers is non-moral, and its work is such that the world had better not have been.

These examples may suffice to illustrate the importance of the distinction between the bare existence of God and the attributes we ascribe to Him. It may seem unscientific to insist so strongly on ethical quality as essential to any really valuable conception of the Divine Being. The scientific man strives to clear his mind of preconceived opinions and foregone conclusions, and to come to nature as an unbiassed inquirer. He takes the universe as he finds it, not as he would like it to be. Ought we not, it may be asked, to address ourselves to the search after God in the same spirit, making no imperious demand at the outset for an ethical divinity, content rather to learn what we can about the Great Mysterious Being at the heart of the universe, whether it come up to our expectations and wishes or not? What effect can any other mood have than to make us biassed judges of evidence, and ready, as a matter of course, to find what we bring? All this is very good counsel. By all means let us be scientifically impartial, unbiassed, presuppositionless, ready to bow before facts and to accept the conclusions they point to. Yet even the scientific man brings to the subject of investigation his guiding hypothesis, and not infrequently also a keen interest in possible practical applications of anticipated discoveries. What he does the theologian also may do. It will, of course, serve no good purpose to foster ideas of God which will not stand examination. But we may very legitimately be eager in the quest for evidence of a God such as is implied in our idea of Providence, when we know that on its result depend the whole character of human life and destiny, and the significance of all history.

Providence being our theme, what is to be our plan? Here at once the question arises: Does the concept of God implied in Providence possess any probability? or, more specifically, What means are available for showing its probability? Now, if there be any such they will be found in man's *position*, *nature*, and *history*. Through man to God must be the line of proof for us. This is indeed the main line of proof for Theism in general in our time. There are, of course, other lines, such as the time-honoured arguments which bear the somewhat technical and repellent titles: ontological, cosmological, and teleological, respectively; the first arguing from the mere idea of God in our mind to the existence of a Divine Being; the second arguing from the existence of the world as a whole, viewed as a contingent event, to a Great First Cause; the third finding in the innumerable traces of adaptation in the world the evidence of a wise Designing Mind. These familiar arguments have had great vogue in the past, and have been deemed conclusive by many devout and thoughtful men. Of late years they have been falling into desuetude. Confidence and interest in them has been steadily waning, even in the minds of Theists. Distinguished apologists still believe in their cogency, and some of them have done good service by restatements, especially of the teleological argument, adapted to the present condition of science. Such restatements will help inquirers to make up their minds as to the real worth of these arguments; for it may be assumed, that if, even as rehabilitated by a Martineau, they are still of doubtful conclusiveness, some incurable weakness must be inherent in them. But, apart from the question of logical cogency in the abstract, we have to reckon with the fact that many are not in the mood to listen to these arguments. The *Zeitgeist* is against them. They are felt to be out of fashion; the very terms in which they are expressed sound stale to the modern ear. In these circumstances, one may excusably waive the question of validity, and on grounds of policy respectfully allow these venerable arguments to retire into the background. It is certainly wise in the apologist to rest the defence of Theism on evidence in harmony with the spirit of the time in which he lives. In making this observation I am not to be understood as insinuating a slighting personal estimate of any one of these old arguments, least of all of the third, the teleological — the oldest, the most popular, and the most impressive of all the three. This argument, from the traces of design in the world to a Divine Designer, has appealed to thoughtful men of all schools and in all ages. Socrates, Cicero, Voltaire, Rousseau, Paley, Chalmers, have all in turn seen in the manifold adaptations of nature the unmistakable evidence of a wise, benignant Creator. I should be slow to treat with disrespect reasoning which commended itself to the great minds of the past. We indeed find ourselves in altered circumstances which make it difficult for us to follow, without hesitation, in their footsteps. Modern science, inspired by the idea of evolution, has altered the way of looking at things. It does not deny the existence of adaptation and harmony. On the contrary, every branch of science is constantly multiplying new instances, or throwing fresh light on old ones. But science has introduced a new way of accounting for the relative phenomena. What before was viewed as intentional adaptation, say of an organ like the eye or ear to its environment, is now regarded as an undesigned fitness produced by the reaction of environment on organ. The apparent indications of creative forethought are simply due to the continuous adjustment of inner relations to outer relations of which life consists. What the teleologist calls a final cause is in reality an effect. An ardent advocate of the new way of thinking exemplifies its bearings by the following instances: 'The particular laws of our present universe bring about night, they also cause the phenomenon sleep in animated creatures: these two naturally suit each other, being different results of the same laws —just as any two propositions in Euclid agree together. But to say that either is the final cause of the other is to transfer an idea derived from one part of ourselves, our motives to action, to an entirely different part of ourselves, our primary laws of sensation. The earth is suited to its inhabitants because it has produced them, and only such as suit it live.'[1] The last sentence of this quotation puts the matter in a nutshell. It states the case for evolutionists in a manner they deem conclusive, as against the teleological view of the universe advocated by apologists. Where the teleologist sees an adaptation of environment to organism by an exercise of beneficent intelligence on the part of the Creator, the evolutionist sees a correspondence necessarily resulting from the fact that only the fit survive.

The result of this revolution of thought, brought about by Darwinism, has been a great abatement in the confidence with which the teleological argument is regarded even in theological circles. Sincere, earnest believers in God, who are at the same time imbued with the new scientific view of the universe, are found confessing that 'the old rapid argument from nature to an omnipotent and beneficent Creator

[1] Alfred Barratt, *Physical Ethics*, p. 33. *Vide* also Fiske, *Outlines of Cosmic Philosophy*, vol. ii. p. 398, where the passage is commented on.

was never logically valid.'[1] Others, apparently feeling that the argument for the new and the old ways of viewing the world is nearly equally balanced in other spheres of inquiry, turn to the region of the beautiful and the sublime as one in which teleology can still find a firm footing.[2] Yet the naturalistic evolutionist may not have been quite so successful in banishing teleology from the universe as he imagines, or as his theistic opponent has been willing to concede. When Romanes wrote his *Candid Examination of Theism*, he triumphantly declared that 'in the one principle of the persistence of force we have a demonstrably harmonising principle whereby all the facts within our experience admit of being collocated under one natural explanation, without there being the smallest reason to attribute these facts to any supernatural cause.'[3] But what says the same scientist in his *Thoughts on Religion*, published after his death? There he lays down these positions: That if there be a personal God, no reason can be assigned why He should not be immanent in nature, or why all causation should not be the immediate expression of His will; that every available reason points to the inference that He probably is so immanent; that if He be so, and if His will is self-consistent, all natural causation must needs appear to us 'mechanical'; and that therefore it is no argument against the divine origin

[1] Aubrey L. Moore, *Science and the Faith*, p. 193.
[2] J. H. Kennedy, *Natural Theology and Modern Thought*, p. 144.
[3] P. 161.

of a thing, event, etc., to prove it due to natural causation.[1]

So it turns out, if this later view of Romanes be correct, that teleology and mechanism are not by any necessity mutually exclusive. All may be mechanism, yet all may also be teleology. Mechanics may be merely God's instrument for working out His ends. Mechanical evolution may invalidate teleological arguments based on particular instances of adaptation, by showing that there is another way of explaining the correspondence which the teleologist had not thought of. But its verdict, even in such cases, can at most be only a 'not proven.' And when one takes a large view of the question of Purpose in the universe, and asks, for example, not, 'How are we to explain the adaptation of the ear to sound waves in the atmosphere?' but, 'What account is to be given of the fact that the age-long process of universal evolution terminates in *man*?' the verdict cannot even amount to a 'not proven.' Here, at least, purpose comes in; and if here on the grand scale, why not elsewhere, and everywhere, on the small? Mechanics, persistent force, everywhere, and teleology there at the same time. Such is the view, not merely of theistic apologists interested in the Christian theory of the universe, but of a non-theistic philosopher like Hartmann, as I shall take occasion hereafter to point out.

Through man to God, I said, was to be our method,

[1] P. 121. To the same effect in *Darwin and After Darwin*, vol. i. p. 414.

and our chosen line of proof. We are to take our stand, not on detailed teleology, where the scientific verdict may be 'not proven,' but on the larger field where the severest scientific judgment cannot well resist a verdict of 'proven.' In other words, to justify the idea of Divine Providential Purpose, we plant our foot, in the first instance, on *Man's Place in the Universe*. To define that place must, accordingly, be our first task. I will try in the next lecture to describe man's position, not merely in terms of a traditional creed, or of what might be deemed antiquated Biblical representations, but in accordance with the ascertained results, or even the precarious hypotheses, of recent evolutionary science. Here happily there is no conflict between the two authorities. The Bible sets man at the head of creation; science does the same thing with added emphasis, assigning him that place not merely as, in virtue of his endowments, the most distinguished of the creatures, but as the crowning result of the evolutionary process by which the known world in the long course of ages came to be. The leading representatives of evolutionary philosophy are not yet agreed in regard to the extent to which man has been evolved, some limiting the process to his body, others extending it to his soul. Men jealous for moral and religious interests may regard with suspicion the more advanced doctrine, as endangering cherished convictions. But in some respects, as will more clearly appear as we proceed, the view that man is wholly the child of evolution is to be preferred even in a theistic interest. Therefore, while not dogmatising on disputed questions, we can afford to keep step with the more advanced section, and to state man's position in the universe in terms conforming to their boldest contentions.

When we have done this, our next task will be to consider the theistic inferences from man's place of sovereignty. That place certainly suggests, if it does not compel, important inferences. For example, such as these: That the Being who is the ultimate ground of the universe, 'the First and Only Cause,' in the language of Lord Gifford, had man in view from the beginning; intended the evolutionary process to arrive at him, and guided it all along so that it should arrive there. Again, that that Great Being values supremely the attributes characteristic of the latest arrival — reason, will, which, if not a monopoly of man's, are at least his emphatically, by way of preeminence. Values, that is to say *possesses;* therefore the ultimate ground of the universe is not mere blind force, but a Being endowed with intelligence and volition — a Spirit. Yet again, that He who had man in view from the beginning of the long creative process will continue to have him in view after he has come into existence, so as to develop to the full the possibilities of this new type of being. That the new type, from the day of his arrival, will be in fact all that he has it in him to be is, of course, not likely. What precisely was the primitive condition of man may be a nice, difficult, and even delicate question, but it is safe to say that it would be such as to leave room for development, growth, progress, from a germinal, rudimentary humanity to a humanity rich in knowledge, inventions, culture, virtue; an evolution within the human analogous to the earlier one which had carried the creation on from the fiery mist to the human. And if God was in the earlier evolution, *a fortiori* He would be in the later. He would not rest content when at length He had reached the type He had had in His eye from the first, saying, 'This is good,' and take no interest in its future fortunes. If there was a Providence in the lower evolution conducting it upwards towards man, much more may we expect to find a Providence in human history, conducting man towards the realisation of his ideal.

The theistic inference from man's place in the universe will engage our attention in the third lecture. From that topic we might proceed directly to consider the traces of Providential Action in the history of mankind collectively and individually. But preparation for *receiving* the doctrine is desirable. There are causes of doubt, hindrances to faith, preoccupying thoughts, which make the idea of a Providential world-aim hard to accept. Three sources of unbelief may be specified: Views of God incompatible with such an aim; facts of human life pessimistically interpreted which seem to give the hypothesis of a Divine care for man the lie; cynical estimates of human nature rendering belief in man being an end for God impossible. It will be worth while to devote a lecture to each of these sources of unbelief in Providence. There is ample matter for reflection in connection with all the three. It is by no means difficult to make out a plausible case against Providence under any one of them. It has not been found impossible by philosophers to conceive a God who is below caring for man, or for all the interests man represents. I have alluded to some such conceptions already in another connection. Spinoza's absolute substance, Schopenhauer's irrational will, Hartmann's 'Unconscious,' with both will and intelligence, each offers us a God of this type. It will not be necessary to subject these three types of Deity to elaborate discussion; a comparatively slight characterisation will serve our purpose. Hartmann's curious Divinity will receive the larger share of attention, not only because it is the newest of the three, but more especially because it goes so far along theistic lines that one wonders why it does not go further. It makes important concessions for which we are thankful, while sensible of its grotesqueness and absurdity in other respects.

No one needs to be told how easily human life and human nature can be utilised in the service of unbelief. Evil physical and moral, what a portentous, omnipresent fact! In view of it who can believe that a benevolent or moral purpose is being worked out in human history? Man! what is man, in the wide universe, in his beginnings, in his present average condition, or even at his best, that God should be mindful of him?

And yet I trust that, in spite of all appearances to the contrary, it will be found not impossible to verify our thesis on the great scale and on the small; in the history of humanity at large, and in the experience of the individual. The proof on the large scale will occupy two lectures: one dealing with the evidence that there is in the world a Power making for righteousness, the other setting forth the benignant aspect of Providence as a power overcoming evil with good, and working out through all events, toward or untoward, a beneficent plan. Divine Providence in the individual life will form the subject of a single lecture.

To one who believes in the reality of a Providence in human affairs, it must be an interesting and profitable subject of inquiry whether it be possible to ascertain any general laws of its working, any methods which God in His Providence employs for the accomplishment of His ends. I should like to make a humble contribution to this study. Exhaustive treatment is here, of course, out of the question. One can offer only samples of what is known, and what is known may be little compared with what is yet to be discovered. Three principles, then, have a wide range of application in Providential Action: Election, Solidarity, Sacrifice. Election: God chooses races, nations, individuals, not for favour but for function, to do service to the world, to promote progress in thought, in art, in government, in religion. Solidarity: men are not dealt with as isolated units; for woe, for weal, they are a brotherhood closely knit together by parentage, by heredity, by a social organism, by ties of race and nationality. Sacrifice: suffering in some form is common to all men, and often seems to be meaningless, the mere accident of lot. But there is a suffering which befalls the best men, the heroes of the race, the pioneers of advancement, suffering for truth, righteousness, humanity. It is not an accident; it is not meaningless. It comes by law, and it serves a high purpose. It is the appointed cost of progress. Sacrificial lives are redemptive lives. Of those who so suffer the world is not worthy, yet they are its saviours.

Such are the topics which are to engage our attention in our first course of twelve lectures. They will deal in the first place with the philosophic presuppositions of a providential order, and in the second place with some generalisations based on observation regarding the modes in which that order manifests itself. It might seem that when these have been disposed of, enough will have been said on the theme. And yet, who that has once undertaken to speak on so momentous a matter would care to dismiss it, without making at least a partial rapid survey of the history of human thought concerning it? One would like to know how the question of Providence presented itself to men in different lands and ages, familiar with the facts of life, and given to earnest reflection thereon; especially to men belonging to peoples among whom the ethical consciousness reached a high measure of intensity — such as the ancient Indians and Persians, the Greeks, and above all the Hebrews. Such knowledge might not only gratify intellectual curiosity, but prove helpful to faith. *Consensus* in fundamental religious convictions always tends to confirm individual belief. Even an eclipse of faith, such as is exemplified in the despair of Buddhism, may have its wholesome lessons. Crude theories of creation and providence, like the Persian dualism, may serve as a warning against superficial solutions. Wise words spoken millenniums ago may be found to contain flashes of insight hitherto only imperfectly appreciated, suggesting possibilities of fruitful investigation along fresh lines. In the latter point of view, the best thought of our own time on topics akin to those which are to occupy us in these lectures may be well worthy of study. Our weightiest ethical teachers have got their inspiration largely from Jesus of Nazareth, or more generally from Hebrew prophets. Their doctrine may be said to be Prophetism and Christianity translated into modern language and applied to modern problems. It may be worth while to consider how far the translation is true to the original, and the application successful. In these sentences I have outlined a second course, whose theme might be sufficiently indicated by the title: *Providence in Pagan, Hebrew, and Modern Thought.*

LECTURE II

MAN'S PLACE IN THE UNIVERSE

WHAT is man? A century ago our pious forefathers would have replied: The lord and king of creation. The latest science confirms the answer. The evolutionary theory as to the genesis of things places man at the head of creation as we know it. It not only admits that this is his position, it proves that it is, sets the fact on a foundation of scientific certainty, making man appear as the consummation and crown of the evolutionary process in that part of the universe with which it is in our power to become thoroughly acquainted.

As stated in last lecture, it is not yet a settled matter that man is out and out the child of evolution. That he is the product of evolution on the animal side of his nature is now generally acknowledged. Any dispute still outstanding relates to the psychical aspect of his being — to his intellect and his moral nature. The evidence here is less convincing, and moreover our interest or bias is divided. We are naturally and justly zealous for man's prerogative as a rational and moral being. It is in that direction, admittedly, that man's distinction chiefly lies, and that he is furthest removed from the lower animal creation. An eminent American advocate and expositor of the evolutionary theory writes : 'No fact in nature is fraught with deeper meaning than this two-sided fact of the extreme physical similarity and enormous psychical divergence between man and the group of animals to which he traces his pedigree.'[1] There is a very legitimate fear lest this divergence be lessened, and the concomitant dignity compromised, by bringing man's higher nature within the scope of evolutionary law. Does evolution, it is asked, give us in unabated fulness and value that which constitutes man's peculiar glory — his intellect, and still more his conscience? More than suspicious that it does not, many are inclined to abide by the position of Russel Wallace, that the application of the idea of evolution in the case of man must be restricted to his bodily organism.[2]

Yet, on the other hand, for one who is mainly concerned for the religious significance of man's position in the universe, the interest by no means lies exclusively on the more conservative and cautious side of the question. Making man in his entire nature subject to evolutionary law (if this can be done without sacrifice of essential truth), presents certain advantages for the cause of Theism. On this view evolution becomes an absolutely universal method of creation whereof man

[1] Fiske, *Man's Destiny*, p. 29.

[2] Mr. Wallace does not deny the continuity and progressive development of the intellectual and moral faculties from animals. His position is that these faculties have not been developed by natural selection, but by some other cause. That cause, he thinks, must be sought 'in the unseen universe of Spirit,' *vide* his *Darwinism*, chap. xv., and his *Contributions to the Theory of Natural Selection*, chap. x., for a statement of his view and the argument in support of it.

in his whole being is the highest and final product. And what we gain from this conception is the right to interpret the whole process by its end. If we place man, in his higher nature, outside the process, we lose this right. If human reason and conscience have no part in the great movement, then their possessor is neither explained by the movement, nor does he in turn explain it. But bring him, soul as well as body, within the movement, and we are entitled to point to all in him that is highest and say : This is what was aimed at all along, this is the goal towards which the age-long process of creation was marching, even towards the evolution of mind and spirit under the guidance of an eternal Reason.

At the very least it may safely be affirmed that so long as the relation of the universe to God is properly conceived and duly kept in mind, the question as to the evolution of man's psychical nature can hardly be a vital one. It is vital that we conceive of God as immanent in the world, and unceasingly active throughout the whole history of its genesis, the ultimate cause of all that happens. That done, it is not necessary in a theistic interest to resist to the death the idea that the human mind is a product of the great continuous movement by which the world, as it now exists, has arisen out of the primitive homogeneous ocean of undifferentiated atoms. The decision come to will affect, not the being of God, nor the reality of His creative agency in connection with the origin of man, but only the method of His working. The alternatives are : Creation of man by laws similar to those according to which other living species have been evolved, or special creation of man, as an exceptional being. The issue may, possibly, have a serious aspect for a believer in the authority of the Hebrew and Christian scriptures; that depends on whether these sacred writings teach or imply any particular theory as to the origin of man. But the issue is not serious for the general interests of Theism. Faith in God may remain intact, though we concede that man in all his characteristics, physical and psychical, is no exception to the universal law of growth, no breach in the continuity of the evolutionary process.

The average Theist, nevertheless, even while accepting this position in the abstract, is conscious of a secret bias in favour of making man *the great exception*. A reason for this it is not difficult to find. If man be a special creation, an immediate, miraculous product of Divine creative energy, his prerogative is safe beyond dispute; if, on the other hand, he fall under the universal rule, it may readily appear questionable. Even in that case it may be capable of vindication; but it will need it, and believers in man's unique nature and high destiny would naturally prefer a view of his origin that rendered such a vindication superfluous. There is a tendency to insist on such a view, even with reference to man's animal nature, in fear lest concession at this point might weaken the defence in connection with the higher nature. But the better informed, feeling the proof to be too strong in that region, hand man's body over to the evolutionist and draw the line there, saying in effect: Intrude not within the sacred territory of the soul; let it be reserved for the direct activity of God.

It is not to be supposed, however, that all who make the soul an exception, do so on purely religious grounds. Some take their stand on scientific considerations. Their plea is, that evidence sufficient to establish the thesis — man evolved in soul as in body — is not forthcoming. One occupying this position may be conceived as saying: 'I have my own firm faith as to man's position in the universe, and his corresponding destiny, which I am ever ready on due occasion to avow and advocate. Meanwhile I put that on one side, and I maintain that simply as a matter of scientific evidence, evolution of intellect and conscience is not proved.'

This is a perfectly intelligible position. It is a position, moreover, which it is well to have stated and vigorously supported, if it were only as a counterweight against the tendency to be too easily satisfied with proof of the thesis. Such a tendency certainly exists. The prevailing inclination is to assume the absolutely universal sway of evolutionary law, as a matter of course. Proof for the evolution of *man!* what proof is needed? Is it not proof enough that evolution is the rule everywhere else? The presumption is that man is no exception, and even if it should be found impossible to muster conclusive evidence for this position, it would be reasonable and scientific to regard it as in a high degree probable. The plea is not destitute of force, yet it is not desirable that the matter should rest there. Believers in universal evolution ought to do their best to establish their thesis in all departments of nature, and especially in those in which it is contested; and one very effective stimulus to exertion is vigorous contradiction supported by argument on the part of those who deny universality. Nothing but good can come of earnest, sustained debate between combatants well-matched in ability and knowledge.

It must be admitted that the advocates of evolution in the mental sphere have not been content with indolent assumption, but have braced themselves up to careful inquiry. The result is an extensive and able literature devoted to the proof that man as an animal, as an intellectual being, and as a moral agent, is the child of evolution. Nor have capable representatives on the other side of the question been wanting. The contributions to the maintenance of the negative on purely scientific lines are perhaps less numerous, but they are such as deserve respectful consideration. It would be out of place here to go at great length into the details of the controversy, and I am as little qualified or inclined, as I am called on, to play the part of umpire between the combatants. It may, however, be well to try and get a general idea of the bearings of the question, in the hope that we may be helped to see more clearly how far we can afford to be dispassionate, and to treat the question at issue as one of fact only, and not of theistic faith.

1. As to the animal nature of man, there is now comparatively little controversy. It is generally admitted that the human body has been evolved. The sources of proof are comparative anatomy and embry-

ology. Man is connected by broad analogies with the whole class of mammalia. His physical structure reveals close affinities with the ape. Even in the brain, where his superiority is conspicuous, the affinity is nevertheless quite remarkable. 'So far as cerebral structure goes,' says Mr. Huxley, 'it is clear that the difference between the brains of the chimpanzee and of man is almost insignificant when compared with that between the chimpanzee brain and that of a lemur.'[1] The testimony furnished by researches into embryonic development is still more impressive. It appears that the human embryo, in the different stages of its growth, presents resemblances to members of the lower animal world in an ascending scale: to the fish, then to the frog, then to the reptile, then to the generic type of the mammalia. These resemblances appear in a somewhat advanced stage in the development. The very early stage has not been investigated in the human subject. But the general result as expressed by Professor Henry Drummond is that 'human embryology is a condensed zoology, a recapitulation and epitome of some of the main chapters in the natural history of the world.'[2] In a few months the unborn child passes through forms of being which represent myriads of years in the evolution of the animal world. This is a fact of curious interest from whatever point of view it may be regarded. At present we are concerned with it as an index of man's subjection to evolutionary law. It is a link connecting him significantly

---

[1] *Evidence as to Man's Place in Nature*, p. 102 (1863).
[2] *The Ascent of Man*, p. 85.

with the lower animal creation. When at birth he sees the light he is *man* superior to all animals, unique in aspect and in possibilities. But before birth he belongs to the humbler world of animal life, and, by passing in rapid succession through many forms of being, shows how one species may pass into another, ever rising higher, from minute living creatures consisting of a single cell to highly evolved forms of animal life like those of the dog and the ape.

2. The question as to the evolution of *intellect* lays under contribution a wide field of inquiry, including investigations into the ascertainable or conjectural mental history of the lower animals, of primitive and savage man, and of children; and, connected with these, the intricate subject of the evolution of language falls to be discussed. The study is not only extensive but abstruse, and it is no easy matter to master the contents of the treatises bearing on it. These contain, not only unfamiliar ideas, but new words to express them. Thus one of the most recent and best-known writers on the subject, the late Mr. Romanes, found it necessary to coin the word 'recept' to denote a mental act intermediate between the elementary act of perception common to men and animals, and the rational act of conception peculiar to man. Percept, Recept, Concept: these terms form a series representing three stages in the evolution or manifestation of mental faculty rising one above the other. A percept is the cognition of an individual object, such as a stone; a concept is an abstract idea of a whole class of objects in which certain common features are

discernible, and to which we attach a common general name. A 'recept' is the result of recognition of things seen before, a mental impression remaining after seeing several things of the same sort, say half a dozen stones. Different objects have different 'recepts' answering to them; stones produce in the observer one 'recept,' loaves another, and the observer is aware of the difference. But why coin a new word, why not be content with the old familiar term, 'concept,' or the still more familiar phrase, 'abstract ideas'? Because the purpose is to describe an attainment of animals which approximates, and in some respects resembles, the process of abstraction characteristic of the human mind, and yet falls short of it. Animals know that a stone differs from a loaf, and therefore do not attempt to eat a stone. Birds know the difference between the sea and the rock round which its waves roll, and they do not attempt to dive into the rock. From their behaviour one might infer that they had abstract ideas of stones, loaves, rocks, and seas, but in reality their mental states do not go beyond spontaneous associations formed unintentionally. They are at most implicit unperceived abstractions.[1]

This, we are to understand, is all the length that animals, even the most intelligent, can go. But man can go further. He can form not only 'recepts,' but 'concepts.' He can consciously and deliberately abstract the points of essential agreement in objects, leaving out of account unessential points of difference, such as size and colour, and so can form a general idea of a

[1] *Mental Evolution in Man*, p. 37 (1888).

class, and distinguish it by a name, such as horse, dog, house. It was, in the view of the evolutionist, a great moment when man first acquired this faculty; the starting-point in a career of indefinite intellectual progress. It was a great step upwards when, to the animal faculty for forming 'recepts' he added the power to form 'concepts.' And yet, great as the step was, it is held to have been only the next step in the onward march of the evolution of intellect. For this position one piece of evidence is found in the fact that children, before reaching the age of self-consciousness, do not rise above the receptual type of thought characteristic of the lower animals. When a child sees a dog he imitates its bark. The exclamation means 'this is a dog,' but the child has no abstract idea of a dog. His judgment is preconceptual, and such as a dog itself makes when it distinguishes between a stone and a bone.[1]

How then did man attain to this invaluable faculty of forming abstract ideas? The answer given to this important question by the advocates of intellectual evolution is: *Through the use of language.* When man acquired the power of speaking then he acquired the power of forming concepts as distinct from recepts. In the phraseology of another investigator in this region, Mr. Lloyd Morgan, the new departure was rendered possible *through the naming of predominants.* Mr. Morgan employs the term *predominant* to serve the same purpose as the term 'recept' preferred by Mr. Romanes. A predominant is an outstanding feat-

[1] Romanes, *Mental Evolution in Man*, p. 203.

ure in an object of perception, such as may arrest the eye or ear of an animal. 'Isolate,' on the other hand, is the term Mr. Morgan employs to denote the product of the process by which human beings select certain qualities and consider them by themselves to the neglect of other qualities. Morgan's 'isolate' is Romanes' concept. And he gives us to understand that man attained the power of forming isolates by naming predominants. 'The named predominant became an isolate.'[1] The naming process, as it were, floated off the predominant features from the objects of perception, and through isolation introduced them into the intellectual sphere.[2]

The concept-forming faculty, then, differentiates man from brute, and it is language that makes that important faculty possible. But whence came language? How did man learn to speak? Are we not in presence of as great a mystery as that which it is supposed to explain? Nay, have we not reason to suspect a *hysteron proteron* here: an inversion of the true order of cause and effect? Language, we are in effect told, made man rational; was it not rather because man had already become rational that he began to speak? Is not language, as Professor Calderwood contends, 'an instrument of thought, an evidence of the presence of thought, a subsequent and consequent of the exercise of rational powers?'[3] I merely throw out these queries by way of suggested criticism, and pro-

---

[1] C. Lloyd Morgan, *Animal Life and Intelligence*, p. 374.
[2] *Ibid.*
[3] *Evolution and Man's Place in Nature*, p. 246 (1st Ed.).

ceed with my exposition. To make the mystery more intelligible and credible, the development of the new talent is represented as taking place very slowly and gradually. It came, we are told, very late in the day of mankind's long history. Man existed on the earth for ages before he could speak in the sense of using articulate language for communication with his fellows. There was a non-speaking man (*Homo alălus*) before there was a speaking man (*Homo loquens*). The earlier non-speaking man could communicate with his fellows, but only through inarticulate, significant signs. Of this primitive stage Mr. Romanes finds a survival in the clicks of the Kaffir, of which it seems there are four, or even six kinds; and the infantile state of child-life is pointed to as a pathetic memorial of the time when even grown-up men were infants.

Another point insisted on to facilitate acceptance of the theory that language was the mother rather than the daughter of reason, is that language was at first a very simple affair. Words did not at first express abstract ideas, but rather named predominants, or expressed preconceptual judgments after the manner in which a child says: That is a dog, by exclaiming, 'Bow wow.' This touches on a question on which students of language differ. Professor Max Müller, reasoning from the data supplied by the Sanskrit language, advocates the theory that the roots of language express abstract ideas, *e.g.* 'cur,' the idea of running. This theory goes contrary to the evolutionary hypothesis, for it presupposes a high power of abstraction at the very beginning of the use of language. The evolutionist gets rid of the obstacle by bluntly denying that the first words were expressive of abstract ideas, and contending that they were more probably of the onomatopoetic type. To the objection: Why then do so many words expressive of abstract ideas survive, while of the onomatopoetic type only a few traces are found? the answer is given: The former survive because they have been prolific of other words, the latter have perished because they were not prolific.[1] And more generally it is pleaded that the historical languages, including Sanskrit, do not show us by any means man's first attempts at speech. They are the final outcome of innumerable crude experiments which have perished, leaving hardly a trace behind. Of the existing languages, those that come nearest the primitive type are the polysynthetic, exemplified by the speech of the American Indians, in which a word represents a whole sentence. The sentence, not the single word, is held to be the original unit of language. Mr. Romanes sums up the result of philological research in these terms: 'Spoken language began in the form of sentence-words, grammar is the child of gesture, predication is but the adult form of the same faculty of sign-making, which in its infancy we know as indication.' According to this view the parts of speech belong to a late stage in the evolution of language. Pronouns came first, but even they were slowly differentiated. Not till ages had elapsed did man learn to say 'I.'[2]

On such grounds as those thus slightly indicated it

---

[1] Romanes, *Mental Evolution in Man*, p. 277.
[2] *Ibid.*, p. 297.

is maintained that 'the human mind itself is but the topmost inflorescence of one mighty growth whose root and stem and many branches are sunk in the abyss of planetary time.'[1]

It will be understood that the development of the human brain would have an important bearing on the evolution of intellect. As the brain grew in mass, quality, and convolution, the powers of thought and speech grew *pari passu*. And conversely the exercise of these powers would react on the brain and stimulate its growth.

Is the case proven? It is a hard question for the jury. Some may be inclined to vote with Mr. Wallace, who admits *continuity*, gradual ascent from intellect in animals to intellect in man, but maintains the necessity of introducing some higher cause to account for the phenomena of human intelligence. Even the history of language gives us pause. What an amazing phenomenon is the Sanskrit language, so rich in inflexional forms, appearing so early in the history of civilisation! It raises the doubt whether languages, like Sanskrit and Greek, are to be regarded as the natural product of the gradually evolving human intellect; whether we ought not to see in them something almost supernatural. Even Hartmann becomes devout when he touches on this theme. 'Language,' he says, 'is the Word of God, the holy scripture of philosophy, the revelation of the genius of humanity for all time.'[2] He sees in such a language as Sanskrit not the work of individual

[1] *Mental Evolution in Man*, p. 2.
[2] *Philosophie des Unbewussten*, p. 256.

minds, but the organic product of a collective mass-instinct, ultimately the work of the great unconscious spirit of the universe, exceeding in skill anything in the way of language-making to be found in later epochs of higher culture.[1]

3. In passing to the subject of the evolution of *conscience*, I remark that the question here is not as to the progressive development of morality within human history. That is now generally accepted. The question is: Has there been an upward movement towards morality as we know it in man, in its crudest form, from the sub-human animal world, and from rudiments of moral feeling and behaviour traceable there, bearing a proportion to the rudiments of reason whereof indications in the same world are not wanting?

It is quite intelligible that reluctance to accept the affirmative answer to this question should be even more decided than in connection with the corresponding question as to the evolution of intellect. And yet evolution in the moral sphere would seem to be a corollary to evolution in the intellectual. Given rationality, morality follows. But this consideration should not supersede inquiry into the kind of conduct to be expected from human beings on evolutionary principles, and how far it deserves to be characterised as ethical.

Some kind of conduct is, of course, to be looked for. *Conduct consists of acts adapted to ends.* On this view conduct is predicable of all living creatures from the worm up to man. All sentient creatures instinc-

[1] *Philosophie des Unbewussten*, p. 258.

tively, or with conscious intent, act so as to promote self-preservation. All action guided consciously or instinctively by this aim will have a certain definiteness and regularity. It will be action subject to the law of what is conducive to well-being. But the action of the lower animal world, subject to this law, is not yet ethical in the human sense of the term. To speak of 'animal ethics' at all, as evolutionists do, may seem a very questionable use of language. But, not to dispute about words, it must be said that *animal ethics* are certainly of a very crude kind. Self-preservation in the animal world means, to a large extent, destruction of creatures of a different species, and even of many animals of the same species. Animal ethics have for their supreme motive, hunger, craving immediate satisfaction, causing conflicts which issue in the survival of the strongest.

But human ethics must rise above the animal plane in virtue of certain features recognised in the evolutionary theory, and legitimately used by it to explain man's moral superiority. Besides the sensitiveness to pleasure and pain common to all creatures that feel, there are, in man, to an extent altogether unparalleled in the lower animal world, reason and sympathy. In the exercise of his reason, man can look to remote advantage, and subordinate present pleasure to what is best in the long run. He can form an idea of life as a whole, and regulate his conduct by the ideal. Hence arise such virtues as prudence, patience, and self-control. Sympathy lays the foundation of another group of virtues of a higher order to which the evolutionist can lay claim. For sympathy in man is an inheritance from his sub-human ancestry. Social instincts reveal themselves in various quarters of the lower animate world — in the ant, the bee, the beaver, in all gregarious animals — and under their influence acts are performed which look like self-sacrifice. What wonder, then, if man can rise above self, subordinating his own individual interest to that of the community, and show himself capable at times of public-spirited, generous, heroic conduct?

Yet another element in human nature, new in degree yet old in kind, is *family affection*. In the creatures that produce offspring by myriads there can be no real parental love. Such love begins with the *mammalia*, which have few young at one time and suckle their young. In man this love undergoes an immense development through the prolongation of infancy due to increase of cerebral surface. The helplessness of the human infant demands incessant maternal care, and its long duration tends to give depth and permanence to maternal affection, which in turn calls forth answering affection deep and stable in the child.[1]

Thus the evolutionist may claim that on his theory he can provide for the development of three sets of virtues, all good so far as they go: the personal, the

---

[1] *Vide* on this, J. Fiske, *Cosmic Philosophy*, ii. 344 ff.; also Drummond, *Ascent of Man*, p. 367 f. Herder anticipated this thought. 'To tame the wildness of men and fit them for domestic life, the childhood of our race had to last long years. Nature constrained them by tender bands, so that they could not scatter and forget, like beasts which soon arrive at maturity.' — *Ideen zur Geschicht der Menschheit*, i. 224.

family, and the social virtues. Whether he gives us all that is demanded by the peculiar sense of moral obligation denoted by the term 'conscience' is another question. There may be ground for suspecting here, as in the case of the relation between language and reason, an inversion of the true order of cause and effect. Through language, says the evolutionist, man has become rational. Is not rationality presupposed in the use of language? suggests the more cautious and conservative thinker. Just so may he deal with the Darwinian attempt to derive conscience from the social instinct. Man feels remorse, argues Darwin, because he is by inheritance a social animal, and cannot help condemning himself when he sacrifices social interests to transient personal indulgence. To this it has been not unreasonably replied that our hypothetical ancestor would have had no such feeling of self-condemnation unless he had had an intuitive perception of the superior excellence of social over selfish instincts. The explanation, that is to say, presupposes the thing to be explained.

One thing must be said in favour of evolutional ethics. They do rise above the level of utilitarianism by the recognition of an altruistic or social disposition as an indisputable part of man's moral inheritance. This further may be claimed for them, that they supply a class of motives which cannot justly be characterised as ignoble, trivial, or impotent. By the doctrine of *heredity*, the evolutionist admonishes men to be careful what they do, seeing immoral actions leave ineffaceable stains, and bear lasting consequences. By the doctrine of the progressiveness of society in goodness taught by most upholders of the theory, he encourages the spirit of hope, and makes it worth while for the lover of mankind to devote himself to beneficent endeavour. On the other hand, by representing progress as very slow, however sure, he instils the lesson of patience, very needful to be learnt by all good men as an antidote to the disappointment which inevitably overtakes those who cherish unfounded expectations of speedy success.

In devout minds a prejudice is naturally created against the ethics of evolution by the fact of their being frequently associated with religious agnosticism. It is unhappily the fact that the advocates of evolution in the moral sphere too often assume an attitude of indifference or hostility to faith in God, the soul, freedom, immortality, the possibility and worth of individual regeneration, the reality and morality of pardon, redemption, etc. Polemics against these and kindred beliefs, occurring in their pages, tempt Christian readers to throw away their works in disgust. It is not wise, however, to assume that this association is other than accidental. Such an assumption must have for its inevitable consequence that we shall feel ourselves compelled to renounce the theory of evolution in its application to man's rational and moral nature, in order to save our faith. So we shall have one instance more of a situation too frequently exemplified in the history of religion: faith interdicting inquiry on scientific methods, in dread of actual or possible results.

Now in this case, as in all cases, it is most desirable, if possible, to make faith independent of the truth or falsehood of scientific theories and hypotheses. And it does seem possible. Man is now a rational and moral subject in a sense predicable of no other living creature in this world. This is a fact beyond dispute. The question may legitimately be asked, How has this distinction been gained? Two answers are conceivable: By evolution, or by special act and favour of God. If evolution, after due inquiry, be found inadequate to the production of so great a result, then we know where we are. If, on the other hand, evolution be found adequate to its production, are we where some evolutionists and not a few Christians *think* we are — in a universe without God? I say no. Why should evolution of intellect and conscience exclude God, any more than evolution of physical organisation? If God be immanent in the universe, then He is in this part of the evolutionary process not less than in all others. Evolution is simply His method of communicating to man the light of reason and the sense of duty. Some weighty words of the late Mr. Romanes from the posthumous publication, *Mind and Motion and Monism*, may here be cited: 'Take again the case of morality and religion. Because science, by its theory of evolution, appears to be in a fair way of explaining the genesis of these things by natural causes, Theists are taking alarm; it is felt by them that if morality can be fully explained by utility, and religion by superstition, the reality of both is destroyed. But Monism teaches that such a view is entirely erroneous. For, according to Monism, the natural causation of morality and religion has nothing whatever to do with the ultimate truth of either. The natural causation is merely a record of physical processes, serving to manifest the psychical processes. Nor can it make any difference, as regards the ultimate veracity of the moral and religious feelings, that they have been developed slowly by natural causes; that they were at first grossly selfish on the one hand, and hideously superstitious on the other; that they afterwards went through a long series of changes, none of which, therefore, can have fully corresponded with external truth; or that even now they may be both extremely far from any such correspondence. All that such considerations go to prove is, that it belongs to the natural method of mental evolution in man that with advancing culture his interpretations of nature should more and more nearly *approximate* the truth.'[1]

Men deeply concerned for the sacred interests of morality and religion may be shy to receive aid from one who writes as an advocate of *Monism*. What does that word mean? 'Why, of course,' the Theist may reply, 'the evolution of the universe psychical and physical from one ultimate substance — matter; in other words, the theory of Materialism.' Now, curiously enough, the author quoted thinks that by his Monism he can refute Materialism, assert the reality of a Divine Mind in the universe, vindicate for the human mind causal power, defend the freedom of the human will, and generally guard all moral and

[1] Page 114.

religious interests. The Monism of Mr. Romanes is a synthesis of Materialism and Spiritualism. It implies that mental phenomena and physical phenomena, though superficially diverse, are really identical, that wherever there is matter there is mind, and wherever there is mind there is matter, and that both matter and mind simultaneously produce both motion and thought. It is an abstruse theme on which one is naturally not in haste to dogmatise. But it may be said that in some form Monism seems to be the natural accompaniment of a thoroughgoing doctrine of evolution. And that a monistic conception of the universe is not incompatible with theistic and Christian belief may be inferred from the fact that it finds an advocate in Le Conte, who is as pronounced in his faith as in his devotion to modern science. This American scientist thus states his view: 'I believe that the spirit of man was developed out of the *anima*, or conscious principle of animals, and that this again was developed out of the lower forms of life-force, and this in its turn out of the chemical and physical forces of nature, and that at a certain stage in this gradual development, viz., with man, it acquired the property of immortality, precisely as it now, in the individual history of each man, at a certain stage, acquires the capacity of abstract thought.'[1]

So we return to the position: Evolution simply God's method of communicating to man the light of reason and the sense of duty. Surely a worthy end-

[1] *Evolution and its Relation to Religious Thought*, p. 313 (2nd Ed.).

ing of the long process of world-genesis! The process, however rude or even brutal, does not disgrace the result. The result rather invests the whole process with dignity and moral significance, and helps us to understand how Deity could have to do with it. The lower stages of evolution seem unworthy of the Creator, but when we think of man with his reason and conscience as latent therein, it becomes conceivable how the Divine Spirit might brood yearningly over chaos, starting the mighty movement by which it was to be slowly turned into a cosmos with man for its crown of glory. Evolution does not degrade man, man confers honour on evolution. Man, considered as in his whole being the child of evolution, instead of being a stumbling-block to faith, is rather the key to all mysteries, revealing at once the meaning of the universe, the nature of God, and his own destiny. To expound this thesis will be our task in the next lecture.

LECTURE III

THEISTIC INFERENCES FROM MAN'S PLACE IN THE UNIVERSE

MAN the climax and crown of evolution — what then? What inferences may we draw from man's place in the universe regarding the Great Being who is beneath and within the creative process, from its commencement to its consummation? That is the theme which is to occupy our attention in the present lecture.

Our appeal, you observe, is to the end of the process. Why, it may be asked, restrict ourselves to the end; why not roam over the whole process in quest of critical points at which the Creator's hand may be directly apparent? Some theistic apologists have in fact done this, as if under an impression that while God may be in the *usual*, He is far more certainly to be found in the *unusual*, where the evolutionary process passes into some new phase and makes a remarkable new departure. Before going on to unfold the argument based on man's position, it may help us to appreciate its comparative value if we first give some account of the leading attempts to plant the foot of faith on what seem crises in the history of world-genesis.

Three such crises have received prominent attention from apologists.

1. Some have sought to find room and need for special Divine activity at the very beginning of the evolutionary process. The contention is that the initial condition, just before evolution commences, is such that no commencement is possible without some action *ab extra*. The starting-point is conceived to be 'a vast diffusion of ultimate units of matter, each like the other in every respect, each subject to equal pressure and tension.'[1] How in such a state of things is differentiation to begin? No other way is conceivable, it is argued, than by the power of God. No great exertion of that power may be necessary. No great force is needed to set a bank of fine dry sand on a steep slope in motion. The touch of a finger at the foot of the slope will suffice to make the motionless mass break into rills. In like manner the sound of a human voice will sometimes cause a snow-slope in the high Alps to rush headlong in a destructive avalanche. Even so a touch of the Divine finger, a word of the Divine voice, may be enough to start the atomic chaos on its evolutionary career. But the point on which those who wield this argument would insist, is that the touch, the word, is needed. A transcendent Divine interposition, however minute, has to take place.

The argument is ingenious, and may be commended to the attention of agnostic philosophers, like Mr. Herbert Spencer, for whose special benefit it is designed. It is obvious, however, that even granting its conclusiveness, on which I confess I do not feel competent

---

[1] C. Chapman, *Preorganic Evolution and the Biblical Idea of God*, p. 151.

to pronounce a confident judgment, reasoning of this sort cannot be of much service as an aid to faith in God, for ordinary minds. It is too abstruse, and it is based on a condition of the universe too remote from that which falls under our observation. It demands the power of thinking *in vacuo*, in an intellectual atmosphere so rare that only experts can breathe in it. The theistic argument based on 'Preorganic Evolution,' whatever its value for its own purpose, can never take its place among the popular proofs for the being of a God endowed with creative power and boundless intelligence.

2. A second crisis demanding Divine interposition has been found in the origin of life. The theistic argument at this point starts from the results of scientific investigation into the question of *spontaneous generation*. As is well known, the generally accepted result of extensive and careful inquiry is that there is now no such thing as spontaneous generation, *i.e.* that wherever life has been seen to appear in connection with experiments, the presence of germs has been detected; and, negatively, that where germs have been successfully excluded, no life has made its appearance. It may therefore be taken for granted that in the present condition of nature no life shows itself where only lifeless matter was before. From this *datum* many theists have inferred that no life ever did, or could, appear where only dead matter had previously been, and that therefore when life first made its appearance in the world the new phenomenon owed its existence, not to the action of natural law, bringing the elements of

protoplasm, separately lifeless, into such a combination as yielded a vital result, but to the immediate causality of the Being who is the Fountain of Life. On the surface the reasoning appears both legitimate and conclusive, and yet, in the name of science, not a few have entered a plea of *non sequitur*. It does not follow, it is argued, that because life does not appear now, so far as can be ascertained, except where life in some form was before, that therefore the first appearance of life in the world must have been something supernatural. We do not know what natural conditions, such as the then existing temperature of the earth, might form the preparation for the new phenomenon, so that on its appearing it should be simply the next step onwards in the regular course of evolution. It is farther contended that, in connection with every phenomenon in the universe however startling and novel, the presumption is that it has its natural causes. From the mere fact, therefore, that at a given stage in the evolving process life appeared, it may be inferred that there were facts in the previous condition of the world to account for it. To make this conclusion more easily acceptable, care is taken to explain what the new phenomenon precisely would be. It would not, of course, be the case of an insect generated in putrefying substances without any assignable cause. It would rather be a case of specks of living protoplasm precipitated from a solution containing the non-living ingredients of protoplasm. Finally it is asked, Why should this seem a thing impossible, except as the miraculous effect of an immediate exertion of Divine power? The difference

THEISTIC INFERENCES

between living and non-living matter is after all not so very great. It is a difference in degree, not in kind. Life, organised matter, is simply a peculiar combination of inorganic matter. Hitherto certainly science has not been able to penetrate the secret of the combination, and to effect it; but we ought not to despair of ultimate success. As Du Bois Reymond puts the case, we ought to see in it nothing more than a 'very difficult mechanical problem.'[1]

Recent theistic writers have been influenced more or less by these considerations, and have been less confident than older apologists as to the cogency of the inference from the beginning of life to immediate Divine causality. It is now deemed unwise to be too dogmatic on the subject. Every Theist, of course, sees in the emergence of life the trace of God's hand, but not necessarily in a miraculous form. The cautious Theist now hesitates to adduce initial life as conclusive evidence of a supernatural agency on the ground that no natural cause is assignable or possible.

3. A third great crisis more than any demanding immediate Divine interposition has been found in the origin of *conscious* life, introducing us into the wonderland of feeling and thought. Here too the Theist has scientific acknowledgments on his side. For the best representatives of science promptly admit that the phenomena of feeling and thought are not resolvable into motions of matter, though they are intimately connected with movements of the cerebral substance. The same

[1] *Vide* Du Bois Reymond, *Über die Grenzen des Naturerkennens*, p. 31.

man of science who pronounced the origin of life only a difficult problem in mechanics declares the origin of consciousness to be a problem absolutely insoluble. Dogmatic Materialists find it necessary for the maintenance of their theory of the universe to assert the contrary, and boldly to treat thought as a mere mode of motion; but they receive no encouragement from responsible scientific authorities. In these circumstances the way to the theistic inference seems open. Every phenomenon must have some cause. If we cannot explain mind in terms of motion are we not shut up to the conclusion that the spiritual world is in essence and origin altogether supernatural, to be accounted for only by the creative activity of the Divine Spirit? But to this reasoning the modern scientist, refusing to step out of the natural, assumes an agnostic attitude, saying: I confess I cannot explain the origin of thought and feeling and consciousness; I even acknowledge that, in my judgment, these phenomena are scientifically inexplicable. But there I stop. I decline to go into the question of supernatural agency. My position is purely negative, viz., that the attempt to discover the natural causes of mental phenomena is hopeless. Such causes may exist, though for us the secret of their nature may remain for ever impenetrable. Present day science fights shy of the hypothesis of a soul, or of a world-soul, and prefers to remain in a position of ignorance.[1]

It is not possible for the Theist by anything he can urge to dislodge the scientist from this agnostic posi-

[1] So Du Bois Reymond in *Über die Grenzen*, etc., p. 37.

tion. But he may be satisfied in his own mind that the phenomena of thought must ultimately have a spiritual origin. We can be quite certain of this at least, that the materialistic theory is impossible. Far from accounting for the origin of mind, that theory leaves us entirely at a loss to understand how there ever came to be such phenomena as thought and consciousness at all. From the materialistic point of view these phenomena are simply by-products, coming into being one knows not how, and serving no purpose, having no more share than the dead in 'all that's done beneath the circuit of the sun.' The chain of physical causality is complete without them, and things would go on just the same if there were no consciousness accompanying brain movements: 'railway trains,' to use the vivid illustrations of Mr. Romanes, 'running filled with mindless passengers, and telephones invented by brains that could not think to speak to ears that could not hear.'[1] One does not need to be a profound philosopher to see the absurdity of a theory which reduces man to the position of a *conscious automaton*. Yet while we are quite sure of our ground in putting Materialism out of court, we are not obliged to dogmatise on the question, whether the phenomena of mind necessarily imply a distinct substratum, and may not rather have arisen in the course of evolution in some quite inscrutable way out of what is called matter. As we have already seen, some theistic scientists, such as Le Conte, decidedly prefer the latter alternative. One can easily understand the bias in this direc-

[1] *Mind and Motion and Monism*, p. 71.

tion. More and more, believers in evolution incline to claim for it universal sway, and regard with disfavour the hypothesis of a dualistic breach of continuity at any point of the process. 'Onwards,' say they, 'let it march, in its inexhaustible energy, from star dust to solid globes, from inanimate being to living matter, from rudimentary forms of life to feeling in animals, and to thought, consciousness, and conscience in man, and all along let the phenomena be but the varied states of one eternal something capable of undergoing the most marvellous transformations.' For one who takes up this position it will not be possible to infer from the mere facts of the appearance of consciousness at a certain stage in the evolutionary process the existence of a cause adequate to its production outside of nature; because for him *ex hypothesi* that phenomenon, like all others, has its place in the natural order of things. But it is open to him to argue from the scope and issue of the *whole*, that the process of evolution has its ultimate ground in a Being whose nature contains or accounts for all that comes to pass, and very specially the last and highest series of phenomena, those belonging to the spiritual life of man.

This seems to be the safe and wise position for all Theists to take up. Instead of looking out for open points in the process of world-making at which to bring in the supernatural power of a transcendent Deity, let us rather believe in the incessant activity, all along the line, of an immanent Deity. If we are not able to compel others agnostically inclined to accept this view, it is much if we find it thoroughly satisfactory to our

own minds. And there is every reason why we should.
In the first place, even agnostic philosophers themselves, like Mr. Spencer, acknowledge a great unknowable ultimate ground underlying the whole process of evolution, and entering as a factor into the production of all that exists. We need not agree with them as to the unknowableness of the ground, but we may most legitimately take comfort from the fact that they are at one with us at least as to its existence. Then, in the next place, the conception of God as immanent in the world, and acting on it throughout its whole history, from within, helps us in some measure to conceive of His action by bringing it into analogy to the relation in which we ourselves stand to our own bodies. When we try, we find it really beyond our power to imagine how the Great Spirit acts on the world. But we find it equally impossible to imagine how we ourselves act on our own bodies. Yet, with all deference to the abettors of the *conscious automaton* hypothesis, the fact is indubitable. I really can, and do, every hour of the day, at will, set the members of my body, my hands and my feet, in motion. This helps me to believe that God's action on the world, whereof He is, as it were, the soul, is equally real and incessant, though utterly incomprehensible. I use the qualifying expression, 'as it were,' in suggesting that the relation of God to the world is analogous to that of soul to body, because the analogy may easily be pressed too far. If God be the soul of the world, asks Du Bois Reymond in effect, where is His brain? This is to take the analogy too literally and prosaically. It should be used solely for the two-

fold purpose of indicating that God's relation to the world is one of immanence and not of mere transcendence, and of making this incessant action on the universe credible, if not conceivable, by representing it as analogous to the action of a human spirit on its material organism.

Before passing from this topic, I may remark that the conception of God's relation to the world as immanent, indwelling, is perfectly compatible with the idea of transcendence. He may be in the world, yet above it. He may act on the world at all times and in accordance with its natural laws, and He may also act on it at particular crises in an exceptional manner, so as to initiate a new departure. I do not know whether any of the points that have been seized on by Theists constitutes such a crisis or not. It is not necessary for me to dogmatise on the question. The beginning of life may or may not have been a stage at which immediate, or transcendent, action of God took place. If it was not, my faith in a God always at work as an immanent cause remains intact. If it was, the occasional transcendent activity is quite reconcilable with the constant immanent activity. At no point in the history of the universe can I compel belief in transcendent Divine action, by abstract reasoning, meant to influence other minds. But such transcendent action, at any point, need be no stumbling-block to my own faith.

But, on the other hand, it must be remembered that it may be the reverse of an advantage to faith to lay an excessive emphasis on the occasional preternatural action of God upon the world. The risk we run by so doing is that of getting into a way of finding God nowhere save in the unusual; *i.e.* of lapsing into *Deism.* The Deist believed that God by a stupendous miracle created the world perfect at the first, then left the machine ever after to itself, to do its appointed work through its own self-acting laws. God's power was thus exhaustively manifested at the creation; since then He has been an otiose Divinity. That crude view is out of date, but the underlying principle may survive. It has been truly observed that 'Cataclysmal geology and special creation are the scientific analogue of Deism.'[1] These also have passed away, but a similar remark might be applied to such survivals of occasionalism as still linger among us. The man who clings eagerly to the primitive impulse that set evolution going, to the origination of life, and to the inspiration of a living soul, as proofs that God exists, virtually declares that in all other parts of the history of the universe he finds no convincing evidence of God's being and power. And what, one may ask, is the good of such a Deity after you have verified His existence to your own satisfaction? He is a far-off, absentee, otiose Divinity. How much better to find God everywhere, than here and there at rare intervals; ever active, not merely rousing Himself out of an age-long sleep to do marvellous things now and then; active in the movements of every molecule as it enters into combination with its neighbours, not less than in the initial push that set all the molecules agoing; revealing Himself as the Fountain of Life in the minutest variations that

[1] Aubrey L. Moore, *Science and the Faith*, p. 185.

condition the development of species, as well as in the fiat by which life first came into being! One can, of course, understand the special interest taken in the more conspicuous activity of the Divine Being for apologetic purposes. In directing attention thereto, the apologist in effect says to the doubter: 'You must admit that here at least God is present.' The prominence given to the occasional and the unusual in the theistic argument is analogous to the insistence on the predictive element in prophecy in the argument of the older apologetic for the truth of Christianity. In both cases, the one-sided emphasis is well meant; nevertheless it is evil in result. In the argument from prophecy on the old lines, the predictive element threw the far more important *ethical* element in Hebrew prophecy into the shade. In the theistic argument, based on critical points in the history of creation, the tendency is to make the evolutionary process as a whole, a God-forsaken, mechanical affair, redeemed from utter godlessness only by Divine initiatives separated from each other by millions of years. The true conception of God's relation to the universe surely is: *God always dwelling in the world and ever active there.*

Always active from the beginning of the evolutionary process to the end, and always looking forward to the end. God ever creating and ever exercising a providence over creation, guiding it towards its consummation — *man*. Here, not at any preliminary stage, is the place on which we should plant our foot, if we desire to know not merely that God is but *what* He is. For from

THEISTIC INFERENCES

man, viewed as the child of evolution and as its climax, we may learn these four things: —

1. That the process of world-making is instinct with purpose — man in view throughout.
2. That purpose guided the evolutionary process so as to insure that it should reach its foreordained consummation.
3. That the object of the purpose being man, the Being who purposes must be manlike.
4. That the purpose which aimed at bringing man on the scene will continue to work towards making the most of man.

1. That creation has a purpose, that there is such a thing as a world-aim, is, to say the least, a very reasonable and credible proposition. I do not say that it is a proposition that can be strictly demonstrated like one of the propositions of Euclid, so that every man, whatever his intellectual bias or moral state, shall be forced to accept it.[1] I content myself with saying that it is a more reasonable and credible proposition than any other which can be enunciated on the subject. Compare it, *e.g.*, with the thesis of Strauss: The world did not proceed from reason, but it has reason for its goal. How much more credible the counter-thesis, that just because reason is the goal of the world-process, therefore it proceeded from reason — mind, thought, spirit,

[1] Professor Seth holds that purpose is involved in the very idea of evolution. 'A speculation which does not see that evolution spells purpose has not made clear to itself the difference between progress and aimless variation. Such speculation rests ultimately on a purely mechanical view of the universe.' — *Man's Place in the Cosmos*, p. 58.

the fountain of all that is! If even the Straussian view is, by comparison, irrational, what shall we think of the materialist conception of reason, consciousness, in man, as a mere *lusus naturae*, not only explaining nothing, but itself inexplicable and not worth trying to explain? Evolution, far from having a purpose, ends in this: A group of unintelligible, useless phenomena; in Hartmann's expressive phrase, 'an insubstantial glimmer resulting from certain constellations of material functions.'[1] Must we not all endorse the sentiment of Romanes when he says: 'Assuredly, on the principles of evolution, which Materialists at least cannot afford to disregard, it would be a wholly anomalous fact that so wide and general a class of phenomena as those of mind should have become developed in constantly ascending degrees throughout the animal kingdom, if they are entirely without use.'[2]

Men of science, as such, are not Materialists, and they will be careful not to commit themselves to such an absurdity as that which the words just quoted so forcibly expose. But while keeping aloof from the dogma that reason is useless, they may equally decline to regard the origination of the rational as the aim of the world-process. They may give the whole question of a world-aim the go-by. They may say: 'What we are concerned with is the physical explanation of the world as we find it. We claim the right to explain man, if

---

[1] Einen substanzlosen Schein, der aus gewissen Constellationen materieller Functionen resultire. — *Philosophie des Unbewussten*, p. 479.

[2] *Mind and Motion and Monism*, pp. 72, 73.

we can, on the same principles as those by which we
explain everything else. And we think we have so
explained him; as a part of nature which has come to
be what it now is by the process which we call evolution.
And there is no more to be said on the matter. We
decline to look at man apart, as if there were something
exceptional about him, if not as to the way in which he
has come to be, at least as to the significance of him,
now that he is here. We refuse to go into questions of
teleology, to inquire as to the aim of the evolutionary
process. We regard that process as explaining all the
phenomena of nature, but the process itself we take as
an ultimate fact, requiring and admitting no explanation. Least of all would it occur to us to isolate the
end of the process from all that goes before, and to find
in it the explanation of the whole. No doubt it is the
end, and, we admit, a very remarkable one. But every
process must have some end, and if the movement be
an advancing one, of course the consummation must be
higher than anything that appears at an earlier stage.'

Perhaps nothing that can be said by one accustomed
to look at things in another light is likely to alter the
views of men in this mood. But it does not follow that
the truths one sees under that light are not worth stat-
ing. I am not one of those who think that it is possible
to compel faith in God by any processes of reasoning
whatsoever. It is possible to remain agnostic in spite
of all conceivable theistic arguments. Yet it is worth
while for the Theist, even for his own sake, to think
out a theory of the universe that shall be helpful to
faith by its consistency and intrinsic worthiness. And

of such a theory man, as the consummation of the evolutionary process, may be made the starting-point, as reflecting the light of purpose on the whole antecedent history of the universe: —

> 'From the grand result
> A supplementary reflux of light,
> Illustrates all the inferior grades,
> Each back step in the circle.'[1]

It looks as if nature herself were inviting us to regard man as, while no exception in *origin*, exceptional in significance. She has hidden the evidence of his parentage. She has thrown down the scaffolding after finishing the building. How much trouble it has given the scientist to find links of connection between man and the lower creation! So far as the body is concerned, the best evidence is that which is carefully concealed from observation, the transformation which a human being undergoes before he is born. Then of the evolution of mind how faint the traces! If we believe in it, it is rather because the presumption *a priori* is in favour of it than because of the detailed inductive proof. It may be that for long ages after the genus *Homo* existed he was by reason of mental imbecility unable to speak, and could communicate only by signs; but the solitary alleged survival of that speechless epoch — *the click of the Kaffir* — is a very slight proof of the fact. Grant the reality of the continuous process, and that in this, as in all other departments, it has proceeded by insensible progression, nevertheless, what we see is a great gulf separating

[1] Browning, *Paracelsus*, p. 189.

THEISTIC INFERENCES 61

man, even at the lowest point of civilisation, from the most intelligent animals. The rudest savage has an artistic *hand*, and a speaking *tongue*. Has this fact no meaning? Does not nature, or its Author, seem to say: 'This is what I was aiming at all along; and now that I have reached the goal I place the final product on a pedestal that he may be well in view, and that you may study his significance. It is nothing less than this, that in him all that went before finds its *rationale*. Evolution of the inanimate and the lower animate world took place because it was to culminate in the evolution of man. Without him the long process of creation would have been much ado about nothing.'

It may indeed seem presumptuous to say that man is of more importance than all the world with him left out; than the biggest objects of nature, the mountain ranges, the seas, the wide fertile plains, or than the heavenly bodies, the sun, moon, and stars, which primitive man worshipped as beings greater than himself. We have a survival of this feeling in the familiar words of the Hebrew Psalter, 'When I consider thy heavens, the work of thy fingers, the moon and the stars, which thou hast ordained . . . what is man?'[1] Here is the key, in part, to nature-worship, man crushed by the overwhelming magnitudes and grandeurs of the physical world. The Psalmist, indeed, was not so crushed. He rose above the oppressive sense of bondage to the *physical*, into the joyous consciousness of the lordship of the *human;* probably not without a struggle with the temptation to succumb. And

[1] Psalm viii. 3, 4.

that is what we have all got to do, and what the theory of evolution, rightly construed, helps us to do. We have to learn that we do not suffer by comparison with the heavenly bodies. Rather they by comparison dwindle into insignificance. When I consider man, final product of the creative process, then say I, What are sun, moon, and stars? Whether the heavenly bodies contain human beings, or intelligent beings of some sort, I know not. If they do, then intelligence, there as here, is supreme. If they do not, then vast in mass, in distance, and in the sweep of their revolutions as they are, these bodies are insignificant compared with the chief tenant of this small terrestrial planet. In themselves, they have no sufficient *raison d'être*. For their own sake it was not worth while bringing them into existence. The reason of their being lies outside them, in their serviceableness to the spiritual universe. The sun, moon, and stars are redeemed from insignificance by illuminating and beautifying the planet in which man dwells.

Similar is the view to be taken of the whole sub-human creation. It has its reason of existence in man, and the moral interests he represents. If man had not been, it would not have been worth while for the lower world to be. If the Creator had not had man in view, the lower world would not have come into existence. This is how the Theist must view the matter. He must regard the sub-human universe in the light of an instrument to be used in subservience to the ends of the moral world. The Agnostic can evade this conclusion by regarding the evolution of the universe as an absolutely necessary and aimless process, which could not but be, which has no conscious reason for being, no purpose to arrive at any particular destination, but moves on blindly in obedience to mechanical law. If it arrive at length at man, why then it must be because it is in the nature of mechanics to produce in the long run mind, and of motion to be permuted ultimately into thought. For us this theory is once for all impossible. We must believe in God, Maker of heaven and earth. And believing in Him we look for a plan in His work. In creation, as in human history, we find at first much mystery and darkness. To what end that all-diffused fiery mist, those igneous rocks, those microscopic protozoa, those hideous 'dragons of the prime'? But stay; here, at the end of the æons, is *man*. It was worth God's while to make *him*, and in the light of this latest creation we can see at least a glimmering of meaning even in chaos, in the apparently useless, the irrational, the monstrous. All these were natural steps in a gradual process that was to have a worthy ending, in which the whole creative movement should find its justification. Man makes the world-process *rational*. With man at the head, every member of the lower creation has its appropriate place, and helps to make a cosmos. Lower forms of life are not to be considered abortions because they fall short of the human. It is enough that the human comes at last along at least one line of evolution. In order that the world may be rational it is not necessary that there shall be in it *nothing but* men. It suffices that there be in it *also* men.

2. Our second inference was 'that purpose guided the evolutionary process so as to insure that it should reach its foreordained consummation.' On this point it is not necessary to dwell, as it is an obvious corollary from the first inference. If there was purpose at all in the creative process, it would be active all through the process. There was *providence* in evolution, looking forward to its end and guiding it towards the end, as well as creation. Indeed, the process was more one of providence than of creation. God was occupied not so much in making new creatures, and originating by immediate activity new departures, as in guiding a world-generating process that was in a sense self-acting.[1] Self-acting so far, but not in a sense that made guidance unnecessary. There were risks of miscarriage, points at which the process might go wrong, possibilities of downward rather than upward, onward movement. There was no absolute mechanical guarantee for advancement, nothing to make improvement, as distinct from deterioration, a matter of course. Providence was there to give things the necessary direction, acting with the certainty of instinct in bee and bird, or of teleological law in an organism, whereby all the parts are constrained to serve the end for which the organism exists. Doubtless the universe is a very different thing

---

[1] In a restatement of the teleological argument, Professor Fraser expresses the above thought in these terms: 'Providential evolution of the universe . . . this rather than sudden creations, or interference with the Divine continuity of events in the providential evolution, becomes the Theistic conception of contrivance in nature, under the modern dynamical conception of the physical universe.' — *Gifford Lectures*, 2nd Series, p. 82.

from an organism like the eye or the human body. A cosmos, we call it, but it is a cosmos wherein multitudes of grotesque creatures may have appeared from time to time more fitted for a chaos than a cosmos. All sorts and forms of being, shapely and misshapen, may have come into existence, and only after innumerable experiments, eliminating the unsuitable, may the creatures worthy to survive have at last been hit upon. This may seem a wild supposition, but I make it that I may have an opportunity of saying that even in such a world of apparently endless fortuity, a providence, teleology, might prevail. There is plenty of the chance element in human history, yet we doubt not that through the ages one unceasing purpose runs. Providence and what we call chance are so far from being incompatible, that some thoughtful men have found in the realm of chance the theatre in which providence is more particularly displayed. 'Those unforeseen accidents,' writes Isaac Taylor, 'which so often control the lot of men, constitute a *superstratum* in the system of human affairs, wherein, peculiarly, the Divine Providence holds empire for the accomplishment of its special purposes. It is from this hidden and inexhaustible mine of chances — chances, as we must call them — that the Governor of the world draws, with unfathomable skill, the materials of his dispensations towards each individual of mankind.'[1] I do not emphasise this view. I quote the opinion simply to back the assertion that 'chance' and providence are not mutually exclusive. I for my part would rather seek traces of purpose in the region of law

History of Enthusiasm, pp. 117, 118.

than in the region of the lawless. Therefore I have no desire to find in the evolution of the world points at which one could say: See, here is a place at which, but for the miraculously guiding hand of Divine Providence, the evolutionary process might have gone wrong, leading the universe, not forward to man, but backward to chaos. There may have been such points, but I am nowise anxious to find them, any more than I am anxious to find points such as the origination of life, at which the *creative* hand of God was indispensable. Enough for me that in the orderly and the disorderly alike, in the necessary and in the accidental, in the law of heredity and in the caprice of variability, purpose, teleology, controlling aim was ever present and active, steadily moving on towards the great goal.

3. Our third inference was 'that the object of the purpose being man, the Being who purposes must be manlike.' The end, that is, explains not only the process of creation but the Creator. It was, we have seen, man in view as the far-off Divine event that gave the Creator an interest in the process, and helped Him, so to speak, to endure its wearisome toil and drudgery. Doth God care for fiery clouds, protozoa, 'dragons of the prime'? He cares for spirit and its endowments — reason, freedom, conscience. But that is as much as to say that He Himself is spirit. God, in short, is like man. Why not, it may be asked, like any other part of the universe? Why not like all parts? If the nature of a cause is to be inferred from the nature of its effects, must not God the cause of all be like all, not to say identical with all; a Being such as Pantheists con-

ceive? So argues Mr. Fiske, who follows Mr. Spencer in thinking that from the process of creation we can learn only *that* God is, not *what* He is.[1] In reply I say that our inference to the spirituality of God does not rest on the category of *causality*. As a cause God stands in the same relation to all beings, and so far as that goes He might be as like one being as another. Our inference is based on the category of *purpose*. Man is not merely one of the infinite number of effects produced by Divine causality, but he is the effect which explains all the rest, the end in view of the Creator in all His creative work. If this be allowed, then it must be admitted that man's relation to God is unique. It is a relation of affinity, because God, *ex hypothesi*, supremely cares for what man distinctively is.

Here I may be allowed to note in passing how far from being out of date is the view of man's relation to God presented in the Hebrew books. By abstaining from elaborate cosmogony, and confining attention to the purely religious aspect of the world, they offer a view which for simple dignity and essential truth leaves little to be desired. 'God said, Let us make man in our image.' This is a flash of direct insight, of inspiration, not an inference from scientific knowledge of the exact method of creation. It is, however, associated with the perception that man's place in the world is one of lordship. In both cases the Hebrew prophet, by religious intuition, grasped truths which our nineteenth century science has only confirmed. Man is lord, therefore man is Godlike: so teaches Genesis. For our

[1] *Outlines of Cosmic Theism*, vol. ii. p. 388.

purpose the statement has to be inverted: Man is lord, therefore God is manlike. The point that needs emphasising to-day is not that man is like God, but that God is like man. For it is God, His being and nature, that we desire to know, and we welcome any legitimate avenue to this high knowledge. And man's place in nature is accredited to us as our surest, if not sole, source of knowledge, teaching us not merely that God is, but more especially what He is: viz., that He is spirit like ourselves.

This doctrine has in its favour the *Consensus gentium*. Everywhere and always men have conceived their gods as manlike, *spirits*. Animism was the primitive religion. Much error has been associated with this fundamentally right thought; inevitably, however lamentably. The only cure for the error by which men have imputed to the Divine human passions and vices, is growth in the ethical ideal. The purification of religion keeps pace with the elevation of morality. From the abuses of the past we must not rush to the conclusion that the notion of God being like man is false, and that the great thing is to get rid of anthropomorphism, in Mr. Fiske's ponderous phrase, the 'deanthropomorphisation' of the idea of God. The *desideratum* rather is to conceive God not as like what man is, or has been at any stage in his mental and moral development, but as like what man will be when his development has reached its goal. There has been a rudimentary likeness all along, from the day when man became in the incipient degree *human*. From that day forth man was, however imperfectly, rational and moral; and when we say that

God is manlike we mean that God is a rational and moral being; and we say this because God's end in the creation was the production of a rational and moral being, like man.

4. Our last inference was 'that the purpose which aimed at bringing man on the scene will continue to work towards making the most of man.' It may be assumed that there will be something more to do. It would not be in accordance with the principle of evolution, and with the analogy of nature, if man were at the outset all that it is in him to be. Our expectation *a priori* would be that man, to begin with, was man only in germ, in skeleton, in outline, in fruitful possibility, rather than in realised fact. Assuming provisionally that such was the case, our position is that the Maker of man would be interested in the realising of the possibilities of man's nature, as a father is interested in the rearing of his child. He will not stop when He has reached the human; He will work on, cultivating to the utmost the humanities. He may rest when the creative process has reached the human stage, and say 'it is good,' but it will be only to make a new start in a rational and moral evolution incomparably more interesting and momentous than the physical evolution foregoing. We therefore expect to find traces of God in history, working as a just and beneficent Providence on the great scale and on the small. Hegel complains of a peddling view of Providence which recognises its action in individual life, but not among peoples, or in humanity at large, regarding history as a chaos, and the attempt to discover a plan there hopeless, not to say

presumptuous. Against this view he maintains that history is a rational process, and that it is competent and incumbent to seek in the world a design which shall enable us to comprehend evil and reconcile the thinking spirit with its existence.[1] One cannot but sympathise with the great philosopher's attitude, though the task he undertook may be more difficult than even he imagined. Perfect rationality it may be as impossible to find in history, as it is to find perfect morality. But that history is wholly chaotic, without even drift or tendency towards the true and the good, who can believe? If darkness broods over the scene, there is at least light shining in the darkness.

[1] *The Philosophy of History,* Bohn's translation, p. 14.

LECTURE IV

NON-MORAL DEITY, OR THE GODS OF MODERN PESSIMISM

BEFORE proceeding to the verification of the hypothesis of a just, beneficent Providence in history, enunciated at the close of last lecture, we are to consider the main sources of doubt, as indicated in the first lecture. The first of these is, views of God incompatible with an ethical world-aim; conceptions of God as a non-moral deity *below* caring for man, and the interests man as a moral personality represents. This is the theme of our present lecture.

It is needless to spend time in showing that a rational and moral world-aim is excluded by Materialism, for which the only possible divinity is the pantheon of eternally existent atoms capable by their motions and combinations of producing a universe. For the Materialist, as we saw, thought, consciousness, is only a curious phenomenon, a *lusus naturae*, a sort of phosphorescent light thrown off by brain tissue, a thing possessing no causative virtue, to be entirely discounted in explaining the physical universe, and wholly unworthy to be the chief end for which the world exists. So contemptuous an attitude towards the rational and moral is not indeed assumed by all Materialists.

Strauss is a conspicuous exception. He held that though the world did not proceed from reason, it is nevertheless on the march towards the highest reason; and contains traces at once of a rational, an æsthetic, and a moral order which demand a worshipful recognition not less earnest and reverential than that which the Theist offers to his God. In this respect the author of *The Old and the New Faith* was certainly better than his theory.

Our present concern is with men who really believe in a God, and in a God endowed with mental attributes, yet not in a God for whom moral distinctions and interests possess significance. I have in view chiefly the German philosophical representatives and advocates of modern pessimism who have introduced some strange new divinities as the objects of a pessimistic cult. Spinoza was no pessimist, and if I make a brief preliminary reference to his idea of God, it is not without apology for placing him in so inferior and uncongenial company, and simply as an aid towards the better understanding of the metaphysical nature of a type of deity so foreign to our habits of thought that we can with difficulty imagine anybody taking it in earnest.

The God of Spinoza, then, is the One self-existent, absolute Substance out of which all being flows in two parallel but non-communicating streams of things which are extended, and things which think. The primal substance possesses the attributes of both these classes of things. God is matter and has extension, he is mind and thinks. But God's thought is not like human thought. The Divine intellect resembles the human only in name, not otherwise than the celestial sign of the dog resembles the animal called dog which barks. Yet it remains the fact that Spinoza does ascribe to the absolute substance intellect in some sense, and likewise will, and assigns to these attributes a function in the production of the universe. But not in a sense that can satisfy Theists. For Spinoza's deity produces all things without aim, as if his will were an uninformed blind unconscious force. Design, purpose, teleology, has no place in the universe. But this does not imply that the universe is a blundering, imperfect piece of work. Spinoza has no fault to find with the world. Let the fact be noted, for herein he differs utterly from the more recent philosophers to be hereafter spoken of. He thinks the world, as it is, perfect. Whatever is real is perfect; reality and perfection are the same thing. But is not there much evil, as we call it, in the world; physical evil, moral evil, bad men, fools? Yes, doubtless, replies the imperturbable philosopher, but it takes all that exists to make a world, and everything that exists has its reason of existence, its own place, and is good in its place. God produced all that His infinite intellect was able to conceive, without choice, by necessity, therefore bad men as well as good men, fools as well as sages. This implies, of course, that moral distinctions have no reality for God, and Spinoza makes no pretence of thinking to the contrary. God, he teaches, has no resentment against the evil and foolish, seeing he brought them into existence. And men, he thinks, should imitate God in this respect, and take the evil of all sorts in the world with philosophic calmness, not vexing themselves because so much sin and sorrow exists. They should neither approve the good nor disapprove the bad, nor indulge in morbid sympathy with human suffering. He who rightly understands that all things follow from the necessity of the Divine nature and happen according to the eternal laws of nature, will find nothing worthy of hatred, mockery, or contempt, nor will he commiserate any one, but as far as lies in his power he will endeavour to live jollily, as they say, and to be glad. Thus Spinoza is as remote as can be from the mood of modern pessimism. He is a thoroughgoing optimist, having for his motto, Whatever is, is good. Merging the ethical in the physical in his conception both of Deity and of human nature, he is content with things as they are, and looks on philanthropic schemes for the amelioration of the world as illusory.

Elaborate criticism on the Spinozan idea of God is unnecessary. It obviously excludes a providential order in any real valuable sense. Spinoza's God is simply *natura naturans*, nature blindly working without cease in the production of the things which make up the sum of being; eternally creating without consciousness and without purpose. Of course this deity is indifferent to moral distinctions, yet it (we cannot properly say 'He') is not on that account to be blamed as if it were immoral. It is simply non-moral, acting without knowing what it is doing. Whether men, imitating this deity by a habit of moral indifference, would be equally blameless is another question. The temper of Spinoza was that of the Stoic. As the mood of one whose lot was hard, it may be regarded with indulgence, but when deliberately cherished as the model frame of mind, and commended to others as the final lesson of the highest wisdom, it cannot be too energetically repudiated. The nobler mood is surely that which cannot reconcile itself to evil, especially to moral evil, which hates it and fights it wherever it meets it, which believes that it can be successfully fought in the individual and in the race, and is ever ready to sacrifice life in the heroic warfare. But this ethical temper needs the support of faith in an ethical God.

In classing *Schopenhauer* among the setters forth of strange, non-moral deities, I am aware that I should speak more exactly, if I represented him as one who believes in no God at all. He is an Atheist rather than a Theist, or even a Pantheist, of any known type. With Pantheists, as he tells us, he has in common 'the one and all' (ἓν καὶ πᾶν), but not the one as *God* (πᾶν θεός). His 'one and all' is the will (*Wille*), and will is the essence of the world rather than a god. Yet Schopenhauer's will takes the place assigned to God in other systems. It is the ultimate reality, the thing in itself, the source of all things, that of which the world we know is the mental representation.

This will, Schopenhauer's substitute for Deity, takes the place of extension in the system of Spinoza, the material attribute of the absolute substance. Schopenhauer follows recent science in conceiving *force* as the essence of matter, and the ultimate principle in the universe. Adopting that view, he identifies the force which, under various forms, works everywhere in the universe, with *will*, that is with the form of force of which we are conscious in ourselves, and which we are accustomed to call will-power. This extension of the term he justifies by a poetic simile. If the first morning-dawn shares with the rays of full midday the name of sunlight, why should not every form of force — mechanical, chemical, electric, bear the same name as that we employ to denote the highest type of energy, that which in the light of conscious thought is guided by an aim?

Nothing is gained for Theism by this adoption of a spiritual designation for the power everywhere at work in the universe. The imposing generalisation does not level up cosmic force to the human, but levels down human will-force to the cosmic. The will of which Schopenhauer sees traces everywhere is blind, mindless. Spinoza endowed his absolute substance with thought as well as with extension; Schopenhauer drops the former attribute from his conception of the ultimate reality, viewing mind as purely phenomenal and accidental, having no part in the inner essence of things. The omnipresent will of which the world is the objectification is a dark, restless, resistless striving towards existence whereof the actual universe of being is the result. How there came to be such a blind Titanic force our philosopher does not pretend to know. There it is; and *hence all our woes*.

For, in the opinion of Schopenhauer, the existence of the world is a pure and unmitigated calamity. It would have been infinitely better had there been no will to exist, or if it had never left the rest of the 'blessed nothing.' Why so; why should the world be so bad; why should existence be a calamity? Because, replies our philosopher, the basis of all will is need, want; hence pain, the pain of unsatisfied desire, inherent in desire, inseparable from it in human experience. Will and pain are close companions wherever, as in man, there is capacity for feeling pain. There is no pain in rocks, or so far as we know, in plants, because there the condition of its existence, feeling, is wanting. Pain comes in with animal life, and the higher the type of animal the more acute the pain. Therefore man, at the head of the animal creation, is the great sufferer, and among men the man of genius has the honour to be the most miserable of beings. Pain, the great fact in human life, — such is the dismal gospel of this new philosophy, — pain, the only permanent and positive element in our experience. Pleasure, fleeting and negative, a momentary gratification resulting from the satisfaction of desire; pain not to be escaped from even by the removal of wants, a life without objects of desire being a life of utter emptiness and insufferable *ennui*.

At this point the contrast between Spinoza and Schopenhauer is great. If, as we saw, Spinoza is an optimist, Schopenhauer is a pessimist of the extreme type. If the temper of the earlier philosopher is cheerful, that of the later is despairing. Correspondingly different are their respective practical philosophies. The counsel of the one being: 'Live jollily,' that of the other is: 'Reduce life to a minimum, extirpate desire, restrain the will to live, enter on the narrow way of asceticism.' In short, as John the Baptist was Elijah reappearing, Schopenhauer is the sage of ancient India, Buddha, *redivivus*. For both, the one path of escape from the misery of the world is renunciation. According to Schopenhauer this is not only our sole refuge, but our highest *duty*. Resignation! behold the final goal, the inmost essence of all virtue and sanctity, and the true means of redemption from the world. If we neglect to follow this course, what was to begin with our misfortune becomes our sin, and the misery we suffer becomes its penalty. The will to live is immoral, and the pain it inevitably entails is its just punishment. And so it comes to pass that there is in the world an eternal righteousness asserting itself not in any uncertain, hesitating, blundering way, but firmly, surely, and infallibly rendering unto every man according to his work. Therefore it is the imperative behest of wisdom to renounce the will to live. But why stop there; why merely subdue the will to live and to enjoy life; why not put an end to life outright and be done with this sorry existence? Because, replies Schopenhauer, suicide differs most widely from the denial of the will to live. Far from being denial of the will, it is a strong assertion of will. The suicide wills life, and is only dissatisfied with the conditions under which it has presented itself to him. He thus surrenders not the will to live, but life, because it is not to his mind. The true surrender is that which shuns not the sorrows of life merely but its joys. Therefore live on, but live as the hermit, as one dead to the world, indifferent to its pleasures, and hence free from its pains, from the torments which visit all who give full rein to desire.[1]

What now is to be said of this strange, dismal philosophy which saw the light in the beginning of the present century? In the first place, that whether we like it or not, it is one of the theories of the universe open to our choice if we cease to believe in Theism. It is always well to have a clear perception of the alternatives. If then we abandon a theistic view of the world, *i.e.* faith in an *ethical* God, this is one of the revival views which to-day compete for the vacant place in our creed. I imagine the feeling of most of us will be that we had better bear the ills we have than fly to others that we know not of. Better try again to construe the world on theistic principles, however hard the task, than find in Schopenhauer's *Wille* the key to all mysteries. But this is a mere *praejudicium;* thorough thinkers desire to know what is to be said of this theory on its merits. I cannot here go fully into this matter, but I may venture to make two remarks. The question may very legitimately be asked, in the first place: By what right is the action of the law of cohesion in molecules, or of the law of gravitation in the planetary system, identified in essence with that of the human will? And secondly, supposing that identification be allowed, why should will in any of its manifestations be dissociated from intelligence? Why must the world-will, except in the case of men, be blind? Why should wisdom, reason, not be everywhere, as well

[1] *Die Welt als Wille und Vorstellung*, vol. i. p. 471. Haldane's translation, vol. i. p. 514.

as will, working in concert with it, directing its energy, so that it shall not blindly produce a world that had better not have been, but rather give rise to a veritable *cosmos?* In wise men will-power associated with reason takes the beneficent form of self-restraint. Why should not the ultimate reality be a will of this kind, not content with producing existence of any sort, but aiming at a world that could be pronounced good.?

Our verdict on the pessimistic philosophy of Schopenhauer must ultimately rest not on speculative but on empirical grounds. It is an attempt at a theoretical justification of radical discontent with the world as it is. Its method is avowedly inductive. It starts from the facts of outer and inner experience and tries to find their *rationale*. The real question therefore is, Has the author of the theory under consideration read the facts truly, or has he looked on them with jaundiced eyes? Is the world as bad as he makes it; is human life as miserable as he represents it to be? That is a jury question on which every one is able to form a more or less intelligent opinion. It is not a question for philosophers only; the common man may without presumption answer it for himself, and his judgment may be sounder than that of the philosopher. There is not much room for doubt that the particular philosopher called Schopenhauer has judged very unsoundly. His indictment against the world and against human life is a gross exaggeration, in which the personal equation plays a great part. It is a good instance of the 'vigour and rigour' to which, according to the late Mr. Matthew Arnold, German theorists in general are prone. It is a

THE GODS OF MODERN PESSIMISM

good instance also illustrative of an observation made by Max Nordau in his work on *Degeneracy*, that philosophic systems simply furnish the excuses reason demands for the unconscious impulses of the race during a given period of time.[1] In this country most men may be content with the unconscious impulse, not troubling themselves about the defensive theory, but in Germany they cannot live without a theory. The pessimistic mood is widely prevalent at present, how widely may be guessed from the extensive circulation of Hartmann's ponderous volume on the *Philosophy of the Unconscious*. In his lectures on anti-theistic theories, Dr. Flint expresses the fear that the disease will spread in this country, and confesses despondency as to the prospect of its soon passing away.[2] Probably his apprehensions are well founded. In any case the question raised by this pessimistic literature is one of present urgency and undoubted importance, on which it behoves all thoughtful men to make up their minds. It is the question, What is the worth of life? This topic will occupy our attention in next lecture.

The philosophy of Hartmann is a much more elaborate, plausible, and attractive scheme of thought than that of Schopenhauer. His idea of God is a great improvement compared with the crude repulsive conception of the earlier philosopher. He sees no reason for making the Deity a Being of one attribute. To Schopenhauer's will he adds intellect, thus reverting to the position of Spinoza, who assigned to the absolute substance the two attributes of thought and extension.

[1] P. 416.   [2] P. 292.

But, for Hartmann, intellect in God is much more of a reality than it was for Spinoza, who, as we saw, held that intellect in God is no more like intellect in man than the dogstar is like a dog, and that all thought, in so far as real, is to be found only in men. Hartmann endows the Divine intellect with a liberal allowance of marvellous attributes. It has clear sight (*Hellsehen*) and foresight; it is omniscient and all-wise; it is infallible — without hesitation, without need of reflection, without fatigue perceiving the true and the fit; it exercises an unsleeping providence over the universe, using every natural cause as a means for its great designs, and exercising its care not merely over the whole, but over every individual part however minute, being omnipresent as well as omniscient. This looks very like the God of Theism; there is, however, one outstanding point of difference. The intellect of God, as compared with that of man, is *unconscious*. But when all the achievements of the 'Unconscious' are considered, it almost seems as if the lack of consciousness were an advantage rather than a defect. Hartmann, indeed, distinctly claims that it is, and represents the clear-seeing intelligence of the unconscious Supreme, with its eye infallibly fixed on its aims, and eternally grasping, in one view, all aims, means, and necessary conditions, as infinitely superior to the lame, heavy tread of conscious discursive reflection obliged to tend to one thing at a time, and dependent on perception, memory, and occasional inspirations.[1] He puts upon the unconscious thought of the Great Spirit the stamp of superiority

[1] *Philosophie des Unbewussten*, p. 536.

THE GODS OF MODERN PESSIMISM 83

by calling it *superconscious*, and virtually asks Theists what they have to complain of if he offers them a Being who, while unconscious, possesses an omniscient, all-wise, superconscious intelligence which teleologically determines the content of the creation of the world-process.[1] Certainly if that were all the difference between his idea of God and that of Theism, there would not be any very serious ground of quarrel. But that is not the only or the chief point of divergence, as we shall see in due course.

Before we come to that, however, it may be well to linger for a few moments over this new name for Deity, *The Unconscious*, that we may familiarise ourselves a little with the grounds on which it rests. In Hartmann's pages it appears as the final result of an elaborate inductive inquiry carried on throughout all departments of nature. This inquiry ought to appeal fully as much to men of science as to theologians, both because of its inductive method, and because of its extensive exhibition of scientific facts which they alone can duly control and appreciate. Hartmann finds traces of unconscious thought everywhere, and specially in the body and in the soul of man. In the body: in physical functions, in reflex action, in the healing power, in the formation of organs, in the instincts which play so extensive a part in the lower animal world. In the soul: in sexual love, in artistic feeling and production, in the origin of language, in thought, in the perceptions of the senses, in the history of the human race. In the former region the facts are

[1] *Philosophie des Unbewussten*, p. 537.

not to be accounted for, Hartmann thinks, by merely mechanical action. There is teleology, action with an aim unconsciously conceived; markedly so, *e.g.*, in the case of instincts, really so in all cases. The thought of the end to be accomplished is not in our brain or consciousness, but it is there all the same, in the part concerned, or rather in the mind of the great Unconscious. As regards the spiritual region, I have already, in a previous lecture, had occasion to refer to Hartmann's theory of the action of unconscious thought in connection with the origin of language. I need not repeat what I said then, nor do I deem it necessary to go into any further detail, though some of the illustrations are very tempting, *e.g.* those drawn from the traces of inspiration in human thought, and of unconscious prescience in human history. With reference to the last-named sphere, Hartmann quotes with approval words of Schiller which speak of a far-reaching vision which sees long before whither the freedom of man is being led in the bonds of necessity, and how the self-seeking aims of individuals are unconsciously tending towards the service of the whole.[1] How far he is right in such views is not at present the question. What we are now concerned with is to understand his way of thinking.

Unconscious thought sporadically present in all parts of the world, accessible to observation, is supposed to be proved by this elaborate inductive process. Granting that the thesis has been established, what then? Does the process of proof justify the application of the epithet unconscious to one being, to God? Not, certainly, as

[1] Page 342.

a matter of course, and of that Hartmann is well aware. He thinks it necessary to lead proof that the sporadic manifestations of the unconscious all coalesce in an ultimate unity, and that the unconsciousness is not merely in the human subject but in that ultimate unity. The ultimate unity is God, and the unconsciousness of the ultimate unity means that God is without consciousness.

An unconscious Deity — is such a conception of sinister significance for the world? In view of the other attributes ascribed to the Deity one would say, No. Yet Hartmann is a pessimist, if not of so truculent a type as Schopenhauer, still a decided and thoroughgoing one. How does the pessimism come in? Just as it came in in the case of Schopenhauer, *from experience*. Hartmann, like Schopenhauer, is thoroughly discontented with the actual world, and he shapes his philosophy to square with the supposed facts. Hence two supplementary propositions, hitherto unnoticed, concerning his unconscious, yet in other respects well-endowed, Divinity. The great unconscious One has no regard to *morality*, and in the origination of the universe only His *will*, not His intellect, was active; so that, though he knows well what he is doing in the world as it actually exists, he did not know what he was doing when he made it. In our philosopher's judgment, if the Creator had known what he was doing, he would not have made the world, for he would have known, as Hartmann knows, that all possible worlds are bad, our world, though the best possible, as Leibnitz maintained, being no exception.

That morality has no significance for God is not an

obiter dictum in Hartmann's system. The position finds frequent expression in the *Philosòphie des Unbewussten*. Thus in one place it is stated that the predicates, moral and immoral, are creations of consciousness, and do not belong to the Unconscious, and that nature so far as unconscious does not know moral distinctions.[1] Elsewhere we find such statements as these: Morality and righteousness have significance only from the standpoint of individuation, *i.e.* they belong only to the world of appearance.[2] Pleasure and pain are wholly real, and the Unconscious is the common subject of them, feeling them in the collective individual consciousness; on the other hand, morality and righteousness are simply ideas of consciousness. Morality and righteousness, as such, cannot be aims in the world-process — they can at most only be secondary aims in subordination to the higher aim of happiness. Immorality (resulting from egoism) is an unavoidable evil without which individual existence is impossible; therefore the demand for a direct Divine interest in righteousness is a theological mistake, which for the sake of a wholly insignificant advantage would continually throw the world out of the groove of its laws.[3]

It thus appears that, in the judgment of Hartmann, morality, righteousness, as such, has no independent value for God. In a world admittedly full of teleology, the moral interest, which theologians have been accustomed to esteem worthy to be the *supreme* end, has no place at all as an end, or at most a quite subordinate place. The great unconscious Being, in-

[1] Pp. 230, 232. [2] P. 639. [3] P. 641.

deed, is more interested in immorality than in morality, for immorality springs out of egoism, and egoism, selfishness, the struggle for existence, is inseparable from individuation. These views are revolting enough, but time need not be wasted in giving expression to pious horror. What I am concerned to point out here is the sinister influence which the doctrines enunciated must exercise on our estimate of the evil that is in the world. They shut us up to pessimism by depriving us of the best means of explaining evil, I mean physical evil — suffering, sorrow, pain. We can no longer say, even in the broadest sense, that physical evil is to be understood in the light of moral evil, and to be regarded, at least in many cases, as its penalty. This theistic theory implies that the moral interest is, for the Ruler of the world, supreme, and that physical evil, to any extent, is abundantly justified when it can be shown to be subservient to the great ethical world-aim. If, as Hartmann declares, this theory be false, then our whole Theodicy falls to the ground.[1]

So much for the dogma that the Unconscious has no regard to morality. Hartmann teaches, further, that the world was created by will unguided by intellect. Hence, we are to understand, it came that there is a world. If intellect had been consulted it would have interdicted creation. It could not have helped to make

[1] A position similar to that of Hartmann seems to be taken up by Mr. Bradley in his recent work, *Appearance and Reality*. 'The absolute,' he tells us (p. 533), 'is not personal, nor is it moral, nor is it beautiful or true.' *Vide* a criticism of this work by Professor Seth in *Man's Place in the Cosmos*.

the world created a better one. The world is as good as it can be, nevertheless it is very bad. All possible worlds are bad; a universe of manifold existence is inherently evil. It embraces among its forms of being *men*, which means a world full of sin and misery. The one redeeming feature in this dark and dismal state of things is that men are *conscious*. The chief use and final cause of consciousness is to find out the true condition of the world, its inherent and incurable vanity; and, when the discovery has become universal — all men, in some distant generation, convinced that life is not worth living — to bring the world to an end by simultaneous suicide, involving the Unconscious and all his works in a common ruin. The discovery is necessarily a slow process. But be of good cheer, we are already well on the way; certain well-known illusions lie behind us, and if we be still subject to other illusions, it cannot be very long till the dawn of disillusionment arrive. Our redemption draweth nigh.

The history of the world, according to our philosopher, is the history of illusions successively blinding men's minds for generations, then at length found out and abandoned. All forms of illusion have reference to the attainment of *happiness*. Three stages have to be passed through before the final truth is known. The first stage is the idea that happiness is attainable in this earthly life by each individual. Such was the belief of the Jewish, Greek, and Roman world. The experiment was thoroughly tried, and the result, general insight into the truth proclaimed by the preacher, 'All is vanity.' That it could not be otherwise our author tries to show by a detailed examination of all possible sources of pleasure: health, youth, freedom, family, friendship, honour, religion, morality, immorality, science, art, hope. The second stage of illusion is the idea that happiness is attainable by the individual in a transcendent life after death. This belief gained currency through the Christian religion, which arrived on the historic stage just when it was needed to rescue the old Pagan world from the deep disgust at life into which it had fallen, when its eyes had been opened to the illusory character of all happiness in this sublunary scene. The new belief was very good as an *interim;* it gave fresh zest to life as long as men could accept it as the truth. But now Christianity is pretty well played out. It dies hard, doubtless. Few have the courage to say openly they are done with it. Even Kant, Hegel, and Schelling tried to persuade themselves that the Christian faith was theirs. Among the faithless only one has been faithful — courageous enough to break finally with the religion of heavenly hope — Schopenhauer. But, we are assured, he is the pioneer showing the way all must sooner or later go. Secular energy steadily gains the upper hand, Antichrist spreads all around, and soon Christianity will be but the shadow of its mediæval greatness, and become once more what it was at its origin, the last consolation of the poor and sorrowladen.[1]

And what next? Yet another final stage of the illusion: the idea that happiness will be realised in the future of the world-process. This is now the faith

[1] P. 728.

coming into fashion, the natural accompaniment of the theory of evolution. 'The life of man,' so the Time-spirit whispers in the ears of our generation, 'has been bad in the past, it is bad enough still, and as for the hope of heaven it is a dream. But, courage! things are steadily mending; there is an immanent development going on which must issue sooner or later in an improved condition of social life, and in a higher standard of morality. Let this hope be your comfort under personal disappointment, your *succedaneum* for a vanished heaven, your stimulus to exertion in the generous work of hastening on the good time coming.' The author of the philosophy of the Unconscious is sorry to find himself in a minority of one here. He does not believe in the good time coming, in a heaven ahead of us, any more than in a heaven above us. He does not expect either social or moral improvement in the distant future. Culture will not bring contentment, nor will immorality diminish. There will be no improvement even in science and art. The future will give us, instead of geniuses, respectable mediocrities. He does not expect, he does not even wish, people to accept this unpleasant forecast. Let the illusion last as long as it can. He even expresses a pious belief in a Providence which will take care that the anticipations of the quiet thinker shall not disturb the course of history by gaining premature currency. Nevertheless, the modern prophet of pessimism has full faith in his solitary vision. It will come true, though fulfilment may tarry. Slowly, reluctantly, men generally will be forced at last to admit that this late-born hope is also an illusion. And then?

The long reign of illusion ended, mankind, not this man or that man, but humanity at large, will sigh for absolute painlessness, nothingness, Nirvana, annihilation.

Such is the attempt made by Eduard von Hartmann to provide modern pessimism with the support of a speculative theory. Whatever one may think of its truth or tendency it were unjust and ungenerous to withhold the praise due to ingenuity, vivid presentation, and unflinching audacity. But we cannot afford to leave the matter there. Vague, evasive commendation must not take the place of wholesome criticism. It is necessary to come to terms with pessimistic philosophers, that we may know just how we stand. A few critical observations, therefore, may fitly close this lecture.

1. My first observation is, that if there be truth in pessimism, some such philosophy as this must be forthcoming as its theoretical substructure. Every dominant mood of feeling, or prevailing way of life, implies a congruous theory of the universe. Therefore you cannot afford to laugh, or be shocked, at the philosophy, and yet indulge in a pessimistic mood. If you will think out your position to its last consequences, this or something like it, something possibly worse, is what you must come to. You must believe not in *no* God, but in a *bad* God, in a God with a will without intelligence, or with intelligence and without morality. The universe, left to the action of its own mechanical forces, without a God to guide them, need not come out so bad as the pessimist finds it. Strauss was a materialistic Atheist, but he believed, nevertheless, that the

world is good, and that in it is being realised more and more a threefold order of reason, beauty, and goodness. It needs a God like that conceived by Schopenhauer or Hartmann to make a world as bad as the present world is supposed to be. Therefore, if the Deity offered to faith be unacceptable, the pessimist will do well to subject his view of life to careful revision.

2. I am not disposed to make it my chief ground of quarrel with Hartmann that he represents his Deity as *unconscious*. I do not think, indeed, that the epithet is duly grounded, but if it pleases the author it may be allowed to pass as, *in itself*, comparatively innocuous. The adoption of this attribute as the most appropriate designation of the Divine Being is simply a conceit. Unconsciousness may be a characteristic of Deity, but it can hardly be the most important one. To those who are unfamiliar with the idea of unconscious thought, it may well appear impossible to understand how it can have any place among the attributes of a Being admitted to be intelligent. If it be an absurdity, however, it is not quite an original one on Hartmann's part. He has had predecessors here, as he is careful to point out, including among them Leibnitz, Kant, and Hegel, to the first named of whom he gives the credit of having communicated to him the first impulse to the investigations whereof the *Philosophy of the Unconscious* is the fruit. He might have gone even further back in quest of sanction for his pet idea. It finds a place in the ancient philosophies of China and Greece. Yang and Yin, the root principles of the universe, in the philosophy of China,

work without consciousness, producing effects in which are embodied the highest reason. In his *Intellectual System of the Universe*, Cudworth shows that the conception was not unfamiliar to the ancient Greek philosophers. The plastic force of nature, which he borrows from them, and discourses on at great length, is pretty much the same thing as Hartmann's Unconscious. The one like the other acts without 'express συναίσθησις, con-sense, or consciousness of what it doth';[1] it is a 'drowsy, unawakened, or astonished cogitation.'[2] Yet it works with all the ease, skill, and certainty which Hartmann claims for his Unconscious. 'Whereas human artists are often to seek and at a loss, and therefore consult and deliberate, as also upon second thoughts mend their former work; nature, on the contrary, is never to seek what to do, nor at a stand,' 'it never consults nor deliberates, never repents nor goes about, as it were, upon second thoughts, to alter and mend its former course.'[3] In one point only Cudworth differs from Hartmann. He does not commit the mistake of confounding the plastic force of nature with God. He conceives it simply as an instrument in the hands of a Being endowed with a perfect mind. Any other view he regards as monstrous. To make *ratio mersa et confusa*, a reason drowned in matter, and confounded with it, the supreme governor of the world is, he thinks, 'to invert the order of the universe, and hang the picture of the world, as of a man, with his heels upwards.'[4] 'If,'

[1] Vol. i. p. 343.
[2] Vol. i. p. 345.
[3] Vol. i. pp. 334, 335.
[4] Vol. i. pp. 353, 372.

he argues, 'there be a Φύσις, then there must be a Νοῦς: if there be a plastic nature, that acts regularly and artificially in order to ends, and according to the best wisdom, though itself not comprehending the reason of it, nor being clearly conscious of what it doth; then there must of necessity be a perfect mind or intellect, that is, a Deity, upon which it depends.'[1]

But be this as it may. Hartmann's Unconscious may or may not be an absurdity, with the additional drawback of being a stale absurdity revived; it is in any case by itself, as already indicated, an innocuous absurdity. The unconsciousness of Deity is not responsible for the pessimism of the system. This is apparent from the contrast at this point between Hartmann and Hegel. I suppose we may admit that Hartmann was entitled to claim Hegel as one of his forerunners in ascribing unconsciousness to Deity. In Hegel's system the Absolute Spirit is unconscious to begin with, and reaches consciousness only in man. But Hegel was no pessimist; on the contrary, his view of the world was pronouncedly optimistic, the *real* being for him the *rational*, and the trend of history being steadily towards the realisation of the moral ideal. For Hegel the divine and human are identical, the human the perfect revelation of the divine; and if in the idea of the human, reason seems to receive undue prominence, it is not a reason divorced from, or indifferent to, *morality*.

3. This last remark leads up to the damning sin of Hartmann's philosophy. It treats immorality as a

[1] Vol. i. p. 371.

necessary accompaniment of individual life subject to the supreme law of the struggle for existence, and offers us a Deity for whom moral interests are of no account. The former of these positions is a cynical assumption; the latter is speculatively unjustified. Why, it may be asked, should morality not be an end for Deity? Hartmann complains of Schopenhauer for conceiving of the ultimate principle as mere will without intelligence. May we not with equal right complain of him for conceiving of the ultimate principle as will plus intelligence but minus morality? Both alike are wrong, if man is to be the chief source of our knowledge of God. Schopenhauer remarks that since the oldest times it has been customary to speak of man as a *microcosm*, a little world; but that he has inverted the thesis and exhibited the world as a *macranthropos*, a large man.[1] He has done this very imperfectly, even if the inventory of human endowment were exhausted by the two words, '*Wille*,' '*Vorstellung*,' will and thought. Still more imperfect is his account of the universe if to will and thought be added conscience as an essential element of human nature. Hartmann does far more justice to the second ingredient, thought, but he is equally at fault in reference to the third, conscience. I fear the reason of this neglect in both cases is that neither philosopher takes this highest element in earnest. This criticism applies with special emphasis to Hartmann. The carnal man is for him the *normal* man. Man, in his view, is simply a hungry animal constantly hunting after enjoyment, bent evermore on giving effect to the will to

[1] *Die Welt als Wille und Vorstellung*, vol. ii. p. 739.

live and to live happily, pursuing this aim at all hazards, and by all means, reckless of the evil consequences that may result to others. Baffled in one direction he seeks happiness in another. Discovering that happiness for himself is unattainable in any direction, by an instinct of sympathy he hopes that at some future time his fellow-men will be more fortunate, and when at last he clearly discerns that neither here nor hereafter, neither in the present age nor in any future age, can happiness be more than a dream, he makes the grave proposal to the assembled human race: 'Brothers in misery, let us together leave this wretched world, and make one sublime simultaneous plunge into the eternal dark.'

4. On the alleged illusoriness of life something will be said in another lecture. Meantime this criticism of Hartmann's philosophy may wind up with one additional observation on his conception of a non-moral Deity. Hartmann believes in inspiration. He discovers traces of the Unconscious at work in the thoughts and productions of men of genius: poets, musicians, and the like. What of Hebrew prophets, and kindred spirits among other peoples? Were they too not inspired, if not with an exceptional or exclusive type of inspiration, at least with an inspiration of a very real kind? But what was the burden of their prophecies? *Righteousness*, the moral order of the world. God asserting His presence in human affairs as a just, beneficent power. Have their sublime utterances on these great themes no objective truth or value? If they have, then are they true messages from God,

true revelations of God, intimations that He does care for righteousness, that He cares for nothing more, that for Him righteousness is the supreme interest in this world. This faith concerning God, the wisest and best men in all ages have cherished. All things considered, it is a better creed than that offered to us in the name of modern pessimism. Many of us are familiar with Richter's famous dream, in which a universe without God appeared as an eye-socket with the eye taken out of it. It is a hideous picture. But there is something more hideous: an eye-socket with an eye in it, fixing on you the demoniac gaze of raving madness. It is the frenzied eye of the pessimist's divinity.

But why, do you ask, turn upon us this evil eye, to haunt us in our dreams? Such deities as you have spoken of, no English mind, even though pessimistically inclined, could so much as imagine, far less seriously propose for the acceptance of the world. Why not leave these pessimistic deities to receive such homage as they can command from the speculative Teutonic intellect that gave them birth? It is too late to speak of this. We are not so insulated in our spiritual situation as many wish. The new gods are already known to our younger thinkers, some of whom are devoting themselves with religious ardour to the propagation of belief in them. Besides, the pessimistic temper is infectious, and spreads like a spiritual influenza. An antidote is needed, and knowledge of what it all comes to may serve the purpose. I want to compel practical pessimists to think a little on the theoretic presuppositions of their pet mood. The ultimate question is:

Is the Being at the heart of this universe good, or is He evil? Blind will, or benignant will; non-moral intelligence, or wisdom allied with righteousness — which is it to be? 'If the Lord be God, follow Him; but if Baal, then follow him.'[1]

[1] 1 Kings xviii. 21.

LECTURE V

THE WORTH OF LIFE

In last lecture we saw that the gods of pessimism are theoretical inventions to account for a bad world. The question now therefore naturally arises: Is the world as bad as it is called?

The problem, What is the worth of life? has only recently taken a prominent place in the reflective thought of philosophers and moralists. This fact of itself is almost sufficient to justify the suspicion that modern pessimists have, under some unhappy influence, fallen into gross exaggeration; and that their type of thought is properly to be regarded as a morbid phenomenon, a kind of *fin du siècle* disease, for which a physician, rather than a refutation, is wanted. Thus viewed, it doubtless has its causes, not merely in the idiosyncrasies of individuals, but in tendencies of the age which it might be instructive to investigate. Of course the disease, if we may without disrespect call it such, is not absolutely new; few diseases physical or mental are. Like the recent scourge of influenza, it is an old disease revived in a malignant form, as old indeed as the time of Buddha. Yet antiquity does not alter its character, or give it the right to assume airs of authority. We may dare to form our own independent estimate of the world, and we must strive to do so as sanely, soundly, and unbiassedly as possible. This, however, is no easy task. We are all apt to find what we bring. We are all more or less the children of our time. In the eighteenth century it was difficult to be anything but an extreme optimist; at the end of the nineteenth century it is perhaps as difficult to be an optimist even of the mildest type. Our judgment is liable to variation with age, health, experience. The same man may be a pessimist in youth, and an optimist in feeling and tendency in advancing years. 'Age,' says Hegel, 'generally makes men more tolerant; youth is always discontented. The tolerance of age is the result of the ripeness of a judgment which, not merely as the result of indifference, is satisfied even with what is inferior; but, more deeply taught by the grave experience of life, has been led to perceive the substantial solid worth of the object in question.'[1] The state of health makes a difference in our estimates as great as that between a cloudless and a clouded sky. A youth diseased in body and morbid in mind visits a particular part of the country and finds it a bleak, flat, treeless plain. He revisits it forty years later, and, to his surprise, discovers that during all that time he has been under a delusion, and that the tabooed spot is neither bleak, nor flat, nor treeless. This is a parable from impressions of physical nature teaching the possibility of a similar experience in the moral world.

The truth here, as so often elsewhere, lies between

[1] *Philosophy of History*, Bohn's translation, p. 37.

two extremes. Unqualified optimism is as false as unqualified pessimism. By the law of reaction the one tends to produce the other. Given a deistic optimism in one century, you may expect as a matter of course a cynical atheistic pessimism in the next. The synthesis of the true elements in both makes the nearest approach to the reality of things. It can therefore serve no purpose, simply to ignore, laugh at, or denounce sombre views of the world, and in particular of human life. We must take them seriously and deal with them wisely. The first thing we have to do is to lay to heart the fact that *Ethical Agnosticism* prevails. By that phrase I mean scepticism as to the reality of a moral order in the world, or of a Providence steadily directed to the realisation of the right and the good, based on the confusion observable in the world suggestive of the reign of chance, blind fate, or even of diabolic will, rather than of a benignant, righteous, gracious God. It is a significant symptom of widespread tendency when this pessimistic mood reveals itself in the literature of fiction, the chief intellectual pabulum of the million. In how many minds must the cynical, sinister phrase, 'The President of the Immortals had ended his sport with Tess,'[1] awaken an ominous echo fatal to all living faith in a Father in heaven! That is a sentiment worthy of Job's wife, and in full accord with the teaching of modern pessimistic philosophy, and it would not have been uttered unless the writer had believed it would bring him into touch with the secret thoughts of many hearts. Without doubt

[1] *Tess of the D'Urbervilles,* by Hardy, at the end.

many in our time are in the mood to go to Schopenhauer's school and learn of him. The sentiment of the Psalmist: 'Truly God is good,' is no longer an axiom commanding unhesitating assent. Many are saying in their hearts: 'The existence of a good God is about as improbable a dogma as one can imagine. There is little in the state of the world, physical, social, or moral, to support it, much that seems irreconcilable with it. We do not pretend to have any theory to account for things as they are; the whole matter is a dark mystery to us, and we are content to leave it so, and to get through life as best we can, glad at last to make the final plunge into eternal nothingness. But, pray, do not mock our misery by offering us that farthing-candle of faith in Providence to guide us through the gloom.'

Ethical Agnosticism prevails: that, I have said, is the first thing to be laid to heart by the wise man. A second fact to be reckoned with is that the pessimistic mood is far from being without apparent justification. There is much in the world to foster a gloomy, hopeless temper. There is an immense amount of wretchedness and wrong in society, and so long as these prevail, a very earnest disbelief in a benignant Providence may be expected to reveal itself on an extensive scale. It is by no means so easy to believe that God is good as people whose life course runs smoothly imagine. For such the sentiment of the Psalmist is a commonplace. 'God good! why, certainly; who ever doubted it?' Strange to say, it has been doubted by the best, noblest, most religious men, even by Hebrew prophets, by all those, indeed, who have ultimately most firmly believed it. The prosperity of the wicked and the tribulations of the righteous were the stumbling-blocks of the Hebrew bard who said at last, with emphasis, '*Truly*, God is good.' He marvelled at the worldly weal of the frankly bad, and at the woe of the sincerely good. An additional source of temptation is supplied in a third type of men, whose character is an amalgam of wickedness without the frankness, and of goodness without the sincerity. These are men who are both religious and worldly, orthodox and unjust; who confess with unction that God is good, and all other usually accepted theological truths, yet neither do justly nor love mercy; who can even interest themselves in saving souls, yet by their conduct do their best to ruin both the souls and the bodies of their fellow-men. This type of character is a great temptation to unbelief in God, especially in the case of young men who love truth, honour, and humanity, and hate hypocrisy. It tempts them to become Atheists that they may have nothing in common, not even the affirmation that there is a God, with men whose character they despise, and whose conduct they detest. Mr. John Morley writes: 'It is hard to imagine a more execrable emotion than the complacent religiosity of the prosperous.'[1] This is strong language, but think with what bitter emphasis the sentiment must be still further accentuated in the hearts of those who have suffered wrong at the hands of these prosperous ones!

[1] *Rousseau*, vol. i. p. 317.

In attempting to estimate the worth of human life, we must have a *standard of judgment*. Valuation based on merely personal, subjective, random impressions can have no value. What then is to be our standard? Is it to be hedonistic, or is it to be ethical? Is the question to be settled by summing up the pleasures and the pains and striking a balance, or are all experiences to be valued in relation to that which is distinctively human, the rational and moral elements of our nature? I cannot hesitate as to the answer. In inquiring into the worth of human life, we must remember that it is the life of a *man* and not of a mere animal we are considering. This point of view is imposed on us by our hypothesis that man, as a rational and moral being, was an end for God in creation. It was only under that aspect of his nature that we found him worthy to be the aim and crown of the creative process, and it is only under the same aspect that we can fitly estimate the value of the life of this latest arrival. The bearing of experience on the moral interest must always be the dominant, if not the exclusive, consideration. It may in its own place be an interesting enough inquiry how far the life of man in this world is on the whole a happy one, containing considerably more pleasant than unpleasant sensations. But if that were all that was involved in the present question, it would hardly deserve the serious attention of a busy, earnest man. Human life is more than pleasant sensation. That can never be the highest good for man, but at most only something superadded. The distinction of man as compared with the lower animals does not lie in this, that, in an equal space of time, he has a larger amount of pleasurable feeling than any of them. It might, with more truth, be said to consist in a far greater capacity for misery due to his endowment with reason and conscience. Man's capacity for misery, even to a tragic extent, is one of the evidences of the dignity of his nature. It is due to his having a soul, a spiritual nature, with its own special needs, which, if not attended to, take their revenge by overtaxing bodily appetites, so turning the pleasure of natural use into the torment of unnatural excess.

While these things are true, and never for a moment to be left out of sight, it is nevertheless the fact that, even on their own hedonistic ground, pessimistic estimates of life are by no means criticism-proof. Throughout, they are characterised by special pleading, distortion, exaggeration. Among the favourite theses of pessimistic philosophy, are such as these : Life is essentially suffering; will means restless, tormenting desire ; pain alone is real, pleasure is negative, consisting simply in the removal of antecedent pain ; where there is not the misery of unsatisfied desire, there will be the greater misery of *ennui*. All these propositions are but plausible falsities, joint birth of a bad psychology and a jaundiced mind. Life essentially suffering ! On the contrary, the fuller the life the greater the joy. It is so in the physical sphere. Fulness of life here means *health*, and health means buoyancy, freedom from all the unpleasant sensations of pain or languor connected with diseased organs or low vital tone. But we may be told that this freedom from unpleasant sensations characteristic of the healthy man is not itself positive pleasure, but only a state favourable to enjoyment, the foundation on which a life of happiness may be built up. As well might one say that pure, colourless light is not light, or that water is a worthless beverage because it has little taste, or that air is an unimportant element because it is invisible, or that the motion of the earth on its axis, or round the sun, is an unreality because it escapes observation. This so-called neutral base is really the best of it, of far more importance as an element in our cup of gladness than the occasional excitements to which sensualists restrict the name of pleasure. Highly emotional conditions are transient, and it is well that they are. Our nerves soon succumb to the strain of prolonged excitement, not less in the case of pleasure than in the case of pain. Best for us is the unemotional state in which we enjoy existence without feeling or consciousness, happy yet not knowing why. Such is the fact, and the fact is significant. It means that 'not enjoyment and not sorrow is our destined end and way.'

The identification of will with desire is bad psychology, though it very well serves the pessimist's purpose to make life a synonym for misery. Desire is irrational, will is rational. Desire presses blindly on towards a particular gratification, will regulates desires, restraining some, allowing others to attain their object; and in so far as it successfully performs this task, it prevents rather than causes misery. It is a great moral crisis in a man's life when he deliberately and seriously addresses the energy of his will to the task.

It is what in religious language is called 'repentance' or the renewal of the will. Schopenhauer has his own theory of repentance. 'Repentance,' he says, 'never proceeds from a change of the will (which is impossible), but from a change of knowledge. The essential and peculiar in what I have always willed I must still continue to will; for I myself am this will which lies outside time and change. I can therefore never repent of what I have willed, though I can repent of what I have done; because, led by false conceptions, I did something that was not in conformity with my will.' The discovery of this through fuller knowledge is *repentance*.[1] There is a fallacy here arising from the confusion of desire and will. Even in a morally altered life old desire remains. Our characteristic impulses, weaknesses, besetting temptations, pass over from the old into the new roots of evil which, if allowed to grow up, will trouble us again. And it is just the function of our will, enlightened by experience, to prevent these roots from springing up. The adoption of this repressive attitude towards desires and passions and the vices they engender, is the new element which enters into our will in repentance. And so, while desire repressed and curbed remains, the will changes in the moral crisis.

The negative nature of pleasure is another mistake in pessimist psychology. Pleasure is surely something more than mere momentary relief from a more abiding state of pain! There are pleasures pure and real which have no pains as their antecedents. 'Where,' asks Mr. Sully, 'is the want, the longing, preceding the

[1] *The World as Will and Idea*, vol. i. p. 382.

innumerable, agreeable sensations which are excited in us during a walk on a bright spring morning?'[1] Hartmann indeed concedes that there are such pleasures, herein differing from Schopenhauer. But he maintains that they are few compared with the pleasures of the negative sort, consisting in relief to pain-causing desire. Whether they be few or many depends a good deal on the individual. To not a few men blessed with good health and good simple habits, it is a true pleasure to open the eyes on the light of day after a refreshing sleep during the hours of unconsciousness. This is a pleasure not preceded by desire. Hartmann confesses that he has never found waking and rising the pleasure it is alleged to be. This may be his misfortune, due to lack of physical tone, or it may be his fault. One cannot help suspecting the competency to judge of the pleasurableness of life on the part of one who writes as Hartmann does about the drawbacks connected with certain other enjoyments which are more than reliefs to antecedent pain, those, viz., connected with the fine arts. Fatiguing pacing up and down the rooms of the picture-gallery, the heat and crowding of theatres and concert-rooms, the risk of taking cold, the tiring of the eye and ear, all the more annoying that you have to pay for the whole entertainment when the half is as much as you can enjoy:[2] what grave annoyances! how obvious that even in the enjoyment of art the pain outweighs the pleasure! Really, when it comes to this, one begins to feel that in the case of this would-

[1] *Pessimism*, p. 219.
[2] *Philosophie des Unbewussten*, p. 703.

be representative of pessimistic philosophy we have to do with an effeminate person rather than with a healthy-minded man, and that the proper way of treating him is to laugh at him rather than to answer him. It would be easy to cancel all the purest pleasures of life by such paltry grumbling; those, *e.g.*, connected with travel, which occupy so large a place in modern experience. Sweet is recreation after toil; what delights nature, by its mountains and valleys, lakes and rivers, forests and wild-flowers, singing birds and rippling streams, brings to eye and ear! But then the drawbacks: sea-sickness, the custom-house, crowded trains, disagreeable companions, luggage gone astray, unseasonable hours of starting, rainy days, mists hiding the glorious view which you painfully climbed to the mountain top to behold!

Pain, then, is not the one great reality of human life. I add that however extensive the *rôle* it plays, pain is not a pure unmitigated evil. It serves beneficent ends. It cannot indeed be fully understood till it is viewed in relation to the moral and religious elements in man's nature, and there may continue to be something mysterious about it even then. But at least some light can be thrown on this dark region by a consideration of the service pain renders to man as a sentient creature. One broad fact often remarked on is that the susceptibility to painful sensations has a preservative use in the economy of nature. The pains of want, hunger, thirst, fatigue, etc., as Dr. Martineau puts it, '*work the organism.*'[1] 'Painful sensations,' remarks Professor Le Conte, 'are only

[1] *A Study of Religion*, vol. ii. p. 81.

watchful vedettes upon the outposts of our organism to warn us of approaching danger. Without these the citadel of our life would be quickly surprised and taken.'[1] Attempts indeed have been made to show that the vedettes might be dispensed with; but while, again to use the vivid language of Dr. Martineau, we cannot go so far as to say that 'among the infinite reserves of things, there is no alternative possibility,' yet 'so far as our range of conditions goes, the objection to pain is an objection to sentient life, and proposes not to reform, but to abolish all but the vegetable realm of natural history.'[2] Pain thus belongs to the natural normal order, not only in human life, but in all animal life. So does *death*, the most formidable evil we have to encounter. Creatures subject to the law of growth must decay and die. Birth has death for its correlate. This fact alone might reconcile us to the repulsive experience, and there are other considerations which come in to help us to contemplate it with composure. Successive generations make room for each other. In this view not only the fact of death, but the brevity of human life, — the trite theme of many lamentations in the literature of our race, — is far from being an unmixed evil. 'The days of our years are threescore years and ten, or even by reason of strength fourscore years; yet is their pride but labour and sorrow, for it is soon gone and we fly away.'[3] Sad fact, doubtless, yet there is another side

---

[1] I regret that I cannot give the reference.
[2] *A Study of Religion*, vol. ii. p. 82.
[3] Psalm xc. 10, R.V.

to the picture which cannot have been in view of these French optimists of last century who included in the glowing prospect of human progress the indefinite prolongation of life, say to the extent of three or four hundred years.[1] Consider for a moment what that would mean. What intolerable obstructives to the very progress in which this preternatural longevity is conceived to be an element would these ancients of three hundred years be! They would wish all things — science, art, machinery, social customs, religious belief and practice — to remain the same as when they were in their prime. The younger generation, those who desire the world to move on, have trouble enough with seniors even as it is. If the length of human life were doubled or tripled, life for the pioneers of humanity would become hardly worth living through the oppressive conservatism of a too numerous and ultra-venerable body of elders.[2] Let it not be imagined, therefore, that we have any cause to envy Methuselah. We are much better as we are. This is an instance illustrating the importance of looking at physical evil in connection with ethical interests. From a merely natural point of view we might all be inclined to unite with the French optimists in their wish for the indefinite extension of man's time on earth. With all deference to the pessimist, life, in spite of all its drawbacks, is sweet,

[1] So Condorcet and Fourier. *Vide* Flint, *The Philosophy of History*, pp. 338, 410.

[2] *Vide* on this my Article in *The Expositor* on the 90th Psalm (vol. ix. 1879), also the elaborate statement by Martineau in *A Study of Religion*, vol. i.

and the longer our lease of it, one would say, the better. But take the higher goods of life into account, and at once you begin to see that there is room for doubt, and by and by it becomes apparent that the generations of man must not linger too long if progress is to be attained. Man must come and go in quick succession if the river of humanity is to flow on in ever-increasing fulness of spiritual vitality.

Before passing from the topic of death, let me glance for a moment at the form in which it comes to many creatures in the lower animal world, viz., not by natural decay, but through the predaceous instincts of carnivorous animals. This has ever appeared to thoughtful minds a peculiarly repulsive feature in the economy of nature, hard to reconcile with the beneficence of the Creator. We seem here to see Schopenhauer's 'Will' asserting itself with brutal indifference to the torture it may inflict on sentient beings. Yet even on this dark aspect of nature, Dr. Martineau, whose whole treatment of the subject of pain is very fertile in instructive suggestion, has contrived to throw some relieving rays of light. The point he makes is that you have to choose between the predaceous system and a world full of death caused by the poison of putrefaction. 'Withdraw altogether the carnivorous habit, and the whole stock of the world must become graminivorous.' Then 'how would you dispose of the bodies of the dead animals?' Do you say that 'in order to have an herbivorous world, we might ask for the corresponding alteration in the laws of putrefaction'? That would mean 'a reconstitution, on new bases, of the whole chemical legislation of the world.'[1] Thus it appears that on a connected view of things beneficence may be discovered even here.

And if here where not? Is there really any stringent reason for denying the thesis of the old Hebrew Psalmist, 'The earth is full of the goodness of the Lord'?[2] Is there not, as Dr. Chalmers alleged, an extensive capacity in the world for making a virtuous human species happy?[3] Nay, is there not a capacity, which has by no means remained an unrealised possibility, for making men happy to a large extent irrespective of virtue? God is a magnanimous Being. 'He hath not dealt with us after our sins.'[4] 'He maketh His sun to rise on the evil and on the good, and sendeth rain on the just and on the unjust.'[5] Hartmann's elaborate demonstration that the hope of man to find happiness here on earth is a delusion is not conclusive. It is simply a plausible show of argument in support of a *foregone* conclusion. Therefore this so-called first stage of the 'illusion' does not lie behind us. The 'illusion' lives and prospers still, and it will continue to do so while the world lasts. Mankind is not yet driven by despair into the next world, or into the distant future of this world, as the only available anchorage of hope. Life is good, not evil; healthy life is full of joy; the world that appeals to eye and ear is the source of a

[1] *A Study of Religion*, vol. ii. pp. 95, 96.
[2] Psalm xxxiii. 5.
[3] *Natural Theology*, vol. ii. chap. vi.
[4] Psalm ciii. 10.
[5] Matthew v. 45.

pure delight that does not pall with years ; work is no curse, rather the want of it is ; a harsh climate is not a calamity, it makes a manly, hardy, energetic race ; love to young man and maiden is sweet and blissful still ; home is home in all the centuries ; true friendship is still possible.

But virtue or vice, morality, ethically right conduct, or the reverse, makes a great difference. It is only when we pass into this higher region that we are able to estimate duly the worth and the unworth of human life. It is only then we understand to what an extent physical evil is interwoven with moral evil. So we come back to the point from which we started, viz., that if you wish to judge truly of the value of life we must contemplate it, not from a merely hedonistic, but from an ethical point of view.

One broad fact stares us in the face here : That much of the suffering that comes on men is the direct effect of their evil-doing. Many sorrows overtake the wicked : disease, disgrace, untimely death. There is no room for complaint on this score, no perplexing problem for the man who wishes to justify the ways of God. Things are as they should be. The sufferings of the evil-doer are the penalty of his folly and crime. It is well that there is a penalty. The penalties of transgression witness to the dignity of human nature and to the reality of a moral order in the world. They show that man was meant to be something higher and better than a slave of appetite and passion, a mere puppet of Schopenhauer's blind will. If there were no penalties attached to self-indulgence and lawless living, one might legitimately doubt whether the Divine Being cared for morality. The severer the penalty the more certain it is that there is such a thing as a moral government of God in this world.

Yet this is only half the truth. The punitive experiences of moral offenders are not exclusively penal. They are likewise redemptive in purpose and tendency, and not unfrequently in effect. Divine justice is tempered with mercy. The furies of judgment are also angels of grace that would conduct the foolish back to wisdom. Penalties are at the same time chastisements, stripes for scourging out the brute nature and making room for the spirit of a man. 'Thou hast chastised me, and I was chastised as a bullock unaccustomed to the yoke: turn thou me and I shall be turned; for thou art the Lord my God.'[1] As the pain of hunger stimulates to exertion in order to procure food, so the dire pains of sin stimulate to repentance.

If it were only sinners that suffered in this world, the task of justifying Providence would be easy. But there is another phenomenon of a more perplexing character — suffering falling on the *righteous*, not merely as well as on the sinful, but sometimes even more than on them, often, too, inflicted by their hands. This fact seems to raise doubts as to the reality of a moral order, and to throw all things into confusion. It puzzled sages of ancient times in Palestine, China, and Greece, and raised in their minds questions they were not able to answer. Thanks to Jesus Christ, we understand the matter better now. But even apart from the

[1] Jeremiah xxxi. 18.

light thrown on the subject by the teaching of Christ, there are certain truths that might disclose themselves to close observation, and that were indeed partly discerned by the unknown author of the fifty-third chapter of Isaiah, and by Plato. One is that the suffering of the righteous is not an accident, but rather happens by law; not a specially dark feature in a moral chaos, but a recondite aspect of a moral cosmos. A second truth is, that this suffering is not in vain, but has redemptive value. These two truths we shall have an opportunity of considering at a later stage. Meantime, there is a third truth to be added to them which may appropriately be commented on here, this, viz., that the suffering of the righteous is not without compensation to themselves, especially when they understand the law of the case, and loyally adjust themselves to it. This crowning truth has not been plain to all who have been alive to the fact that the suffering of pre-eminent goodness is a uniform experience. In a dialogue between nature and a soul Leopardi makes nature say: 'Go, my beloved child. You shall be regarded as my favored one for very many centuries. Live; be great, and unhappy.'[1] This is an echo in modern literature of the thought of Euripides: 'I have never heard it said that sons born to mortals of divine paternity were happy.'[2] Leopardi regarded the fact stated as one of the most convincing arguments in support of a pessimistic theory of the universe. The unhappiness of nature's noblest children unrelieved, and serving no purpose — how can a good God preside over such a

[1] *Essays and Dialogues*, p. 36.   [2] *Ion.* v. 510.

world! But the unhappiness is not unrelieved. With the outward unhappiness goes inward *Blessedness*. When the suffering endured ceases to be regarded as an untoward fate involuntarily endured, and is freely accepted as an incident in a heroic career, then all heaviness of heart departs, and pain is transmuted into pleasure. The heroic temper is cheerful, buoyant, exultant. It can mount up on wings like an eagle, it can bound like a chamois from rock to rock on the Alpine mountains. 'Rejoice and be exceeding glad,' said Jesus to the persecuted, hinting a fact in terms of an exhortation. And He ought to know. He speaks with the authority of an expert. His first disciples caught His spirit, and knew how to exult in tribulation, and many Christians since the apostolic age have learned the high art. But the mood is not confined to Christendom; witness Socrates and the serenity with which he met death. It is the mood of self-sacrificing love all the world over; of every mother who devotes herself to her offspring, and counts all hardship endured in their behalf a very light affliction. Herein lies the 'mystery of pain' that, in association with love, it ceases to be an evil. 'The pains of martyrs, or the losses of self-sacrificing devotion, are never classed among the evil things of the world. They are its bright places rather, the culminating points at which humanity has displayed its true glory, and reached its perfect level. An irrepressible pride and gladness are the feelings they elicit: a pride which no regret can drown, a gladness no indignation overpower.'[1]

[1] Hinton, *The Mystery of Pain*, p. 12.

Only with this highest truth does the apology of pain reach its triumphant climax. The three points stated before — that pain stimulates to self-preservation, serves as penalty for transgression, subjects those who have erred to a salutary discipline — are all true and important, and together go a considerable way towards justifying the large place which suffering holds in human experience. But not till it has been seen that in a world where evil abounds, pain is inseparable from love and welcome to love, does perplexity vanish. Then we perceive that love needs pain for its highest self-manifestation. Then also complaining is rebuked by the manner in which love takes pain. If the noblest do not lament over their afflictive experience, why should others repine? Is our repining not a proof that we have not been initiated into the highest kind of life? Does not our extreme sensitiveness to pain reveal some moral defect, some blindness as to the true nature of happiness? 'Doubtless, we are right to loathe and repudiate pain, and count its endurance an evil. To be happy is good: to feel pain is evil and the sign of evil. . . . But the question is, What is the happiness God has meant us for, the happiness to which human nature is fitted, to which it should aspire? Should it be that from which the painful is banished, or that in which pain is latent? Should pain be merely absent, or swallowed up in love and turned to joy?'[1]

If we were initiated into this life of love, we should not need to fly to another world in quest of a happi-

[1] Hinton, *The Mystery of Pain*, pp. 38, 39.

ness we could not find here. This earth offers peculiar facilities for enjoying the bliss connected with self-sacrifice. You do not need to leave the world to escape from Hartmann's first phase of illusion. You require only to discover the secret of the blessed life, now and always, here and everywhere. This is the life which Christ called *eternal*, because it is the true life, and which He did not locate exclusively in heaven. It is the life which makes a hereafter credible and desirable. For one who possesses this life now, the life beyond will not be an absolute novelty. It will simply be a case of present life going on. In any case, whether there be a heaven or not, it is the best life going, the life of wisdom and goodness, and of peace independent of circumstance.

The question of *Progress* is a vital one for those who believe in a beneficent Providence. It is characteristic of pessimism to meet the thesis that the condition of the world is steadily advancing with a blunt, unqualified denial. The hope of a good time coming is for Hartmann simply the final stage of illusion. By this view he places himself in antagonism not merely to Christian belief, but to the convictions of the most prominent advocates of evolutionism. Spencer and Fiske expect the social condition to go on improving. They are optimists for the distant future. And the evils of the present they can bear with a patient mind, regarding them simply as incidental to the stage of social evolution at which we have arrived. 'The physical ills with which humanity is afflicted,' writes

Mr. Fiske, 'are undoubtedly consequent upon the very movement of progress which is bearing it onwards towards relative perfection of life, and moral evils likewise are the indispensable concomitants of its slow transition from the primeval state of savage isolation to the ultimate state of civilised interdependence. They are not obstacles to any scientific theory of evolution, nor do they provide an excuse for gloomy cynicism, but should rather be viewed with quiet resignation, relieved by philosophic hopefulness and enlightened endeavours to ameliorate them.'[1] Into the question in dispute between pessimists and optimistic evolutionists I cannot here enter; I confine myself for the present to a point on which these antagonists are agreed, viz., the non-reality of a living beneficent Providence. This, Fiske, in his *Cosmic Philosophy*, affirms as resolutely as Hartmann does in his *Philosophy of the Unconscious*, and the grounds on which he rests his position are worth noticing. If, you naturally ask, one can put such calm trust in the course of evolution, why not equal confidence in a living God? The answer in effect is: Because in the one case you have to do with an impersonal unconscious tendency, in the other with a personal conscious will, from which you are entitled to expect more, even the instant removal of evil, a millennium *per saltum*. Such is the gist of the following arraignment of Providence. 'A scheme which permits thousands of generations to live and die in wretchedness, cannot, merely by providing for the well-being of later ages, be absolved from the alterna-

[1] *Outlines of Cosmic Philosophy*, vol. ii. p. 404.

tive charge of awkwardness or malevolence. If there exist a personal creator of the universe who is infinitely intelligent and powerful, he cannot be infinitely good; if, on the other hand, he be infinite in goodness, then he must be lamentably finite in power or in intelligence.' God, that is, cannot be allowed time to do His beneficent work : He must make the world perfect at once.

Is this a reasonable demand ? It is certainly a very sweeping stipulation. It really amounts to this, that God, as theistically conceived, is incompatible with evolution in any sphere of being. God can, and ought to, make the universe with a wave of the hand, with a word of His mouth. Why should millions of years elapse before man comes on the scene ? If this creature was so good in God's eyes as to be the reason for the creation of the world, why not create both stage and actor off-hand ? And if man, in his ideal form, was so fair in God's sight, why bring him into being at the first in a state far short of the ideal, as evolutionists believe, with the bare rudiments of humanity, just one short step in advance of the brute, so that thousands of years would be necessary to make him out and out a man with fully developed rational and moral powers ?

But the demand for summary action, while really striking at the very idea of evolution, has reference chiefly to the social aspect of the process. It is here the shoe pinches. The tediousness of evolution anterior to man's arrival might be excused, but, after that, ought not the Creator to have accelerated his pace, and to have moved on rapidly towards the grand consummation when men, the world over, should 'brothers be,' with all that goes along with that?

It must be admitted that there is a difference between the earlier merely physical, and the later social and moral evolution, in respect to the measure in which they try faith. Pious men of old did not know enough of the method of creation to be able to make any reflections on the former, but they did have experience of the slow movement of Providence in human history, and their recorded utterances show that it created in their minds surprise and disappointment. They often exclaimed, 'O Lord, how long!' It did not in their case go the length of unbelief in a living God, to whom to appeal, but that is what it is coming to now. Agnostics say, 'It is useless to exclaim, useless to pray; so far as appears, there is no "Lord" to pray to, or that can give seasonable, effective succour. Bear, therefore, patiently if you can, the ills of life, and hope that it will fare better with later generations than it has fared with you.' Not much of a gospel this! Is there no better? Cannot we combine the old faith in Providence with the new faith in a slow, secular, social evolution?

Evolution does not appear to introduce any new element into the problem beyond a clearer perception of the exceeding slowness with which the world moves on towards goodness. At no time in the world's history have men of deep earnestness and profound moral reflection expected the consummation soon. It is only persons of sanguine temper and shallow thought who in any age imagine that evil is going to disappear from the earth in a year or two. But now that the evolutionary theory of the universe has taken possession of men's minds, it has become more than ever impossible to think that by any amount of faith, prayer, or effort, the bringing in of the kingdom of heaven into this world can be made other than a slow, insensible movement, at the rate, say, of a single great step in a generation, or a century, or in some cases even a millennium. This is now understood more clearly than ever it was before. But this clearer vision of the slow rate of movement does not introduce any new principle into the question at issue. The real question is, Is any delay whatever compatible with the idea of Providence? Should not a good God, with adequate power, make the world what it ought to be, at once? Now the best men of other ages did not find themselves shut up to this conclusion. And let us not lower the value of their judgment by imagining that for them a living God and a Providence were fixed elements of a traditional creed which for even the freest minds was above criticism. The book of Job is a standing proof to the contrary. The author of Job was capable of any amount of audacity in the way of questioning accepted beliefs. He could put into his hero's mouth such a sentiment as this: 'It is all one; therefore I say, He destroyeth the perfect and the wicked. If the scourge slay suddenly, He will mock at the trial of the innocent. The earth is given into the hand of the wicked: He covereth the faces of the judges thereof; if it be not He, who then is it?'[1] If not He who then? The

[1] Job ix. 22-24, R.V.

ancient thinker could not anticipate the answer of the modern Agnostic that it is not a 'He' but a great unconscious law of progress with which we have to do. But he could ask the question. It was present to his mind, as a possibility, that the state of things to be observed in the world was due to the fact of there being no living or righteous God above the world, and ruling over it in justice and mercy. If, nevertheless, he held fast his faith in such a God, it was not in servile subjection to a traditional creed, but with free, personal conviction victorious over daring, radical, possibly protracted doubt.

If the evolutionary theory in one respect increases our burden, in another it lightens it. The burden is made heavier by the perception that æons must elapse before the kingdom of goodness come in power. But it is lightened by the inspiring thought that the world is marching on towards the desired consummation with the certainty of a law of nature. Of old it might be doubted whether there was any certainty in the matter. The world seemed given over to a reign of chance and caprice. If relief came, it came apparently by special, miraculous providence, catastrophically, not by the sure action of an immanent law. On that view, faith might occasionally gain great confirmation, but it was also liable to crushing disappointment. If the Lord turned back the captivity of Zion, the mouth was filled with laughter and the tongue with singing. But if the Lord did not visit His people in mercy, but brought wrath upon them to the uttermost, what then? Now, faith is less liable to extreme fluctuations. It looks at things on the large scale, and has less to hope for, so far as the single generation is concerned, and also less to fear. Catastrophes, crises, may come now as of old, and in these, devout souls will continue to trace the divine hand. But whether they come or not, the world marches on, and that is our comfort and stay. The heart may bleed over the miseries of mankind, yet it will cling to the hope that these miseries will not last for ever.

Still the questions come back, Why last so long, why last at all? How is the lasting reconcilable with the idea of a good God, and with an optimistic view of the world? Why cannot the moral ideal be realised at once? The answer must be, Because *process* is essential to morality. To realise the moral ideal *per saltum*, by an act of omnipotence, is to annihilate it; it is to turn the moral into something merely physical. To introduce the category of power into this region, as if it were equal to all demands, is to ignore the nature of the region, to forget that a will or a heart is not a thing like a lump of clay that can be moulded, or a mass of rock that can be broken in pieces. Moralisation is possible only in accordance with the nature of morality, *i.e.*, in the exercise of freedom, through struggle, effort, experience, all demanding time as an indispensable condition, even for the sanctification of the individual, still more for the humanisation of the community, or the race. It is true indeed that for one who contemplates the history of the world *sub specie aeternitatis* time and process are eliminated. Ideal and reality, root and fruit, seed and tree, beginning and end, then become one. For God the moral ideal is eternally realised. Hence He might see in man perfect goodness the day he was created, though in him at that initial stage were found only the rudiments of goodness, the fruitful germ out of which a thoroughly disciplined moral character had to be slowly evolved. To the mystic temper of religion the same divine mode of contemplation is congenial. For it also the ideal is the real, and distinctions between beginning and end, now and then, are abolished. The good are perfectly good, the regenerate man knows no sin. This mode of viewing things has its own value, but used exclusively and carried out consistently it would mean the abolition of time, history, change, process, finitude, all swallowed up in the categories of the infinite and the absolute. Alongside of it, to balance it and make it have any significance, must be placed the ethical mode of viewing the world for which process is not only real but indispensable. In the moral world, process has its drawbacks; it implies defect, error, suffering, hopes deferred making the heart sick. But not otherwise can the goal be reached. And what an interest attaches to the sublime, though tragic, process of moral evolution! Who would exchange the historic method of human redemption for a magic transformation which should in the twinkling of an eye make all things new? The former supplies to devout reason a subject for admiring study; the latter, if it were possible, would simply stupefy. Process in the moral world commends itself at once to the scientific and to the ethical spirit. It is in analogy with all that we find elsewhere in the universe, and it is in accordance with the nature of morality. Heart and conscience may cry out against it; the heart because of the misery that follows sin, the conscience because the goal is still so far away. But the heart's pain and the wound of conscience are themselves among the chief forces working for the grand consummation. 'And this process of learning goodness, this gradual realisation by man of an ideal infinitely high and absolute in worth, throws back a light which illumines all the pain and strife and despair, and shows them all to be steps in the endless "love-way." The unrealised, though ever-realising good, which brings despair, is the best fact in man's history; and it should rightly bring, not despair, but endless joy.'[1]

[1] Professor Henry Jones, *Browning as a Philosophical and Religious Teacher*, p. 268.

LECTURE VI

THE WORTH OF MAN

In the fourth lecture we saw that a fruitful source of unbelief in Providence may be found in conceptions of God which make Him a Being beneath caring for man and the interests man represents. We are now to consider a complementary cause of doubt, viz., ideas of man which make him a being beneath the notice of God.

That contempt of man, however originating, and in whatever manner it may manifest itself, directly tends to breed scepticism in a providential order, needs no proof. The best historical illustration may be found in the opinions of the heathen philosopher Celsus, as reported by Origen in his reply to an attack made by him on the Christian religion. That controversial work, bearing the name of Ἀληθὴς Λόγος, the True Word or Discourse, has perished, and we are dependent for our information as to its author's views on Origen's accounts; but the position of an antagonist could not be safer in any hands than in those of that church Father, whether we have regard to his intelligence or to his candour, and we may implicitly rely on the accuracy of his representations. From these we gather that Celsus was a very capable and very formidable opponent of Christianity. His statements regarding man's worth have the great merit of being perfectly frank and unreserved. They are very brutal, but just on that account all the more significant. They form a prominent part in an elaborate argument against the doctrine of an Incarnation of God in the person of Jesus Christ, with a view to the redemption of man from moral evil. Celsus denied that doctrine on three general grounds: first, because it degraded God, by subjecting Him to change; second, because it unduly exalted man, by making him the object of God's special care; third, because it had in view an unattainable end, the cure of moral evil. It is in connection with the second of these positions that his peculiar anthropological theory finds expression.

Celsus bluntly denies that man has any exceptional place in the gracious thoughts of God. Whatever providence there may be, is, in his judgment, common to all creatures, on equal terms. Man has no more claim to be a special object of Divine care than bats or ants or frogs or worms. As a matter of fact he does not receive more attention, as a matter of right he is not entitled to it. What, one is ready to exclaim, not even in view of his rational, moral, and religious nature? No, stoutly rejoins Celsus, not even in view of that. He has the hardihood to maintain, not that reason, morality, and religion are matters of secondary moment, but, admitting the value of these things, that in respect of these high endowments, man is not superior to the other animals. He has no monopoly of language, art, virtue, or religion. The ants can talk to each other when they meet; the bee can build its cell with exquisite skill; the elephant is a pattern of fidelity, and the stork of filial piety. Even religion is not above the capacity of the animal world. Birds have the prophetic gift of foreseeing the future, and their very movements are a revelation of things to come, to those who have skill to interpret them. They can divine, and they supply data for the diviner. In this connection we can better understand what at first sight appears the wanton, whimsical, cynical degradation which man suffers at the hands of Celsus. That this pagan philosopher was in the mood for exaggeration and banter when dealing with this topic is more than likely, but in the main he meant what he said, and he was not alone in saying it. Porphyry agreed with him in ascribing more importance to animals, specially to birds, than to man,[1] and both did this in connection with divination. For the diviner a bird was more important than a human being. How natural, at a time when his art was a momentous reality, that men should get into the way of regarding the living creatures which furnished its materials, as holy, religious, near to God, awe-inspiring!

Celsus lived in the second Christian century, and it is probable that his own faith in the practices of divination was not strong, and that he simply used a popular belief for a controversial purpose. Perhaps the deepest source of his unbelief in Providence was sympathy with the theology of Epicurus, who conceived the Gods as dwelling apart in high Olympus, and giv-

[1] Porphyry, *De abstinentia*, vol. iii. p. 5.

ing themselves no concern about the lower world. In his philosophy, as befitted his age, Celsus was an eclectic, his thoughts reminding us here of Plato, there of the Stoics, at another place of 'the philosophers of the garden.' But his chief master seems to have been Epicurus. Origen states that in his other works he showed himself an Epicurean, but that in his polemic against Christianity he concealed his connection with the school of Epicurus, lest the avowal of it should weaken the force of his argument against those who believed in a providence and set God over all. If this was, indeed, his intention, he has been only partially successful. The Epicurean connection is very imperfectly hid. The Celsian God is the Epicurean God. 'God,' he says in one place, 'is good, honourable, happy, the fairest and the best; but if He descends to men He becomes subject to change — from good to bad, from the honourable to the base, from happiness to misery, from the best to the most wicked. Let no such change be ascribed to God.' This is quite in the spirit of the Epicurean theology, whose gods were happy, imperishable beings that could have nothing to do with the affairs of the universe or of men. From this idea, echoed by Celsus, to that suggested by the phrase in the New Testament: 'The glorious gospel of the blessed God,' or, the gospel of the glory of the happy God,[1] what a distance! The happiness of God, on the one view, is apathy; on the other, it is associated with sympathetic suffering and self-sacrifice. The superiority in moral grandeur of the Christian conception is obvious.

[1] 1 Timothy i. 11.

It thus appears that Celsus was doubly disqualified for accepting the Christian belief in providence: by his theology as well as by his anthropology. He believed in a God who was incapable of caring for anything, while he conceived of man as a being not worth caring for, not more important than any of the other creatures which together make up the universe. 'If,' he says, 'thunders, lightnings, and rain be indeed the work of God, which is doubtful, they are made just as much for trees, grass, and thorns as for man; if plants grow for man's benefit, they grow for the benefit of the brutes as well; nay, even more, for we obtain our food with labour and difficulty, while the wild beasts get theirs without sowing or ploughing.' This is in the spirit of Spinoza, who recognised no degrees of value in the universe, and confounded reality with perfection, deeming all things modes of the one absolute substance, and in that sense divine, but one thing as divine as another. For Celsus as for Spinoza, God was the one and all; all creatures, as modes of the absolute, were in his view legitimate objects of worship; but just because all was divine no particular being seemed to him entitled to any preference, not even man. Man, as he conceived him, was not a being made in the image of God, or a son of God, or a chief end for God, or of more value to God than the inanimate and lower animate creations.

But Celsus belongs to long-past history, and our concern is with present-day faiths and unbeliefs. The question we have to consider is, Under what forms are we now tempted to cherish a contempt for man which tends towards scepticism as to the possibility of his being in any real sense an end for God? This question let me now endeavour to answer.

Contempt for man may manifest itself under three forms:—

1. Contempt for man even at the best.
2. Contempt for man in the average.
3. Contempt for man at the lowest and worst, in rudimentary moral conditions or in degenerate states.

1. A true respect for man, such as may form the basis of earnest faith in a like respect for him on the part of God, requires three things: a lofty moral ideal, belief in its approximate realisableness in this world, and belief in the permanence of the moral universe. Not one of these conditions can be dispensed with. Thus a low-pitched ideal which conceives of happiness as the *summum bonum*, and of virtue simply as the safest way to the goal, surely tends to undermine respect. The chief end of man, thus hedonistically conceived, may be realisable enough, but is it worth realising; when it has been realised can it command the sincere esteem of thoughtful men, not to speak of God? Recall deistic views of man and the contempt they have bred! The Deist did not indeed himself despise man and the ideal of humanity, but he may be justly accused of making them appear to others despicable. Man naturally good, not without faults, but these such as spring from the appetites and passions of the body, for which the spirit cannot be held responsi-

ble. Even with these faults the average man has every reason to be well pleased with himself, and to cherish the comfortable conviction that he is an object of complacent regard for the Divine Being. What more natural, then, that God should contemplate with indulgence at least, if not with entire approval, the behaviour of men who on the whole live such good lives? And how can Providence be better occupied than in making such worthy people happy? A pleasant creed, this, for those who are ignoble enough to be able to receive it. But a morally vulgar creed like that of the Deist must inevitably provoke sooner or later a sceptical reaction. Is the *rôle* of supreme dispenser of happiness to morally commonplace men a God-worthy one? Is there not a risk that a Providence thus occupied may fall into disrepute? Be sure of this, that if faith in a divine care of man is to retain its hold of earnest minds, you must make man worth caring for, and rightly conceive the purpose of the care. Pitch your ideal of man high, and assign to God the supreme aim of helping man to reach that ideal. Then, though 'happiness' may not be a very prominent feature in human life, your faith will not fail, because you perceive that through sorrow lies the way to wisdom.

But a high ideal, however lofty and austere, will not sustain faith, unless it be conceived as realisable, at least approximately, by man in his place in this world. The assumption that this is impossible underlies *asceticism*. The implied postulate of the ascetic mode of life is that you cannot be good under normal conditions as a member of society; that goodness is possible only for one who withdraws from secular positions, duties, and relations. This theory strikes at the root of all faith in a providential presence of God in human history. God is only in the monk's cell, the devil is everywhere else. By and by men begin to wonder if God be even in the monk's cell. If the monk be a saint, the only really good man in the world, how is it that the Supreme Being who loves him alone has nothing better for him than a cell? But *is* he a saint, is he indeed better than other men, is he not in some ways, perhaps, a good deal worse? In that case God is not even in the cell. God is in fact nowhere. In the world is frank wickedness, in the monastic retreat is only hypocrisy; the devil rules, and God and Providence are banished from the universe.

What is the remedy for such desolating atheism? Unreserved acceptance of the truth that goodness is practicable in society, as well as in the desert; nay, in society only, not at all in solitude; for in this connection it is emphatically true that it is not good that man should be alone.

> 'You 've seen the world
> — The beauty, and the wonder, and the power,
> The shapes of things, their colors, lights, and shades,
> Changes, surprises, — and God made it all!
> — For what? what's it all about?
> To be passed over, depised? or dwelt upon,
> Wondered at?'

The answer of all who believe in God must be: —

> 'This world 's no blot for us,
> Nor blank; it means intensely, and means good.'

In his pessimistic philosophy, Schopenhauer has presented the creed of asceticism in a new form. Goodness, said the old ascetic, is not compatible with remaining in the world. Goodness, teaches Schopenhauer, is not compatible with retention of *personality*. You can become kind, noble, benignant, like Buddha, only by rending the veil of Maya, the *principium individuationis;* by ceasing to think of yourself as an individual, realising that all individuals are essentially one, thus serving yourself heir to all the sin and sorrow of the world, and, burdened with the dismal inheritance, contemplating annihilation with complacency. Sanctity means no will to live, and that means ultimately no world, and no God.

The new form of the theory is as false as the old. Personality is as necessary to morality as is society. We must be 'selves' before we begin to be moral. The moral ideal consists in *self-realisation*, giving full effect to all that is contained in the idea of a self, which turns out to mean, not egoistic self-assertion against all others, but on the contrary due recognition of, and respect for, the 'selves' of other men with all that is involved therein. This is sane, and at the same time Christian, ethics. Schopenhauer, conscious of the grandeur of Hebrew religious thought, sought in it backing for his cynical philosophy, and claimed Christ and the apostles as on his side. The construction he puts on their teaching is but a misleading plausibility. They were not pessimists, though they did severely judge the actual moral state of man in the light of a high ideal. Their ideal was very lofty, but they believed it could be realised. They believed it could be realised approximately, not in heaven only, nor in solitude, but in this world, and in society. And with this faith they found it easy to combine firm belief in a Divine Providence making all things work together for good to them that love God.

Such faith in man and in God needs yet another support — belief in the permanence of the moral universe. Some of the teachings of modern science make this difficult. I do not here refer to the conscious *automaton* theory, according to which mind and its phenomena are reduced to by-products, and all that is peculiar to man dwindles into cosmic insignificance. Neither do I allude to the vastly enlarged view of the extent of the universe through which the earth with its inhabitants becomes as a grain of sand on a vast mountain. I have in mind rather the outlook for the remote future set before us by scientific prophets, who by the aid of mathematical calculations, predict that, the order of nature continuing as it now is, the ultimate issue must be a perfect balance of force, implying the total cessation of change, universal death. Mr. Huxley, endorsing this view, remarks: 'The theory of evolution encourages no millennial expectations. If for millions of years our globe has taken the upward road, yet, some time, the summit will be reached, and the downward route will be commenced.'[1] The prospect forces on us the chilling thought that man, with his rational and moral nature, can hardly be a chief end for the cosmos and its Maker, but at most only a by-end. In a dialogue between Nature and an Icelander, Leopardi puts into the mouth of the former this grim sentiment: 'If I by chance exterminated your species

[1] *Evolution and Ethics*, p. 85.

I should not know it.' It does not follow, indeed, that even in that case we should cease to believe in the worth of humanity, and give up striving with all our might to justify the belief by the realisation of the moral ideal, even though the time allowed us for the task should be, as Mr. Huxley hints, a period barely 'longer than that now covered by history.'[1] That distinguished scientist advises this heroic course, summoning all brave men to play what may be described as the part of Athanasius *contra mundum*, the microcosm man waging an unequal, yet not hopeless, battle for morality against the macrocosm brutally indifferent to morality. Such, doubtless, is our duty; yet, with the chill prospect of annihilation before us, we must labour under an oppressive sense of cosmic discouragement, apt to end in surrender at discretion by adoption of the cosmic view of morality as a mere by-end. In the long run there will be but two courses open, either to abandon our high-pitched theory as to the absolute worth of the rational and moral, or, holding on at all hazards to that theory, to remodel in accordance with it our conception of the destiny of the cosmos, and dare to believe that the Maker of the world has somehow provided against the destruction of the human, either by an immortal existence elsewhere, or by guaranteeing the stability of man's present abode. It is interesting to note that some of the most ardent advocates of evolution feel keenly the need of some such refuge for faith. Mr. Fiske, *e.g.* says, 'For my own part, I believe in the immortality of the soul, not in the sense in which I

[1] *Evolution and Ethics*, p. 85.

accept the demonstrable truths of science, but as a supreme act of faith in the reasonableness of God's work.'[1] He professes himself unable to believe that God made the world, and especially its highest creature, simply to destroy it, like a child who builds houses out of blocks just for the pleasure of knocking them down.[2] Not less strongly Le Conte writes, 'Without spirit-immortality, this beautiful cosmos, which has been developing into increasing beauty for so many millions of years, when its evolution has run its course, and all is over, would be precisely as if it had never been — an idle dream, an idiot tale signifying nothing.'[3] These utterances do not settle the solemn question of human *destiny*, but they do illustrate the logical value of faith in human *worth*. The question is, Which are to have the upper hand — physical or ethical categories? Give physical theory the first place, and the ethical must go to the wall. Give precedence to the ethical, and it will compel faith in a physical universe conformed to its requirements.

2. Thus far of contempt for man at the best. We have next to notice that form of contempt which has for its object, average or ordinary humanity. Those who are guilty of this fault cannot be charged with undervaluing ideal humanity. On the contrary, it is their high and reverend esteem for the ideal, and for the few favoured sons of men who approximately realise it, that makes them contemptuous in their estimate of the un-

---

[1] *The Destiny of Man*, p. 116.
[2] *Ibid.*, p. 114.
[3] *Evolution and its Relation to Religious Thought*, p. 329.

distinguished multitude. The late Mr. Thomas Carlyle was a conspicuous offender here. We are all familiar with his description of the English people as consisting of 'twenty-seven millions, mostly fools,' and with the very uncomplimentary account of the American people which he puts into the mouth of Smelfungus. 'What have they done? They have doubled their population every twenty years. They have begotten, with a rapidity beyond recorded example, eighteen millions of the greatest *bores* ever seen in this world before.'[1] Of course a certain allowance must be made for the exaggeration of a humorist not given to measuring his words, whose heart was more kindly than his tongue or his pen. Yet that these whimsical estimates represented a fixed serious conviction is shown by Carlyle's whole method of dealing with history. History meant for him the biography of great men.[2] Not common men, or the masses of men and the influences by which they are being slowly raised to higher levels of intelligence, goodness, and comfort, were the objects of interest for him, but the few exceptional men here and there, who have risen above the common level, and who compel attention by the greatness of their thoughts and deeds. Carlyle sincerely, passionately, reverenced humanity, but his reverence took the form of *hero-worship*, having for its negative side disdainful indifference to all who were not heroes.

Now hero-worship is not an evil thing. We have certainly no reason to complain of this modern cult as

[1] *Latter Day Pamphlets*, No. 1.
[2] *Lecture on Heroes*, p. 1.

practised by its chief apostle, for to the enthusiasm it inspired in his mind we owe some splendid works which have permanently enriched our literature, such as that in which *Cromwell* figures as the hero. Hero-worship, by comparison with certain other cults, is even a positively good thing. Unbounded admiration for men who have been great in wisdom, character, and conduct, is surely a higher thing by far than servile homage paid to brute force in the person of an Oriental despot, or to money in the person of a modern millionaire. Still this new religion, whereof Carlyle is the prophet, is, at its best, a one-sided thing; it is very apt to become an unjust and inhuman thing, and it tends to unbelief in God's care for man. It does not indeed deny Providence, but it virtually recognises it only in the careers of those who belong to the intellectual and moral aristocracy of the human race. Its doctrine of Providence is a new form of the Calvinistic doctrine of election. Neither in the old form of the doctrine, nor in the new, is the idea of election baseless. There is such a thing as election in the case both of individuals and of nations. Election, as we shall see, is one of the methods by which Divine Providence accomplishes its beneficent purposes. But in no case does election mean a monopoly of Divine favour enjoyed by the elect. They are chosen for the good of others, not for the benefit of themselves only. And a philosophy or a theology which overlooks this great truth is unwittingly sapping the foundations of faith in Divine Providence. That faith cannot permanently hold its ground on the hypothesis that the Divine Being cares only for the few, and that salvation here or hereafter is meant only for a remnant, or an exclusive very select company of favoured ones. There must be a Providence over all, if we are to continue to believe in a Providence over any. Such a universal Providence does not preclude the recognition of a very special or signal Providence in the career of exceptional men. The hero is emphatically a chosen one of God, and it is easier to trace Divine leading in his history than in the obscure lives of humbler men. But heed must be taken not so to emphasise that leading as to obscure the still more important truth that God careth for the little and dwelleth with the humble. For if this vital truth be allowed to fade out of our minds, the end may be unbelief in Divine care for any man however great. For, after all, what is the difference between the least and the greatest among men in the view of a transcendent Deity? In His eyes the inhabitants of the earth are all alike 'as grasshoppers.'[1]

The only hope of sure abiding faith in Providence is the abandonment of this figment of a far-off transcendent Deity, much concerned about His Majesty, and just deigning to recognise the few tall figures among the myriads of men; and the substitution for it of a God who by His providence and His grace is immanent in humanity, bearing its burdens, sympathising with its sorrows, grieving over its errors, and ever working towards a better time. Affirm the transcendency if you will, it has its relative truth; but do not forget the immanency. 'I dwell in the high and holy place, with

[1] Isaiah xl. 22.

THE WORTH OF MAN 143

him *also* that is of a contrite and humble spirit, to revive the spirit of the humble, and to revive the heart of the contrite ones.'[1] The aristocratic Deity hero-worshippers believe in is a poor Divinity compared with the sublime conception of the Hebrew prophet. Do you offer me a God who takes notice of the great man? I prefer a God who hath respect unto the lowly.[2]

It is well on the whole that hero-worship is on the wane, and the 'service of man' on the increase. It is well that history has ceased to mean simply the biography of great men, and has become the sympathetic study of the corporate life of the million, noting its condition from age to age, and recording with humane interest the signs of advance, comparing one century with another. There is nothing to be said against looking out with eager quest for the prophets, righteous men, and great actors of the race. But do not forget that he that receiveth a prophet, or righteous man, or saint, in the name of prophet, righteous man, or saint, is also worthy of recognition. Prophets and the like are very venerable persons, but one who honestly respects them, even so much as touches his hat to them, is not to be despised. The moral order of the world does not despise him. A man who has just enough goodness to reverence goodness in another is not far from God, and God is not far from him. Even a cup of cold water given to a weary, way-worn saint will not miss its reward. How many are equal to that service who are far from being saints themselves! Think of them thankfully, hopefully! Preach hero-worship and saint-

[1] Isaiah lvii. 15.   [2] Psalm cxxxviii. 6.

worship by all means: both have their use, if also their baleful abuse. But regard kindly the worshippers as well as the worshipped. Believe that God regards them; that He regards those in whom is the smallest fragment of the good, as well as those rare souls who have travelled far towards the goal of perfection. This is Christ's doctrine; but it is also the doctrine of right reason, and it is the necessary presupposition of all true faith in the worth of man to God.

3. We pass now to the third form of contempt for man, that, viz., for man at the lowest and the worst: for primitive man, for the savage and the criminal, in comparison with whom even the so-called 'fools' of civilisation are wise and good. If even the average man of civilisation be deemed contemptible, the classes just named may seem beneath contempt, utterly unworthy of notice, to be simply forgotten, if one is not to despair of humanity altogether, and to become an utter unbeliever in God's care for the human race. And in truth it cannot be denied that these classes, especially the *second* and the *third*, present to the believer in Providence a sufficiently dark problem which cannot be satisfactorily disposed of in a few paragraphs. I am not going to attempt a solution here. I leave the savage and the criminal on one side meantime, and propose to speak a kindly word for the primitive man whose unrecorded life filled up the long blank space of thousands or tens of thousands of years before civilisation and history began, whose religion was *animism*, whose tools were made of flint and stone, and who was slowly learning to say 'I.' Theologians have hardly

begun to recognise his existence yet, and are even gravely in doubt whether they can afford to do so. Whether he ever lived on this earth is still a debated question. Science, geology, and anthropology affirm; theology, interested in traditional dogmas, denies. I do not presume to judge authoritatively between them. I only venture to express the hope that theology does not need, in the interest of the Christian faith, or of a high esteem for the Scriptures, to foreclose the question, but can afford to treat it as a simple question of fact. It is always best when faith is able to take up this attitude; and it has happily been found possible to do so in many cases in which at first it was supposed to be impossible. I shall go on the assumption that this case will turn out to be no exception, and provisionally take for granted that 'primitive man' is not an imaginary being, but from the most recent tertiary period to the earliest dawn of history has been an actual denizen of this earth. And the question we have to consider is: Must we as upholders of the worth of man be ashamed of this ancient type of humanity? Is it possible to take any rational interest in him; is it credible that God could take an interest in him? A negative answer to this question would be of serious import. It would mean that, for long ages after it came into existence, the human race had no value or moral significance for God, no share in His providential guidance, no place in His gracious plans. Such a conclusion would be hard to reconcile with an adequate conception of Divine benignity. Thoughtful men, devoted to the Christian faith, are beginning to feel the pressure of this question. Thus the brilliant author of *The Christ of To-day* writes : 'The consciousness of history as of unmeasured extent, and as embracing countless multitudes of the human race, inferior, doubtless, in every way to the men of to-day, but upon whose sacrifices and rude civilisation, representing worlds of struggle and suffering, the modern age has built, and without which even genius itself would be comparatively helpless, is one of the great forces that are calling for a new conception of salvation. It is impossible to believe that the unmeasured worlds of prehistoric man that are at present rolling into the vision of the nobler spirits, and whose wonderful contributions in the way of brain and muscle and rude inventions, of the indispensable preliminaries of civilisation, are receiving wider and more reverent recognition, do not stand in the eternal loving thought of God in Christ.'[1]

For the author of these sentences, it will be observed, primitive man is far from being an object devoid of interest. He claims for him that he has made 'wonderful contributions.' And this is really no exaggeration. Primitive man and his achievements, as these are made known to us by archæology, are indeed uniquely interesting. His work possesses the interest that belongs to all beginnings of things that have grown to greatness. In the prehistoric times were laid the foundations of art, language, morality, religion. Then man began to employ the *hand*, that distinctive organ of the human body, as a tool-making and using instrument. The tools made were doubtless very rude — flint knives,

[1] Gordon, *The Christ of To-day*, p. 15.

stone hatchets, and the like. Nevertheless there they were, first attempts in a new departure, promise of better things to come, their very defects stimulating to invention with a view to improvement. Then also man began to use the tongue as an organ of *speech*. The origin of *language* belongs to that prehistoric time. Doubtless the first efforts at speaking were of the crudest sort; but the very earliest attempt in this direction, however rudimentary, was of infinite significance for the future intellectual history of mankind. And what immense strides had been made in the creation of language before the dawn of the historical period! Men learned at length to say 'I' and 'thou,' distinguishing themselves from one another, and from the outside world. Specialists tell us it took thousands of years to get this length. It was well-spent time. What a great thing for a man to become conscious of himself as a personality distinct from the world! But this is not all. Before the historical period, men had produced such highly developed languages as the Sanskrit, an achievement which even to a Hartmann, appears little short of miraculous, demanding the special aid and inspiration of the Great Unconscious Spirit of the universe.

To the same prehistoric age belong the first beginnings of *morality*. With man came into this world the beneficent peculiarity of exceptionally helpless infancy, making protracted demands on a mother's care. The human infant created society, yea, even the rudiments of the kingdom of heaven. It gave rise to the family, the social unit, to permanent relations between father and mother, parents and children. This unit, the social cell, grew by affinity into an aggregation of cells, forming a tribe whose members were knit together by common affection, common interests, and a sense of mutual obligation.

Once more in this prehistoric time are to be sought the rudiments of *religion*. But how can we know what were the primitive man's thoughts of God? The method of writers on 'Primitive Culture' is to gather facts about the religious ideas and customs of savages, and to transfer them to the prehistoric time, going on the assumption that savage religion is not a degeneracy but a survival. The method has not been allowed to pass unquestioned. Vigorous protests have been entered against the hypothesis that to all intents and purposes the savage and the primitive man are identical, that the savage of to-day *is* what the primitive man *was*. And it is obvious that in some respects the identification is inadmissible. For example, the primitive man was an originator, the savage is the child of inherited custom. 'The primitive man, just because primitive, although endowed with a good intellect, heart, and will, could have no traditions, acquisitions, or habits, no words except those which he invented, no tools or rudiments of art not of his own devising, no beliefs not attained by personal exertion.'[1] Then the savage is an unprogressive man, stagnant in thought and conduct, remaining the same as his forefathers from generation to generation. Primitive man, on the other hand, so far as we have the means of

[1] Flint, *Philosophy of History*, p. 659.

ascertaining the facts, was progressive: he went on improving in speech and in tool-making. But with this caveat let us concede that in religion the savage of to-day fairly well represents the primitive man. What follows? That the religion of the primitive man was what Mr. Tylor has called 'Animism,' a belief, that is to say, in the presence of spiritual beings everywhere in nature, in men, in beasts, in plants, and even in inanimate objects. A crude, childish faith, doubtless: crude in its psychology, in its natural philosophy, and in its theology, yet with all its crudeness not without points of interest for philosophic reflection. In the first place, it was something that men began to ask themselves questions concerning the difference between a living and a dead body, concerning the nature of the shapes which appear in dreams, concerning the mystery of death and what lies beyond. Once entered on that path of inquiry, the human mind would not rest until it had arrived at the idea of a *Great Spirit* of the universe, who is to the world as a whole what the soul in a human body is to an individual man. Then it is worthy of note that the primitive philosophy of nature was *spiritualistic*, not *materialistic*, as one might have expected. At this point the beginning and the end of human thought meet, for the tendency of modern philosophy is more and more to find in spirit the ultimate explanation of the universe. Spirit is also the last word in religion as in philosophy. God is a Spirit, said the author of the Christian Faith, and our deepest modern thinkers have nothing better to put in the place of that great word. But the wild man of the woods and the caves anticipated the oracle when he saw spirits everywhere: in individual plants and animals, in a group of individuals like a forest, in the great, wide world. Despise him not for the crudity of his thought; he was on the right road.[1]

We do not despise the primitive man; no one, imbued in any measure with the modern scientific spirit, can despise him. Does God then despise him? Must we conceive God as too holy to be able to contemplate with any complacency the rudimentary rational and moral state of primitive humanity? To some such feeling is probably due the tenacity with which the religious spirit clings to a conception of the pristine state as one of perfection, the first man bearing God's image not only potentially, but in full realisation, in respect of knowledge, righteousness, and holiness. It is specially natural to cherish this idea as of vital moment when man is viewed as a direct product of the immediate creative causality of God. What God has to do with only at a distance and at second hand may be imperfect, but must not that which proceeds from His own hand, without the intervention of second causes, be absolutely faultless, as good as it is in its nature to be? As I said before, I have no wish to pronounce dogmatically on the question of fact. But

---

[1] This is acknowledged even by Mr. Herbert Spencer in the concluding volume of his *Synthetic Philosophy*. He says, 'A germ of truth was contained in the primitive conception — the truth, namely, that the power which manifests itself in consciousness is but a differently conditioned form of the power which manifests itself beyond consciousness.' — *The Principles of Sociology*, vol. iii. p. 170.

I venture to hint that the inference from Divine Holiness to the necessity of an absolutely perfect pristine state is mistaken. If holiness is no barrier to intimate relations between God and man, throughout his history as a sinful being, why should it postulate sinlessness, moral completeness, to begin with? Besides, is not the whole conception of Divine Holiness underlying the argument legal rather than evangelic, worthier of Judaism than of Christianity? Is it not truer, I say not to the teaching of Christ merely, but to our own best ethical insight, to lay the emphasis rather on the condescension, the grace, the benignity of God, and, in the light of that, to hold it possible for Him to take a kindly interest even in the rude primitive man of anthropological science? Think of the affectionate, tender interest taken by fathers and mothers in the faint early dawn of reason and conscience in their offspring! All beginnings in the use of faculty in childhood possess intense interest for those who have arrived at maturity: first attempts at speech, walking, thinking, judging between right and wrong. Is this very human enjoyment beyond the reach of the Great Being whom we call the Father in heaven? It was indeed beyond the reach of the Zeus of Greek Tragedy, whom Æschylus represents as inflicting merciless punishment on Prometheus for services rendered to primitive humanity, which showed the Titan god to be the better deity of the two.[1] But not so thought the Hebrew prophet, who likened God to a *nurse* in the suggestive words, 'I taught Ephraim to go.'[2] May we

[1] Vide *Prometheus Vinctus*, 440-514. [2] Hosea xi. 3.

not extend the scope of the pathetic metaphor, and conceive of God as the nurse, not of Israel only, but of primitive man, teaching him to go, to walk erect on two feet, instead of on four, to use his hands in the making of tools, to use his tongue in the creation of language, to use his reason in the explanation of what he saw happening around him, to use his moral sense in discerning between good and evil? If ever there was need for Providence it was then. When our children grow up, they become to a certain extent independent of parental care, but in the early years, that care is indispensable even for the preservation of life, not to speak of higher culture. So with primitive man. His Maker had to take special care of him then, to keep him alive in an inhospitable world, full of trackless jungles and uncultivated wildernesses tenanted by wild beasts, and to promote the development of his human capabilities. And, that the providence exercised over the childhood of humanity did its work well, is evidenced by the goodly manhood it reached in the earliest civilisations, of which ancient history, and still more ancient unearthed monuments, bear record: those of India, Egypt, China, Babylon, with their languages, arts, wisdoms, religions; imperfect, rude in many respects, yet not without elements of real, permanent value.

The conclusion, then, at which we have arrived is this: Cynical underestimates of the worth of man are to be rejected, whether these refer to man at his best, to man in the average, or to man in the rudimentary condition. And we are to believe that God cares for

THE WORTH OF MAN

man in all the stages of his long history, in all the phases of his development, in all samples of his common humanity, whether good or bad. God cares for the beginnings of man because He cares for the end. He sees the end in the beginning, the ripe fruit in the root, the oak in the acorn, the perfect man in the rudimentary man, the ideal of humanity in the crudest specimen of actual humanity. Therefore He might pronounce the verdict 'very good' on the new thing which had appeared in creation, the *human*, on the very first day of its appearance, assuming that the phenomenon presenting itself to the Divine eye was not man with all his possibilities realised, but simply man with those rational and moral capacities which constitute in the abstract the Divine Image. The first man, even so conceived, was a son of God, and the appearance on the stage of this new divine type of being gave to the morning of the sixth creation day a quite unique significance. The dawn of that day was conscious of its importance as ushering in the epoch of the human, to which all the earlier epochs had looked forward. The Creative Spirit rejoiced in that dawn, albeit not ignorant what a tragic affair the long day of humanity might turn out to be, God said, ' Better the human with all its possible tragedy than a world with man left out of it.' And from the bright morning He looked forward to the far distant evening when the storms should be past and the sky serene, and man at last should have become a son of God indeed, perfected through suffering and even through sin.

Because God takes into account possibilities, He can

care even for the degenerate and the depraved. 'The worst person in all history,' it has been boldly said, 'is something to God, if he is nothing to the world.'[1] That degeneracy may go to a hopeless point even for God may be possible, but it very often seems to have reached that point in the judgment of men when, to the Divine eye, there is still some redeeming feature; under the hard, rocky surface of evil habit, a store of water that, reached by the boring tool of pain, might spring up an artesian well of eternal life. 'Recall Christ, brother of rejected persons, brother of slaves, felons, idiots, and of insane, diseased persons.'[2] Christ hoped for those who were given up in despair. Christ's sympathetic hopefulness, methinks, is nearer the mind of the Eternal than the hopelessness of less loving, more austere judges, who would deem the world well rid of its bruised reeds and smoking wicks. God loves the human, and His omniscient eye wistfully searches for some small remnant of it, even in men whose life seems wholly bestial or diabolic. He shows His love, not by attempting to make such men happy, — that is neither possible nor desirable, — but by conducting them through a hell of misery to wise reflection and penitent resolve. 'Let the wicked forsake his way, and the unrighteous man his thoughts, and let him return unto the Lord, and He will have mercy upon him, and to our God, for He will abundantly pardon.'[3]

[1] Gordon, *The Christ of To-day*, p. 200.
[2] Whitman's *Poems*.
[3] Isaiah lv. 7.

LECTURE VII

THE POWER MAKING FOR RIGHTEOUSNESS

WE now proceed to consider the verification of the providential order within the sphere of human history. And the first topic inviting our attention is that aspect of Divine Providence in which it appears as a power making for righteousness, on the great scale and on the small, a retributive justice connecting conduct with its congruous lot; in familiar Biblical phrase, rendering to every man according to his works.

It must be understood at the outset that this idea of Providence is only an aspect, not a complete view of the subject. The conception of God as a Moral Governor has the sanction of the Hebrew sacred literature, and, of course, it has relative truth; but it is not the whole truth, nor even the deepest, most important part of the truth. To take it for the whole is to disqualify ourselves for understanding the moral phenomena of history. These can be read aright only by one who remembers that there is more than a single law or force at work; not merely retributive justice, but benign purpose working out its will independently of human misconduct, and also a law whereby goodness suffers at the hand of evil, and so becomes a redemptive power. It was characteristic of the eighteenth century apologists, as represented, *e.g.* by Bishop Butler, to give the Old Testament idea undue prominence. One of the most important chapters in Butler's *Analogy* is that which treats of *the moral government of God.* It exhibits at once the author's strength and his weakness; his strength by the weighty manner in which he asserts and proves the truth of his thesis, his weakness in so far as the whole treatment is dominated by the deistic conception of God as transcendent. For the idea of God as above all things a *Governor*, is vitiated by transcendency. That is to say, it yields a Deity standing in a very external far-off relation to the world. 'Government,' it has been well said, 'especially when conceived after the analogy of the ancient monarchies, has an element of externality about it, which fails to express that union of the organism with its members which is the true figure under which we conceive God's relation to the world of men and things.'[1]

Yet, as already remarked, this idea has a relative, partial truth which cannot be ignored without damage. While it is certainly true that God has never dealt with any human being on the basis of mere justice, that 'He hath not dealt with us after our sins,' that He is ever striving towards overcoming evil with good, yet the history of the world amply proves that it is no empty threat which is contained in the prophetic words: 'I will visit you for your iniquities.'[2] And though the truth embodied in the threat be but a fragment of the whole doctrine of Providence, and, when taken apart,

[1] Hyde, *Outlines of Social Theology*, p. 36.
[2] Amos iii. 2.

a mere abstraction, yet it is well to isolate it for separate consideration. The study of it forms a good introduction to the investigation of a complicated problem. It is the best lesson to begin with, because it is the simplest, most elementary, most obvious, most on the surface. Then this truth — God a moral Governor, placed in the forefront, will help us to grasp firmly at the outset an ethical conception of Providence as concerned supremely, not for the happiness of sentient creatures, but for the reign of righteousness. It is well to see at once that the history of the world gives the lie to the doctrine that pleasure is the chief good.

Belief in a Divine Power making for righteousness is not to be waived aside as a mere Hebrew fancy, or as a pet theorem in an antiquated apologetic. Greek poets and Chinese sages shared this faith with Hebrew prophets, and proclaimed it with equal explicitness, if not with the same power and emphasis. And leaders of nineteenth century thought, thoroughly imbued with the modern spirit, and free enough from theistic bias, have asserted the reality of a moral order of the world with a sincerity and intensity of conviction that entitle them to take their place by the side of Butler. Carlyle, Arnold, even Strauss, may be named in this connection. These names are a sufficient guarantee that what we have to do with here is not a theistic dogma, but a fact capable of being verified by observation. Carlyle's idea of God is theologically indefinable. Arnold scornfully relegated the personality of God to the category of the unverifiable. When Strauss proclaimed his faith in a moral order by which the idea of the good was being realised, he was a materialist firmly persuaded that thought is a mode of motion. Yet all three are fit to be cited as witnesses for our present contention. For what we are now concerned with is a fact, not a theological theory. We want to be satisfied, in the first place, that the alleged fact of a moral order in the world *is* a fact. That ascertained, men will make their own use of the fact according to their preconceived theological ideas. For us it will be a verification of the idea of God we took out of man's place in the universe: a Being with a rational and moral nature, and an ethical world-aim. The fact, if it be a fact, will tend to verify our theistic hypothesis. But meantime we need not be ashamed to have Strauss for a companion as far as his creed will allow him to go with us.

Having said this, I may say another thing. If even Strauss is not disqualified by his materialism for being a witness to a moral order, a Hebrew prophet is not disqualified for bearing testimony because his evidence is given in a book containing, in the belief of many, a special revelation. The Hebrew prophets may be admitted as witnesses along with the rest, on the same footing, *i.e.* as giving evidence based ultimately on observation. That is really their position. They looked around on the world, and this was what they saw: a power at work in the interest of righteousness, causing this man or nation to prosper because they did right, bringing ruin on another man or nation because they did wrong. Their testimony is to be taken for what it is worth. No authority need be claimed for it except such as is due to superior powers of observation sharpened by exceptional interest in the subject. It may be that they have stated the case too strongly, too unqualifiedly, and run into a certain onesidedness. That is apt to be the way with prophets. Be that as it may, in any case it would be foolish and flippant to disregard their testimony as that of persons not worth listening to at this late epoch. To the present hour none have appeared in the world more worth listening to on this matter. All competent judges of all creeds — theistic, pantheistic, agnostic, are agreed about that.

In proceeding now to indicate some of the traces of a moral order in the world, a commencement may fitly be made with that which lies nearest to us: the sense of right and wrong which every man has within his breast. This is not only near us, but it may be said to form the very core of ourselves, of our moral personality. And yet we cannot help feeling that in conscience there is something that is not ourselves. The devout Theist listens to its voice as if it were the voice of God. For some Theists this is more than a pious sentiment, even the strict scientific truth. Not otherwise, they hold, than on this view can the note of authority wherewith conscience speaks be adequately accounted for. Among those who in recent times have advocated this opinion, Dr. Martineau occupies a prominent place. He assigns to an act of conscience a power to compel belief in an external source of its authority, equal to that possessed by an act of perception to compel belief in an external world. 'The externality in the one case, the authority in the other, the causality in both are,' according to this able defender of theism, 'known upon exactly the same terms, and carry the same guarantee of their validity.'[1] This seems to be, to say the least, an overstatement. The authority of God is not so obtrusively forced upon our attention in the phenomena of conscience as is the existence of an external world in the phenomena of perception. The appeal, of course, must be to the ordinary consciousness. Now with regard to perception, the fact is that the ordinary consciousness cannot help believing in an external world distinct from, and the source of, sensation. It is only for philosophers, accustomed to habits of severe abstraction and reflection, that an idealistic view of the physical world is possible or conceivable. In connection with conscience, on the other hand, the state of the case is just the reverse. It is only for a man of highly disciplined moral nature, like Dr. Martineau, that God is inevitably and self-evidently present in the voice of the inward monitor. For the average moral consciousness God's presence is, at best, but faintly discernible, if, indeed, it be discerned at all.

Thoroughgoing advocates of the evolutionary theory, as applicable to the whole universe of being, mental and moral phenomena not excepted, think it possible to account for the feeling of authority connected with the moral sentiments without reference to a supernatural source. It is held to have its origin in the various forms of control exercised by the community over the individual. At first this control is felt as coercion, but by and by, according to well-known psychological laws, it

[1] *A Study of Religion*, vol. ii. p. 28.

assumes the aspect of moral obligation. Primitive man was compelled to do certain things by the authority, and in the interest of the tribe, and in course of ages civilised man came at last to feel, in relation to social duties, such as telling the truth, or abstaining from acts of violence or theft, an inward sense of constraint. This is a theory sufficiently plausible to give satisfaction to such as are predisposed to be content with it. Those, on the other hand, whose bias lies in another direction do not find it difficult to criticise it. Dr. Martineau's criticism is sharp and peremptory. 'I can understand how society taking the individual in hand can create a "must" for him; but not how it can create an "ought," and as self-interest, by which alone it works, does not begin to be anything else by length of days, but only becomes a swifter thought, and easier habit of the same type, it is useless to borrow millenniums in order to turn it into duty.'[1]

In another connection, I have tried to show that dogmatism on the applicability of the evolutionary theory to morals is not necessary in the interest of Theism. The remark may be repeated here. If, as Martineau contends, evolution cannot give us what we want, a real sense of moral obligation, then there is an end of the matter. If, on the other hand, it does, then we need not quarrel with the result because of the way in which it is brought about. Even that in which the Theist is chiefly interested, the identification of the voice of conscience with the voice of God, remains intact. God can speak to me through conscience under any

[1] *A Study of Religion*, vol. ii. p. 9.

theory of its origin. The only possible difference is that on one theory, that of Martineau, He may seem to speak immediately and in loud, audible tone, while on the other, that of Spencer, He speaks only mediately, and as from a great distance. In the one case, it is as if one were standing beside me speaking into my ear; in the other, it is as if one were speaking to me miles away through a telephone. Granting the fact to be so, do we suffer serious practical loss? The sound may be fainter, less arresting, but is it not equally distinct to the listening ear? Nay, is the sound necessarily fainter? need it be a case of speaking through a telephone? Is it not the prerogative of religious feeling to make God always near as the real actor, however many second causes intervene between His causality and the effect? The chain of second causes exists for science, but the magic power of faith can bid it vanish. Even so here. The telephone is there for philosophic reason, and the voice is very feeble and ghostly; but for the devout soul God is close at hand, and His word strong and commanding.

Of the peace and trouble of mind that are the inward reward and penalty respectively of obeying and disobeying the voice of conscience I do not speak, but pass on to notice another sphere within which the Power making for righteousness reveals itself. I mean society. It is the interest of society, in self-defence, to constitute itself an instrument for enforcing fundamental moral laws. On this Butler remarks, 'It is necessary to the very being of society that vices destructive of it should be punished *as being so;* the vices of falsehood, injustice, cruelty; which punishment therefore is as natural as society; and so is in an instance of a kind of moral government, naturally established, and actually taking place.'[1] Butler here states a fact, that society necessarily punishes vices inimical to its being and well-being, and draws from it an inference in favour of the reality of a Divine moral government. For us the fact is the thing of immediate interest, because what we are in quest of is facts of this sort serving as verifications of our theistic hypothesis. Now the statement which Butler makes is undeniably true of all societies of human beings, whatever stage of civilisation they may have reached. There are certain elementary moralities without which no society could hold together for any length of time. Primitive men, living together in social groups, could not be very long in discovering some of these moralities, such as, 'Thou shalt not lie,' 'Thou shalt not steal,' 'Thou shalt not kill.' It might take longer to arrive at the important moral generalisation embodied in the precept: 'Thou shalt not commit adultery,' and there may be some foundation for the assertion that the first stage in the relation of the sexes was a state of promiscuity.[2] But even here nature and the exigencies of social well-being might teach men the needful lesson sooner than theorists imagine. At all events, it is certain that one of the most urgent tasks imposed on men associated together

---

[1] *Analogy*, chap. III. § iii.

[2] *Vide* M‘Lennan, *Primitive Marriage*, chap. viii. But see, on the other side, Westermarck, *The History of Human Marriage*, chap. iv., where M‘Lennan's hypothesis is subjected to a very searching criticism.

would be to think out, with all possible expedition, the rudiments of social morality. A *Decalogue*, so to speak, would be as necessary for them as a language. And as we had occasion to remark, in connection with language, what great achievements had been wrought out even in prehistoric times, so it is likely that a tolerably complete table of relative duties had been constructed for itself by each social organism at a very early period. And if, in connection with language, in view of the greatness of early attainments, even a Hartmann is constrained to recognise the aid of that Power whom he calls the Unconscious, shall we not own that primitive man wrought out his table of duty not without the assistance of the Being whom Mr. Arnold calls 'a Power not ourselves making for righteousness'? Israel believed that she received her *Ten Words* from God on Mount Sinai. If that be true in any real sense, then there can be no doubt at all as to the Divine interest in righteousness. In course of ages, Jewish belief in the Divine origin of the law became somewhat attenuated. By that time God had become a transcendent Deity too far above the world to do anything in it, except through angelic intermediaries. But even then God was regarded as the ultimate source of the Law: from God, through angels, to Moses; through Moses to Israel. Translate that into other terms: From God through the moral sense and through the human mind active on the question, how must men behave in their relations to each other? to some man more thoughtful and earnest than his fellows, and through him to the community, and you have a formula which holds true not of Israel only, but of every people that has come to any good in this world.

It is a great affair for any people when it has got the length of having its 'Decalogue.' Israel's faith that her law was God-given was but a due recognition of the supreme value of a code of fundamental duties, and of the truth that when such a code, written or unwritten, has taken its place in the consciousness of a nation, it is for that nation a veritable revelation of God as a moral Governor. Nothing more important can happen to a nation than to attain to this knowledge of duty. A Hebrew Psalmist claimed for his countrymen that they were the only people to whom God had shown His statutes.[1] His claim may seem to some extravagant, but at least he was not wrong in congratulating Israel on possessing the privilege, whether it was peculiar to her or common to her with others.

Laws for the benefit of society are meant to be enforced, and necessarily have annexed to them penalties for transgression. The love of law, the sense of its supreme value, the passion for righteousness, belongs to the few, to a Moses or a Confucius. The mass of men lag far behind; hence crime is ever of frequent occurrence, and infliction of penalty plays a considerable part in the history of communities. This is an ungenial aspect of the Power that works for righteousness. But a legislator who does not care whether his law is obeyed or not, cannot be credited with a passion for righteousness. Severity is an index of moral earnestness. Even merciless severity may be viewed as a

[1] Psalm cxlvii. 19, 20.

tribute to the awful seriousness and fixity of purpose with which the providential order of the world pursues its aim for the moralisation of mankind. At the worst, rigour is infinitely better than laxity.

We pass now, in quest of traces of the retributive moral order, into the wide sphere of universal history. The Power that makes for righteousness appears here as deciding the fate of nations, out of regard to the presence or absence within them of morality or right conduct. The *destructive* action of the Power is the thing that most readily strikes the eye. It was on this that the gaze of the Hebrew prophet was chiefly fixed. He was largely a prophet of judgment. His sombre imagination revelled in the tragic spectacle of great powerful nations, one after the other, precipitated by the vindictive action of Providence into utter irretrievable ruin. It was a mournful satisfaction to him to see that, if peoples and monarchs would not do what was right, the Divine righteousness asserted itself against them as an irresistible destructive force. Yet though his mood was grim, it was not inhuman. He was not insensible to the pathos of the contrast between national prosperity and national decline; between the epoch of creation and the epoch of destruction, between the age of the axe, when the woodman felled cedars on the mountain side, to be turned into carved work for the ornamentation of palaces, and the age of the hammer ruthlessly wielded in the demolition of palaces and temples.[1] The prophetic mood has reappeared in western lands and in modern times, especially at social or

[1] Psalm lxxiv. 5, 6.

political crises fitted to superinduce it. Think of Volney, on the eve of the French Revolution, sitting among the ruins of Palmyra, and seeing in them the emblem of what had befallen all the great historical nations of antiquity in the East. But more remarkable is it to find a man like Mr. Matthew Arnold re-echoing with eloquent impassioned emphasis the words of doom uttered by Hebrew seers: 'Down they come, one after another; Assyria falls, Babylon, Greece, Rome; they all fall for want of *conduct*, righteousness. . . . Judæa itself, the holy land, the land of God's Israel, falls too, and falls for want of *righteousness*.'[1]

'For want of righteousness'—such is Mr. Arnold's deliberate verdict. 'Look a little deeper, and you will see that one strain runs through it all: nations and men, whoever is shipwrecked, is shipwrecked on *conduct*.'[2] So he interprets the general drift of Hebrew prophecy, and with unqualified approval, as appears from the fact of his applying the principle to Greece, which hardly came within the range of prophetic vision. Of Greece, the elect instrument of Providence in the sphere of art, he ruthlessly affirms: 'Brilliant Greece perished for lack of attention enough to conduct; for want of conduct, steadiness, character.'[3] Unspeakably sad, surely! Yet if it be true that conduct, *i.e.* misconduct, was the cause of failure and ruin in the case of Greece, or of any of the other ancient nations, a certain element of comfort need not be wanting. A world in

[1] *Literature and Dogma*, p. 353.
[2] *Ibid.*, p. 352.
[3] *Ibid.*, p. 356.

which ruin is rife as the penalty of moral shortcoming is still a different world from that of pessimistic dreams. The pessimist's world is one in which a non-moral Deity works havoc aimlessly and recklessly. A world in which ruin prevails as the result of sin is one in which a holy will works destruction in the interest of righteousness. Even in the extreme case of a world wholly gone to badness, in the abuse of freedom,[1] and therefore doomed to misery, there would still be this to say, that the universal woe would be a gigantic demonstration of a moral order reacting against unrighteousness. But, it must be owned, the consolation contained in that reflection would be very small. Such Nemesis would be suicidal. The Power making for righteousness would thereby be convicted of impotence. It would show itself as a power unable to insure that there shall be so much as one righteous man in a city or a world, or to do more than insure that unrighteousness shall not go unpunished. On these terms the moral order would utterly break down. What boots a universal deluge if it leave the earth without inhabitants? God must be *more* than a moral Governor rendering to every man according to his works if He is to be even so much.

We are all familiar with the Carlylean doctrine that right is might and might right. Care should be taken not to misunderstand it. Its meaning is not that it does not matter about right; the great thing is to

[1] *Vide* Fraser, *Gifford Lectures*, 2nd series, p. 197, where this case is put.

have might. Such an immoral dogma was not in all Carlyle's thoughts. It means just the opposite, that right is the one omnipotent thing in the world; that wherever right is, might must and shall be. It is a bright, optimistic assertion of the invincibility of righteousness. Applied, it will mean that right was on the side of Israel when she dispossessed the Canaanites; of Greece, when she defeated the Persians; of Rome, when she subdued Carthage, Greece, Judæa; of the northern barbarians, when they broke up the Great Roman Empire; of the Mohammedans, when they overran the Christian world in East and West in their conquering career, and put the crescent in the place of the cross. There can be little doubt as to these instances, except, it may be, in some minds, in reference to the last. The name 'Christian,' it may be thought, ought to have protected Palestine and Spain from becoming Mohammedanised. But mere names, however sacred, count for nothing in the sight of the moral order. It respects only real ethical values. And Christians should not need to be reminded that it is possible for the 'salt' to lose its savour and become the most worthless of all things.

No objection should be taken, therefore, to the action of the righteous Power on this score. Neither should we be scandalised when we observe that it has no respect of persons, no partiality, *e.g.* for favoured races and peoples. The fact is certainly so. Elect peoples, destined to distinction in attainment and service, and chosen for that end, are not exempt from the retributive action of the moral order. Indeed, if there be any difference, they are the most roughly handled. 'You only have I known of all the families of the earth, *therefore* I will punish you for all your iniquities.'[1] So Israel, Greece, Rome, one after the other, must go down. Elect peoples have tragic careers. They are born, grow, decay, die, or even fall a prey to the brute force and greed of barbarians. And there are always good reasons why they should. You may ask, Can we accuse them of misconduct? Israel, for example? Was she less moral than Rome her conqueror? No, but she was *spiritually blind*. She did not know that the old religious order had served its time, and that a new order was due. She had a zeal for righteousness, but she perished through obstinate clinging to an antiquated type. In the eyes of the moral order, lack of spiritual vision is a fatal crime.

But are there no exceptions to the doctrine that right is might, in either direction, no faithful peoples that go down, no faithless, unworthy peoples that live on? Apparent exceptions abound in individual life; may we not look for exceptions also in national life? Is China, for example, not a case in point? Her days have been very long on the earth. What has she done to deserve it? And the Turkish Empire? Is it not about time that it were broken up by the Power that makes for righteousness? Or take the case of Israel. Must we conclude that she was a greater sinner than Babylon because her sons were swept as in a net into captivity? Did the Babylonian captivity not simply mean the weaker succumbing to the brute force of the stronger?

[1] Amos iii. 2.

Would it have made any difference though the conduct of the elect race had been all that its prophets desired? That it would, seems plainly implied in the pathetic lament: 'O that thou hadst hearkened to My commandments! then had thy peace been as a river, and thy righteousness as the waves of the sea. Thy seed also had been as the sand, and the offspring of thy bowels like the gravel thereof; his name should not have been cut off nor destroyed from before me.'[1] But the question *will* obtrude itself: In presence of such great powers as Babylon, Egypt, Greece, and Rome, could the independence and prosperity of Israel, however faithful to God, have been guaranteed by anything short of preternatural interference, such as that which destroyed Sennacherib's army? I fear it must be acknowledged that the problem of Divine Providence is not so simple as Carlyle's theorem supposes; that God's judgments are a great deep; that His way is often in the sea, and His footsteps untraceable; and that the bearing of conduct on lot is only one of the factors to be taken into account. Thus the short-lived nature of the monarchies of Western Asia may be partly explained by the nomadic antecedents of the founders. 'A monarchy formed of nomads,' remarks Herder, 'can hardly be of long duration. It destroys and subdues, till it is itself destroyed. The capture of the capital, or the death of a king, may end the whole robber scene. So was it with Babylon and Nineveh, with Persepolis and Ecbatana.'[2] With reference to the

---

[1] Isaiah xlviii. 18, 19.
[2] *Ideen zur Geschichte der Menschheit*, vol. iii. p. 128.

short duration of the ancient Persian kingdom, which lasted only two hundred years, the same writer parabolically observes: 'Its roots were so small, and its branches so large, that it could not but fall to the ground.'[1] As for Greece, the brevity of its brilliant career has been deemed explicable, without reference to moral causes, by the simple consideration that for Greeks the State meant the single city as distinct from a nation, implying a high-strung enthusiasm which cannot last, and a lack of union disabling for combined action against a common foe.[2]

The extraordinary longevity of a nation like China may be accounted for by the consideration that it grew out of its own roots, rested upon itself, and therefore lasted, the same people essentially, for thousands of years, through all vicissitudes of fortune. Or we may say that China has endured so long because it is an unprogressive nation. It is everlasting as the inert mountains. Other nations have lived their life, run through a brilliant career, then passed away in death. China dies not, because she has never lived.

But such considerations as these, tending to show that the destinies of nations may depend on a plurality of causes, need not weaken our conviction that a very prominent place among these belongs to national morality. This is the truth, and it is wholesome to give to it in our creed about Providence, without too

---

[1] *Ideen zur Geschichte der Menschheit*, vol. iii. p. 77.
[2] E. A. Freeman, *Comparative Politics*, pp. 93, 94. For further remarks on this point, *vide* Lecture X.

much refinement or balanced qualified statement, a very broad recognition, such as that embodied in the doctrine that right is might. One thing, however, we must carefully avoid: resting the verification of the principle on too narrow a historical basis. All judgments based on a few events, or on the experience of a few years, are to be distrusted. Calamity, famine, pestilence, disaster in war, may overtake any people, and it is easy to suggest that it is a Divine judgment on sin. And when such so-called judgments are on a land, the most thoughtless of its inhabitants may for the moment be startled into repentance. But the repentance will be as short-lived as the construction put upon events is shallow. We are on surer ground when the connection between conduct and lot can be shown to be one of natural causality. That proves that the moral order of the world has a deep root in the constitution of the universe. The Power that works for righteousness is not to be seen only, or chiefly, in the unusual, the occasional, the catastrophic; any more than the creative hand of the Almighty is to be traced mainly in the critical periods of the world's evolution, as at the introduction of life. It is more certainly traceable in the steady working of moral causes going on silently through long ages, and at last culminating in a great, stable empire; or, it may be, in the final overthrow of a kingdom which has had a splendid career of power and prosperity. The one way to an enlightened, firm grasp of the truth that there is indeed a moral order in the world is a wide, careful study of history. The text-books for those who desire to master the important lesson are such works as Gibbon's *Decline and Fall of the Roman Empire*, and Carlyle's *History of the French Revolution*. The story of Rome from its Rise to its Fall extends over more than a thousand years. Across the ages covered by the stirring tale is written in large letters, wide apart: 'Verily there is a God that judgeth in the earth.'[1] He who has been able to spell out the mystic scroll has studied to purpose.

The study of history with an eye to its moral significance ought to suggest some important inferences as to the causes on which the fate of nations chiefly depends. These summed up in memorable aphorisms might serve the purpose of a book of Proverbs for the guidance of rulers. I am not going to attempt the ambitious task of constructing such a compendium. I only offer the modest observation, that it may be assumed *a priori* that the fundamental laws of social morality will be found to be very intimately concerned in the matter. The keeping by the people of its 'Decalogue' ought to be an affair of life and death. Truth, justice, chastity, and the qualities that go along with these virtues, must count for much in the destinies of nations. Among the companion qualities may be named: a simple temperate habit of life, courage, modesty. These are conspicuous in the early life of peoples that have taken a great and honourable place in the history of mankind. It is when power and prosperity have been reached that they are apt to be replaced by 'pride, fulness of bread, and abundance

[1] Psalm lviii. 11, R.V.

of idleness';[1] effeminacy, cowardice — sure causes of decline and death. Of these vices, none is more severely condemned, as hostile to national well-being, than *pride*. Many aphorisms are directed against this vice in the Hebrew books. 'Though the Lord be high, yet hath He respect unto the lowly; but the proud He knoweth afar off.'[2] 'Surely He scorneth the scorners, but He giveth grace unto the lowly.'[3] 'Those that walk in pride He is able to abase.'[4] The thought these sentences embody is not a theological dogma; it is an ethical maxim based on observation. It is not the peculiar possession of the Hebrews; the same thought finds a place in the wisdom of other peoples. Greek poets know as well as Hebrew Prophets and Psalmists that pride (ὕβρις) is offensive to the gods. Thus Sophocles says: 'Discretion and humility are the foundation stones of happiness. Wherefore be thou reverent towards the gods; for pride carrieth in her hand a rod of chastisement, and will teach thee humility in the latter days.'[5] Again, 'God abhorreth exceedingly the boasting of a proud tongue.'[6] Yet again:—

'Know this well:
That he who has both fear and reverence
Has also safety. But when men are free

[1] Ezekiel xvi. 49.   [2] Psalm cxxxviii. 6.
[3] Proverbs iii. 34.   [4] Daniel iv. 37.

[5] Πολλῷ τὸ φρονεῖν εὐδαιμονίας Πρῶτον ὑπάρχει· χρὴ δ'ἐς τὰ θεῶν Μηδὲν ἀσεπτεῖν· μεγάλοι δὲ λόγοι Μεγάλας πληγὰς τῶν ὑπεραύχων ἀποτίσαντες Γήρᾳ τὸ φρονεῖν ἐδίδαξαν. — *Ant.* 1347-53.

[6] Ζεὺς γὰρ μεγάλης γλώσσης κόμπους ὑπερεχθαίρει. — *Antigone*, 127, 128. The translation of this and the previous quotation is from D'Arcy Thomson, *Sales Attici*.

> To riot proudly, and do all their will,
> That state, be sure, with all its prosperous gales
> Is driving to destruction, and will fall.'[1]

It would be well for individuals and for communities, both civil and ecclesiastical, to lay to heart this teaching of sages. For it is in accordance with the realities of the universe. It points to one of the laws of the moral world which, doubt it not, act with all the certainty of the law of gravitation in the physical world. But they act also as noiselessly and inobservably to the common eye; whence it comes that men can easily lapse into a state of complete obliviousness as to their existence. The earth is constantly whirling round the sun, but the motion is so swift as to be non-existent for the senses, and we need science to assure us of its reality. Even so with the laws of the moral order. Pride, vain thoughts, self-sufficiency, contempt for others, move steadily on towards humiliation and disaster, but the movement is so unobtrusive, and it is so long before anything happens, that we can easily flatter ourselves there is no danger, and continue to nurse the fond delusion till the catastrophe comes with its rude awakening. So in the case of all laws pertaining to the moral sphere. The moral order moves slowly, slowly; its action for long is unobserved by the many; it arrests attention

---

[1] δέος γὰρ ᾧ πρόσεστιν αἰσχύνη θ' ὁμοῦ
σωτηρίαν ἔχοντα τόνδ' ἐπίστασο·
ὅπου δ' ὑβρίζειν, δρᾶν θ' ἃ βούλεται, παρῇ,
ταύτην νόμιζε τὴν πόλιν χρόνῳ ποτὲ
ἐξ οὐρίων δραμοῦσαν ἐς βυθὸν πεσεῖν.

Translation from Plumptre, *The Tragedies of Sophocles*, 'Ajax,' 1079–1083.

only when the crisis arrives, and when it is too late to escape doom. They only are safe who believe habitually in the reality of the moral order: who are firmly convinced that moral law is not less certain in its action than physical law, and who with prophetic eye can foresee the judgment that is coming, even when the sky is blue and the air serene.

To many not minded to live wisely, the alleged certainty of the moral order is not welcome news. They would rather be told that history is a moral chaos, that in this region nothing is certain, that anything may happen to any man at any time, and that every man must take his chance. For such as are in this mood there is more than enough to supply an excuse for scepticism. Even to those, indeed, who want no such excuse, the state of things may appear to be such as does not justify a tone of confidence as to the reality of a moral government of God in this world. A tendency towards it rather than the reality of it is all they can discover. So Butler, *e.g.* interpreted the situation. He speaks of 'the necessary tendencies of virtue, which, though not of present effect, yet are at present discernible in nature; and so afford an instance of somewhat moral in the essential constitution of it.' 'There is,' he adds, 'in the nature of things, a tendency in virtue and vice to produce the good and bad effects now mentioned, in a greater degree than they do in fact produce them.'[1] Butler could be content with this view, because he expected in another world a perfect realisation of what now exists only in a rudimentary form. It was

[1] *Analogy*, ch. iii. v.

enough for him if the present state of things was such as to show which side God is of, and to make a perfect moral order hereafter credible. How different this depressed and depressing tone of the eighteenth century apologist from that of the Hebrew prophets, for whom the theatre of Providence was this present world, and the drama of history an effective, if not a perfect, demonstration of Divine righteousness! The sympathies of modern thought are with the prophets rather than with Butler. 'Why,' men of our time are inclined to say, 'why, if there be indeed a Power making for righteousness, should it not manifest itself in a decisive manner here and now? Let the world to come rest on its own evidence; but surely that world is not furnished with the best possible credentials, when it is viewed simply as a refuge from despair for those who wish to retain faith in a moral government of God!' The appeal, however, must ultimately be to fact. How does the matter actually stand? Well, with much that Butler says we must all agree. Right has not all the might we could desire. It encounters in many ways vexatious frustration. There are conditions of success which are not always at its command, such as sufficient numbers and union:[1] good men knowing each other, and recognising each other as on the same side, and all together forming a compact band bearing some appreciable proportion to the forces of evil leagued against it. For lack of these, especially for lack of union, the cause of justice and truth has often been reduced to a lamentable state of impotence. Yet it is possible to exagger-

[1] Vide *Analogy*, ch. iii. v.

ate here. Much good may be done even when there is disunion, as we see in the case of the Christian Church. And numbers are not always necessary to power. Some of the greatest movements the world has seen — movements ethical in spirit and on the whole making for righteousness, *e.g.* Buddhism and Christianity, began with one man. In times like those of Butler, when faith is worn out, and enthusiasm is at a discount, and even virtue is of the homespun, utilitarian, unheroic type, men have no conception of the inexhaustible might stored up in epoch-making originators. How can one who has seen a river only when it is shrunk to a tiny rill in a dry bed, dotted here and there with stagnant, unwholesome pools, imagine what it is like when it is in full flood, overflowing its banks and sweeping swiftly over the fields? Yet such floods do come. There are creative epochs when a little one becomes a thousand, and a small one a strong nation. Nothing can arrest the movement; death cannot destroy it; persecution strengthens it; ten persecutions only multiply it tenfold. Then the friends of God do not dejectedly talk of just perceptible tendencies of virtue to produce good effects. They triumphantly sing: —

'God is our refuge and strength, a very present help in trouble.
Therefore will not we fear, though the earth be removed, and though the mountains be carried into the midst of the sea;
Though the waters thereof roar and be troubled, though the mountains shake with the swelling thereof.
There is a river, the streams whereof shall make glad the city of God, the holy place of the tabernacles of the Most High.'[1]

[1] Psalm xlvi. 1–4.

We must keep these creative epochs, with their buoyant temper, in view, in order to have firm faith in a Power making for righteousness in this world, and adequate conceptions of the energy with which it works, its capacity of self-propagation, and its persistency. There have been many such, and there will be more. Those that have been are not yet exhausted, though they have had their periods of low vitality, as was the case with Christianity in Butler's age.

Among the conditions of success in the fight of good with evil Butler specifies, along with numbers and union, *time*. 'Length of time, proper scope and opportunities.'[1] The point to be emphasised, however, is not so much that the cause of right *needs*, as that it has *command of*, time. The future belongs to it. No great ethico-religious movement needs to be in a hurry. It can afford to spend the first generation in simply getting rooted in the minds and hearts of a few susceptible disciples. The more leisurely its pace to begin with, the more certainly will it take possession of the ages to come. And space belongs to it as well as time. If the environment be ungenial in one place, it can retire to another. When persecuted in one city, it can flee to another; and the flight, instead of bringing disaster, may, like Mohammed's flight from Mecca, form the beginning of a new era. The Puritans of England, overpowered here, emigrate to America, to create there a great nation whose future is guaranteed by having such an ancestry.

It may be objected that the instances to which allu-

[1] *Analogy*, ch. iii. v.

sion has been made are all cases illustrating the power of *religion* rather than the power of righteousness. Formally this is true, but in reality what exemplifies the one exemplifies the other. Religion and morality are not two entirely distinct things, but rather different phases of the same thing. They cannot be separated in fact without fatal injury to both. Religion apart from morality is a ghost, morality apart from religion is a carcass. Religion is the soul of morality, morality is the body of religion; the two together form an organic whole. Morality is the outcome of true religion, but it cannot exist in vital potency unless there be an antecedent religion capable of giving it birth. Morality without religion lacks wings, motive power; it is a ship without propeller, or sails to catch the wind. Hence all movements fruitful in beneficent ethical results have a religious origin. The Power in the world making for righteousness works through religion as His instrument. The choice of this instrument only shows that the Power understands human nature. For there is more in man than reason, or 'common sense' — the idol of the eighteenth century, or even than conscience. There is imagination, emotion, the mystic faculty of faith. All these must be brought into play in order to get the highest kind of results. 'All that is within' must be at the bidding of righteousness. Only on these terms can we become heroes in the warfare for justice and mercy. A man is very weak when he serves the good with only a part of his spiritual nature. It is well to have a definite religious creed, if it be sincere, and a philosophic theory of the universe in harmony with that creed. Furnished with these, the man of ethical benevolent bent engages in the fight clad in 'the whole armour of God'; without them he enters into battle, brave possibly, but defenceless, vulnerable. Merely rational morality, a purely ethical organisation, can never do much for the world. Let no man dream that it were good for the world if religion died out. Rather let us listen to those who speak to us in this wise: 'Pain is a fact; religion is a fact; little is known of the past, nothing is known of the future. But that religious effort can do something to diminish pain is a conclusion of certain and incalculable value; and so, whatever may have been the origin of the religious sentiment, whether our souls be mortal or immortal, whether there be a heaven or a hell, the enhancement of the religious faculty must remain the one essential effort, and how this can be promoted the one essential inquiry.'[1]

[1] Kelly, *Evolution and Effort*, pp. 103, 104.

LECTURE VIII

THE POWER WORKING IN AND FOR HUMANITY

PART I. HISTORIC DAWNS

IN last lecture God was viewed as a Power without and above men, commanding the doing of right, and enforcing His commands with penalties — a moral Governor rendering unto every man according to his works. This conception, while not untrue, and not unworthy of separate consideration, is, as was then stated, and as must here be repeated, an imperfect, abstract, partial one, needing to be supplemented by a conception more in accordance with the modern doctrine of Divine immanence. God must be viewed not only as a Power without, but also as a Power within; as a Power working beneficently in humanity, and for humanity; working towards the ever-advancing humanisation of man through the development of the rational and moral possibilities of his nature. For such must be the goal. 'The aim of a thing that is not merely a dead means, must lie in the thing itself.'[1] If there be such a thing as progress in history, it must be towards making man answer more and more completely to the ideal of his nature and position, effectively lord and worthy to be lord of creation.

Herder, *Ideen zur Geschichte der Menschheit*, vol. iii. p. 316.

This Divine working in humanity is the natural corollary from the hypothesis that man was the aim of the creative process. If God worked towards man in the lower stages of the creative process, we expect that He will work on in man, towards adequate realisation of the human ideal. Creation, evolution will go on, now in the human sphere. If there be no trace of onward movement in history, there will be reason to suspect that we were mistaken in our whole conception of man's place in the universe, and of its significance.

But it is important to come to the study of history with rational expectations. Over-sanguine hopes inevitably react in the direction of scepticism. To this it may be due that some who see God everywhere in nature find no trace of Him in history; discovering there nothing but a dreary moral chaos, an unrelieved godless scene of sin and misery. What went ye out to see? God making men good and wise as easily, certainly, and quickly, as He makes crystals and flowers? This were unreasonable. Remember that we are now in the region of human freedom, and that we must not assert the Divine immanence, and bring into play the Divine power, so as virtually to annihilate the nature supposed to be given in man. We are also in the region of reason, and that means, as Kant long ago pointed out, that man must find out ways of doing things, slowly, by trial and error, for himself, instead of acting under the guidance of instincts which exclude at once error and progress.[1] We must be prepared for mistake and

---

[1] Kant remarks: 'It is the will of nature, that in all that goes beyond the mechanical ordering of his animal existence man should

misconduct on a large scale, and while still hoping for advance, we must not be surprised if it turn out to be in spirals, rather than in a straight line. Neither in the moral nor in the rational sphere can God, however willing, do everything for man. Man must be a very real and earnest fellow-worker with God. Human nature must be allowed to retain its river-like fluidity, whereby it tends to wander hither and thither at its own will; and the Divine action must be like the gentle coercion of the banks which constrain the wayward stream to move on, though in a circuitous course, till it finds its way to the sea. Such gentle coercion we may certainly count on. God, we may be sure, will not allow the river of human life to run waste. Whatever error, folly, depravity may reveal itself in human history, counteractive, corrective, redemptive, Divine influence may be expected also to appear in ways possibly that shall give lovers of their kind a glad surprise.

While the world lasts, men will find in history what they bring, according to temperament and theological or philosophical bias. A Hegel will interpret events optimistically, on the principle that here, as everywhere, the real is the rational; a Lotze, losing no

depend on himself, and become partaker of no other happiness or completeness than that which he procures for himself without the aid of instinct by his own reason.' He comments on this thesis to the effect that nature is parsimonious in the use of means, therefore having given man reason she leaves him to work his way with that, discovering for himself means of clothing and defence (without horns or claws like oxen and lions) as well as performing the higher functions of enriching life with enjoyments and developing his own character. *Vide* his essay entitled 'Idee zu einer allgemeinen Geschichte in weltbürgerlicher Ansicht,' *Werke* (Hardenstein), vol. iv. p. 143.

chance of criticising adversely the Hegelian system, will sympathise with those who think that the impression made by history is on the whole melancholy. Without indulging in strong statements, I am content to say, at the outset, that history is not a chaos without any trace of progress or rational significance; that God has not left Himself without a witness in the form of persistent beneficent activity, and that that activity has not been limited to giving rain from heaven and fruitful seasons, but has manifested itself in other and much more important ways. If this be true, as a matter of fact, then the hypothesis of a beneficent providential order may be held as verified.

One who desires to discover the traces of such an order in history naturally bethinks himself first of that portion of history which lies before him as a completed whole in the distant past, and, within that whole, of those parts in which the lesson is most clearly taught. That means turning to the stirring pages of Hebrew, Greek, and Roman story. These certainly are of capital importance for a providential, not less than for a philosophic, view of history. But we cannot afford to leave altogether out of sight those portions of the human race which have not had an eventful, thrillingly interesting career, and to proceed on the assumption that, so far as ancient times are concerned, our view may be limited to the countries situated on the shores of the Mediterranean sea. We must remember that large sections of mankind have occupied, or now occupy, positions which may be described by the epithets: *prehistoric, sub-*

historic, *post-historic*. The first applies to peoples which have had a historic career, and points to the time of obscurity antecedent to its commencement. The second refers to peoples which have not yet had a historic career, and possibly never will. The third describes the conditions of peoples who have run through their historic career, in former generations, and have passed out of day into night.

It is not impossible to take a human interest in all these three unrenowned unsung sections of our race, or to believe that they are not devoid of significance for Divine Providence. Special attraction attaches to the first class. By the nature of the case, of a prehistoric condition, little can be known, but it is sometimes possible to observe a people just emerging out of the darkness of prehistoric night into the daylight of history. We can watch *historic dawns*. Very fair and prognostic of a notable future are some of these dawns, *e.g.* those of the ancient Indians, Persians, and Hebrews, and, many centuries later, of the Arabs and the Germans. A glance suffices to show us how far they have got already, and to suggest hopes of greater things to come.

Look first at the Vedic Indians, settled in the valleys of the Punjaub, say fifteen hundred years before the Christian era. They are acquainted with the arts of agriculture and weaving, and with the use of metals; in possession of a highly organised language; rich in the higher treasures of the spirit: witness the collection of sacred hymns called the Rigveda, indited by Rishis who had an eye for the sublime and the beautiful in nature, and especially for the loveliness of the dawn — *Ushas*. The religion of these hymns is a nature-worship, but of no ignoble type, having for its psychological basis poetic sensibility, as is especially apparent in the hymns to the praise of Ushas, which touch a chord in our hearts to this day. Worship was poetry, and poetry was worship in those primitive times. Amid the polytheism of this nature-worship there is a dim feeling after a higher unity. 'Agni is all the gods'; the many are one. The one may be pantheistically conceived, still there is a groping after the one true God if haply they may find Him. Sin, moral error, is not forgotten in these hymns, though by no means so prominent as in the Hebrew Psalter. Varuna[1] is asked to pardon faults, and to assist in the struggle against evil habit; though the larger number of the prayers are for material good, illustrating the truth of the remark in the Sermon on the Mount: 'After these things (food and raiment) do the Gentiles seek.' Would you say that a people with all these characteristics had been left entirely to walk in their own ways, wholly unguided? Would you not rather say that God was not far from them, and that He had brought them thus far? Of what He had given they may make a wrong use, evolving out of Vedic hymns a baleful Pantheism and Brahminism. The like has happened in the history of other religions, the Hebrew and Christian not excepted; first, a God-given heavenly thing, then a woful de-

---

[1] The hymns which refer to moral faults are mainly addressed to Varuna.

generacy. But good is here if not unmixed with evil, and that no good came of it cannot be said in view of the extraordinary moral intensity of early Buddhism.

Turn your eye now to the other branch of the primitive Aryan race: the ancient Persians, with their religious poems called *Gâthas*, the oldest part of the Zendavesta. What do we find here, in this historic dawn of a people destined to play a prominent part in the ancient history of the world? To begin with, again an agricultural community, but that is not the remarkable feature. Most notable is a Hebrew passion for righteousness; a deep-seated conviction that righteousness is the first, supreme interest of human life. This faith forces on the ancient Zoroastrians the question: How does there come to be so much evil in the world? and gives them no rest till they discover a theory that explains the facts to their satisfaction. The theory is crude enough: a good Spirit created the good, and an evil Spirit, a sort of anti-God, created the evil. But the remarkable thing is the existence of a feeling of the need for a theory, due to an intense sense of the surpassing value of righteousness. How strange to find a people endowed with such a sense in the early morning of its historic career! Surely a Divine Educator has been at work who means good to that people and through it to the world! Even their crude theory will serve a purpose in the education of mankind. It is one way of solving a hard problem tried, found wanting, and put aside; so clearing the ground for something better. The lesson taught by a true, noble passion for righteousness, and by a false theory to support it, remains a permanent gain to the world, though both the people who taught it and their religion pass away.

Our next historic dawn is that of a people belonging to another family of nations, destined to play a not less distinguished part than the Aryans in the history of the world. This dawn, as mirrored in the pages of the Old Testament, the unique literature of the people concerned, shines with supernatural brightness. But for our purpose the supernatural light must be shaded off, and Israel must take her place alongside of other peoples, as an example of the ordinary action of a beneficent Providence in the training of races destined to greatness, before they emerge above the historical horizon. The example loses nothing by ceasing to be exceptional; for, if the light of this dawn be of the common kind, it is peculiarly intense in degree. The essential facts are these: The Beni-Israel have just escaped from Egypt, where they have sojourned for generations in a state of bondage, and they are on the way to a settled abode in Palestine under a leader called Moses. The hero of the Exodus, like Zoroaster, is a man of prophetic insight, and he is contemplating the arduous task of turning a horde of slaves into a nation of law-abiding, self-respecting men. He has two things to teach them: that God is one, and that right conduct is the prime need and interest of life. It will be hard to inculcate these high lessons, but the Egyptian experience may help him. The house of bondage was a severe school, but salutary; an excellent illustration, be it remarked in passing, of how little Providence cares about the misery men may have to endure for a while, when it is to issue eventually in moral gain. The gain was great: an inbred horror of everything Egyptian; of a universal servitude, witnessed to by those huge, overgrown cairns, the Pyramids, which could only be built where human life was cheap, labor compulsory, and the government an iron despotism. Horror also of Egyptian religion with its many gods, its beast worship, and its dismal ideas of the life beyond the tomb. In Moses this anti-Egyptian feeling rises to a passion, and the people have been imbued with it to a certain extent; therefore the heroic task of making them a nation of freemen and of ethical Monotheists is by no means hopeless. What a splendid testimony to the reality of a beneficent providential order steadily pursuing the higher development of mankind! The tongue of this people is peculiar, a remarkable product of the language-making faculty of man; but its moral temper is even more distinctive. And this intense dawn came early in the day, fifteen hundred years before our era. Some have doubted the existence of ethical monotheism, even in rudimentary form, at so early a period in Israel's history, and have even gone so far as to question the existence of Moses. But, if there was a Zoroaster why not a Moses? and if the Gâthas go back to the twelfth or fifteenth century before Christ, why not the Decalogue writ in lapidary style?

Our next dawn carries us forward some two thousand years. It is that of a people kindred to the Hebrews in race and tongue, possibly as old, but remaining in obscurity all that time, and then suddenly appearing above the horizon. I mean the Arabians, whose emergence into the light of history took place in connection with the religious movement inaugurated by Mohammed. They were a people of great qualities and possibilities, 'unconsciously waiting,' as Carlyle remarks, 'for the day when they should become notable to all the world.'[1] There is the fuel for a great fire in their nature, and as the fuel has never yet been used up, it is all there ready to be kindled when the hour of Providence and the man come. They live in a land blessed with a fine, bracing climate, fitted to foster vigorous health and high elastic animal spirits: the sky ever clear, the air pure and strengthening; the air of a sandy desert more vivifying, says Sprenger, himself a Swiss, than the air of the Alps and of the Himalaya.[2] The temperament of this people is full of poetry and passion. There are poetic contests in which the best poets of the different tribes take part, and the poem that wins the prize is suspended by the gate of the Kaaba, visible to all who enter. The passionate nature finds its outlet in perpetual tribal feuds. A wild, restless people, capable of a great career, if only a man should arise to lead them, and a great enthusiasm were to take possession of them, knitting them together by a common purpose and calling into play all their latent powers. Mohammed was the man, and his heart-stirring watchword, *Islam:* submission to Allah Akbar, the one great God, the word that made their wild hearts burn.

[1] *Heroes, Hero-Worship, and the Heroic in History*, p. 223.
[2] *Life of Mohammed.*

Some think that this dawn ushered in a day which was an unmitigated curse and disaster to the world; not an illustration of a beneficent Providence caring for the higher interests of mankind, rather a mystery sorely trying faith. This to me is not easily credible. I sympathise with those who, like Carlyle and Maurice,[1] have tried to show that Mohammedanism is not an unmixed evil, and that it owed its remarkable success, not principally to any of the causes that before their time were much insisted on: not to force of arms, or the credulity of human nature, prone to embrace any plausible imposture, or to plagiarism from the Old and New Testaments, but before all things to the presence of positive and important truth earnestly believed. Mohammed's own religion, in its inception, was a genuine enthusiasm against idols as naught, and for the essential truth that one God is, and that He is the rewarder of those that obey Him and serve Him. It was a religious reform conferring a real boon, in the first place on his own countrymen, morally as well as otherwise. Both in religion and in morals, the Arabians before Mohammed arose were in a very degenerate state. Their religion seems to have been a combination of star worship and fetichism. Among the objects of worship were stones, trees, shapeless masses of dough, also certain female divinities called the daughters of God. The most famous object of worship was the *Black Stone*, kept in the temple at Mecca, called the Kaaba, of very ancient date and fame, built in the shape of a cube, and forming, as Bosworth Smith says, 'a veritable Pantheon

[1] *Religions of the World;* Boyle Lectures for 1847.

of all Arabia.'[1] The morals of the people were low. Drunkenness was prevalent; gambling was indulged in, to the extent of staking even personal freedom; the revolting practice of burying alive female children was not uncommon; women were held in no respect, and polygamy was practised to an unlimited extent. In both respects reform was urgently needed, and the best men in Arabia had for some time been longing for the advent of a prophet. The prophet at length came, saying with a voice thrilling with conviction, 'The idols in the Kaaba are naught,' and denouncing with vehement earnestness prevalent evil practices; and after much initial opposition his message was listened to as the word of the one living, true God. Thus Mohammed did for the sons of Ishmael what Moses did for the children of Israel. Mohammedanism may indeed be called an Arabian Judaism.

The larger question, to what extent the religion of Mohammed has been a blessing to the nations which it overran in its career of military conquest, or to the peoples whom in more recent times it has converted by the more Christian method of missionary propagandism, is less easily answered. Some have laid down the broad position that in no case has Mohammedanism gained, or at least, held ground, where it did not bring something better than it found. Those who hold this view admit that, if Mohammedans had succeeded in conquering the most civilised races of the world and the Christian nations of the west, it would have been a calamity. But they contend that the religion which

[1] *Mohammed and Mohammedans*, p. 102.

took its origin in Arabia, in the sixth century of our era, has done good to the peoples among whom it has taken a permanent hold in Asia and Africa; that it has indeed done for these peoples what it did for the Arabians: made them better than it found them, elevated their religious ideas, and improved their morals, if it has not set before them the highest moral ideal.[1] This is a question to be settled by careful, dispassionate investigation, not by prejudice. It is not inconceivable that in the purpose of Providence the Mohammedan religion might be intended in some parts of the world to prepare the way for something better than itself. Providence does not usually give the best at once. It gives what men can receive: the relatively good as a step towards the better, and the better as a step towards the best. On this method it proceeded in the case of Israel, why not also in other cases such as that now under consideration?

One thing, however, is certain. Islamism can make no rightful claim to *finality*. Wherever it is confronted with Christianity, worthily represented, it ought to bow to its superior worth. A religion which proclaims one Sovereign God is a great improvement on idolatry, but it should give way to a religion which gives to men not merely a Divine Sovereign ruling over them as slaves, but a Father who regards them as His children. A religion which restricts the number of wives to four is an improvement on unlimited polygamy; but even restricted polygamy is a barbarism compared with the

[1] This is the view of Bosworth Smith, vide *Mohammed and Mohammedans*, p. 286.

Christian ideal of monogamy. Once more, a religion which enjoins on slave-owners to be kind to their slaves, is an improvement on a state of society in which the slave is unprotected by the law, and left at the mercy of a master; but no religion can be final which does not so conceive the dignity of man as to make slavery appear essentially evil and inadmissible. In all these respects Islamism comes short, therefore its right of existence, in the view of the providential order, can only be temporary. Mohammedans, however, are not willing to accept this humble position. They have no thought of giving way to a better, no idea that there is anything better to give way to. In this they are at fault, but they do not stand alone. The Jews made the same mistake; adherents of all religions are prone to it. It is always hard to look steadfastly to the end of a religion, long-established, but ripe for abolition.

One more historic dawn offers itself to our view, the last to be named, but not the least fair or prophetic. It is that of the ancient Germans, who appeared above the horizon shortly after the commencement of the Christian era. They have the good fortune to be introduced to our notice by one of the ablest and most candid of Roman historians, Tacitus, in whose pages the character of those Northern barbarians suffers no harm; possibly it is even too favourably exhibited, for the writer is dissatisfied with the manners of Rome, and uses those of the Germans as an instrument of rebuke. In the little book on the *Position, Manners, and Peoples of Germany*,[1] written about the end of the

[1] *De situ, Moribus, et Populis Germaniae.*

first century, the people who were destined to break up the Roman Empire appear in a very attractive light. The men have blue piercing eyes, red hair, large bodies. They are brave; to leave a shield on the field of battle is accounted an indelible disgrace. They love liberty. They choose their kings for their nobility, their leaders for their valour. Their kings are not despots with unlimited power; all matters of great importance must be brought for discussion and final decision before the assembly of the people. Their captains lead by example rather than by authority; swift in decision, well in view, in the van, they command admiration. They are given to hospitality, making no distinction between friend and stranger. They are self-restrained; they do not lament lost friends, they remember them. They are romantic; they do not live together in towns, they till the land apart, and each in his own way, as fountain, plain, or grove takes the fancy. They love song, by which they give expression to their religious faith and celebrate dead heroes and memorable exploits. The women are as brave as the men, and sometimes fight along with them. They are greatly respected by the men, who see in them something holy, and credit them with the gift of foretelling. The relations between the sexes are chaste and pure. Monogamy prevails. Adultery is rare, and is rigorously punished; vice is abhorred, not laughed at. Good morals have more authority there than elsewhere good laws.

Verily a beautiful dawn, full of promise for the future! How shallow the notion that these barbarians were of no account in the moral order of the world, because up till the moment when they attracted the attention of Roman rulers and writers they were unknown to fame! Manifestly a beneficent Providence has been preparing this people through silent centuries for historic service and renown. They might have become distinguished centuries earlier, but they had to wait for their opportunity. They had to wait long for their hour. For they are an old people. They belong to the Aryan stock, and their language is kindred to that of the Vedic Indians. Common words point to a common origin and a common home in a far past time, say two thousand years before the Christian era. They have wandered from the East to the forests of Germany in the course of the ages, and here they are ready for the work assigned to them, with sterling virtues already acquired, and with aptitudes for learning more. If such a people never had their opportunity, one's faith in Providence might be shaken, for it would signify an excellent instrument wasted. But the instrument is ready, and the time for use has come; and in both, and in the correspondence between them, a beneficent providential order is apparent.

These five dawns are all instructive as to the significance in the providential order of the prehistoric life of nations. The last two, from the lateness of their dates, are specially instructive as tending to throw light on the destinies of such portions of the human race as may seem fated to abide permanently in the obscurity of the *sub-historic* condition. Our thoughts here naturally turn to *Africa* — that vast, populous, dark continent which has hitherto contributed so little to the higher life of man; the main distinction of its people being fertility, vigour in the purely animal function of multiplying and replenishing the earth. Carthage and Egypt can hardly be reckoned exceptions. Carthage rose like a great comet in the historic firmament, in its deadly struggle with Rome, under its renowned general, Hannibal. Its armies fought splendidly, but it was well that they were beaten. For Carthage belonged to the bad stock of the Pagan Semites whose religion was a revolting combination of cruelty and lust, human sacrifice and sacred prostitution. My charity is not equal to thinking well of that infamous cult. I am unable to invent apologies for Baal worship. It was unspeakably vile, corrupt, and corrupting, and the one conceivable function of Providence in relation to it is that of asserting against it a judicial moral order, and providing for its destruction. The destroyer in the case of the Canaanites was Israel, in the case of Carthage, Rome. The motives in either case might be far from perfect, but at least, in the hands of Rome, the execution was thorough. Carthage was destroyed, and her memory obliterated.

The feeling awakened by the monumental story of ancient Egypt is one of perplexed interest. The religion of that land has been well called the religion of mystery. Everything connected with it is mysterious, and as such at once repulsive and fascinating. Its sculpture, as combining adherence to proportion in form with a lack of personal expression, especially in the statues of the gods, where the features are stereotyped — noble, but without individuality; its hieroglyphic, which fascinates by the consciousness that mind produced the signs and embodied thought therein, yet repels by the opaque veil which hides the thought from view; its embalming of the dead, which bears testimony to a belief in the life beyond, that touches a sympathetic chord in our hearts, yet repels by the ghastly, vain struggle against the law of corruption exhibited in the mummy.

The Egyptians lived in a perpetual twilight. Properly speaking, they were a people of the prehistoric type, of whom we ought not to have known anything, and of whom we do know something owing to the accident of their coming into contact with historic peoples, and to the recent unearthing of their funereal monuments. Bunsen pronounces them an antediluvian people, and sees in their language and traditions, as revealed in the hieroglyphic records, 'a deposit left by that period which we call the primeval world.'[1] From this point of view, we can judge them more justly, and feel more kindly towards them. We are no longer surprised at the inconsequences, incongruities, and even monstrosities in their religion, which make theorising about it impossible, and compel you to be content to state facts, without pretending to understand. It is the religion of children, and that is enough.[2] Far from being surprised or shocked, you rather wonder that, amid all the crudity and unreason, there is so much

---

[1] *God in History*, vol. i. p. 226.

[2] There is truth in the remark of Herder that the ancient Egyptians were children in thought because they were children in the *expression* of thought. — *Ideen*, vol. iii. p. 121.

that is wise and morally sound in the religious consciousness of this survival of primeval humanity. The judgment of the dead reveals a knowledge of duty which constrains the admission that God was not far from this quaint old-world people, and suggests the inference that the same thing holds true of all prehistoric peoples. That is the chief lesson to be learned from the monuments, and the teaching of that lesson by the inscriptions in her tombs is the one service rendered by ancient Egypt to the providential history of mankind; unless we reckon as another that, by being a hard taskmaster to Israel, she produced in the minds of her bondsmen a religious reaction destined to be very fruitful in consequences. That a reaction or reform in the direction of a more rational religion should ever take place within herself was not to be expected, for the souls of the Egyptians, during their lifetime, were embalmed in the cerements of stereotyped religious custom as completely as their bodies were mummified after death.

Returning from these far-past times to the present, the question may be asked, Is there any likelihood of the dark races of Africa, or of any one of them, becoming an elect instrument in the hands of Providence for signal service to the higher interests of mankind on that continent? At this late era the presumption is in favour of the negative. And yet the fact that the Germans and the Arabs had to wait so long for their opportunity ought to put us on our guard against too confident dogmatism. Doubtless it is not a question of opportunity merely. Endowment has to be considered; even climate. Extremes of heat and cold are not favourable to the development of intellectual and moral energy. The temperate zones, lying between the tropics and the Arctic regions, have been the home of the races which have made their mark in history. Still, Africa is a vast continent stretching from 35° north to 35° south latitude, and it is far from impossible that some of the peoples occupying its healthiest and most bracing tracts of country may waken up to a new life under the stimulating influence of a new social environment. One thing seems certain: that a dawn has already come to Africa, giving promise of a brighter future, if not in the sense of a great career in commerce, literature, or political power, at least in the sense of enjoying to a considerable degree the benefits which European civilisation can bestow. The eyes of all Europe are now turned to the dark continent. Travellers have penetrated to its remotest recesses, so that it is no longer an unknown land. Heroic explorers of the type of Livingstone and Thomson have invested it with a romantic interest, and awakened in devout hearts the hope that their devoted efforts are the promise and pledge of a beneficent providential purpose. The colonising energy of Britain has struck root in its soil, destined to bear fruit, mainly, we may hope, if not wholly good. These things are not unworthy of notice in a study of the providential order of the world. Neither *a priori* theory nor experience justifies the notion that, if there be a Providence at all, it must take the form of making all peoples renowned. Some are fitted to give and some to receive benefit; some to achieve results of which history will take note, and some to play the humbler part of participating in the good effects of their achievements. Peoples who are in the latter position cannot be said to be neglected by the Divine Father of mankind.

This observation facilitates transition to the last topic that falls to be mentioned in the present connection, viz., the position of those peoples whose historic dawn and day are long past, and who are now in the post-historic stage of their existence. The Jews and the modern Greeks supply illustrative instances. Must we think of them as simply reprobate, or as human refuse in which the moral order of the world takes no further interest? By no means. God does not despise them, neither ought we. Doubtless their glory is departed, their appropriate motto is *fuimus;* the races they belong to have seen better days. But what then? They have simply stepped down from the exalted position of those who do signal service to mankind to the lowlier position of those who are served. Whether any people that has undergone this change of fortune can regain the higher position is a question on which it is not necessary to dogmatise. Perhaps the chief obstacles to resurrection are demoralising self-contempt, and unbelief in the possibility of national rejuvenescence prevalent in society. There is no irreversible decree of heaven standing in the way. St. Paul believed that God was not done with Israel. What precisely he expected we do not fully know. He could not, of course, expect Israel to repeat her past history, and do a second time what she had done before. The Jewish people continues to produce great men: some of the most distinguished men of modern times, in various European countries, and in different spheres of life, have belonged to that race. But it can hardly give to the world a new succession of Hebrew prophets; still less can it give us a second Christ. It may, however, learn to appreciate better the one Christ it has given, and that surely would be for its good. That, I think, was what St. Paul chiefly desired and hoped for. May we not hope for it also? How the desirable result is to be brought about is a problem. Possibly not to any great extent by express efforts at conversion by church missions; perhaps rather by the indirect, undesigned influence of the sincere reverence of Christendom for the author of the Christian faith, backed by wiser second thoughts of Israel's sons left to their own reflections.

In any case, it remains true that God has not cast away this ancient elect people. Providence casts away utterly no elect people. There is an Israel, a Greece, an Italy still. They are not what they were, but who can tell what they may become? Meantime they have a share in that goodness of God which is unto all, and in those tender mercies which are over all His works.

LECTURE VIII

THE POWER WORKING IN HUMANITY

PART II. HISTORIC DAYS

MY purpose in this second part is not, as the title might suggest, to sketch the historic careers of the five peoples whose dawns have been described in the first part. I thought it well to take a hasty glance at these dawns, as an aid to due appreciation of the significance, in the providential order, of the prehistoric life of mankind, without meaning to commit myself to speak further of all the peoples then alluded to. At the present time, only one of these will specially engage our attention, along with two other peoples not hitherto named, save in a merely incidental manner. Israel, Greece, Rome — names recalling momentous memories — are to be our main theme, and that with the view of indicating briefly their respective services to the higher interests of mankind. It may indeed seem futile to try to say anything instructive on so great a subject, within the available space. But the task on hand is to point the moral of a tale which does not need to be told, because its general outline may be assumed to be known. Of the three peoples I shall treat in this order: Greece, Rome, Israel.

1. The bright dawn of Greece came with Homer and his immortal Epics. In the *Iliad* and the *Odyssey* we are introduced to a wonderland, among whose surprises are a highly evolved musical language, an inimitable poetic skill in the use of it for the realistic description of stirring events, a warlike people, heroic in temper, versatile in genius, and rich in strongly contrasted individualities; and a pantheon of humanised divinities, presumably transformed from physical deities of an earlier time, but now become very like their worshippers — magnified Greek men and women. Here, we think as we read, is a wholly new type of people, as remarkable as its tongue, a people whose future is sure to be brilliant if not lasting, likely to distinguish itself in many ways — in thought and in art not less than in war; a race of boundless, unique possibilities.

In the light of its subsequent history we see that this people touched the highest watermark of intellectual endowment. One might say that its vocation was to show what human reason is capable of in all departments of intellectual activity. In poetry of all kinds, in architecture, in sculpture, in philosophic thought, in oratory, in historical writing, even in science as represented by Aristotle, the Greeks are still the masters of the world. It is on their achievements in purely intellectual and artistic regions that their fame chiefly rests, but not on these alone. They did epoch-making service also in ethics and in politics. How fruitful in results the moral intensity of Socrates and his memorable counsel to his fellow-countrymen, 'Know thyself,' summoning them to realise the contents and significance of personality! Then what a really great matter it was that, in the person of the Greek, men became imbued with the passion for *freedom*, and had their minds opened to the idea of a State in which a body of free citizens should exercise themselves in self-government! Till the Hellenic race arrived on the historic stage, the world had groaned under Eastern despotisms, in which only one man, the king, was free, all others being his abject slaves. Perhaps the despotic monarchies were natural in their place and time. That they may not bring a reproach on Providence we must try to look at them, not from our modern view-point, but as they appeared to those who lived under them. For the Oriental peoples of antiquity, the absolute rule of one man was a law of nature, and they accepted any evil consequences it entailed with the same patience with which they would endure disasters brought upon them by the elements. What we call a despotism was for them a reign of God, a theocracy. The monarch was God's representative and vicegerent, a god on earth: his will was divine; and if it sometimes showed itself as an evil will, the fact was a mystery to be borne with resignation, not to be complained of. Well for those who had to suffer that they were able to meet their fate in this way! It is, as Herder remarks, consoling to reflect, that for every evil that afflicts humanity there is a balsam that at least soothes the wound.[1] The balsam for the wounds inflicted by despotic arbitrariness was patience. But it was not desirable for the good of the world that that patience should be too long-suffering

[1] *Ideen*, vol. iii. p. 55.

or long-lasting. Devoutly to be wished was the advent of a temper for which despotism should be intolerable. That temper came in an emphatic degree with the Greeks, making one free European man worth many Asiatic slaves, as was proved on the day when ten thousand Athenians defeated sixty times their number of Persians on the plain of Marathon. What a difference it would have made to the fortunes of humanity if victory had inclined to the other side!

That the Greeks did good service by defeating the Persians all will admit. There may be less complete agreement as to the intrinsic, permanent value of their more distinctive contribution for the benefit of humanity within the intellectual sphere. One meets occasionally with depreciatory estimates in unexpected quarters. In the case of a professional theologian, an inappreciative attitude might not greatly surprise us. His point of view is the supreme importance of religion and a true knowledge of God. Bringing to all things the standard of the sanctuary as his guide in judgment, he is prone to ask, What is art but time elegantly wasted? nay, what is philosophy but a vain quest after ultimate truth? He may thus see in Greek philosophy, with all its fascination, as set forth in the Dialogues of Plato, only an unsuccessful attempt to find God, one of many similar attempts made by heathen peoples, serving, indirectly, one useful purpose, that of preparing these peoples for welcoming the true light from heaven when it came. He may assign to the Greek experiment the distinction of being one of the most brilliant and the most thoroughgoing, and acknowledge that in this point of view it possessed high utility. Such is the gist of the following words in the excellent Essay on the 'Preparation in History for Christ' in the well-known work, *Lux Mundi*. 'If man the race, like man the individual, was finally to find salvation by dying to himself, to his own natural man, he could only do this when it had been adequately and magnificently proved, both that he could not save himself, and how splendidly worth saving he was. He must do his best, that he may despair of his best. Do we not feel that this is just what was worked out by the histories of Greece and Rome? They are splendid experiments of human power. Diverse in their method they combine in this result.'[1] There is doubtless relative truth in this view, yet it is by no means the whole truth. Relatively to Christianity Greek genius, in its varied manifestations, full of grace and beauty, was, if you will, an abortive experiment. But relatively to the general providential order, it possessed positive substantive value. This may be said of the Greeks just as it may be said of the Jews. For they also, according to St. Paul, made their unsuccessful experiment, the legal covenant being, in his view, as in that of Jeremiah before him, a failure; the law a mere pedagogue παιδαγωγὸς) conducting to Christ. But Israel did more than that. She lived, through all the centuries, in her best sons, a true life of fellowship with God; she gave to the world the prophets, and out of her midst came forth the Christ who spoke the satisfying word about God. The Greeks also did more than make a vain experiment.

[1] *Lux Mundi*, p. 146.

If there be any reality in the idea of a providential order, a people so gifted as the Greeks, and using their gifts so well, could not appear without rendering an important service to the higher interests of humanity. The service rendered was twofold. First, the Greek genius, by the bare fact of its appearing, legitimised the pursuits to which it was devoted, established their title to have a place assigned to them in human life; next, by the splendid manner in which that genius was displayed, it supplied a model and communicated an inspiration.

As to the former point: there may be difference of opinion as to the just proportion between what we may call culture and conduct in a well-ordered human life. Mr. Arnold, as is well known, assigned to them very unequal measures: to conduct, three-fourths; and to all that the word 'Greek' represents — poetry, art, philosophy — only one-fourth. This is somewhat oracular, but let it pass, the main point is that an appreciable fraction of value is assigned to these interests. Surely with good reason! What are the psychological roots of poetry, art, and philosophy? The keen sense of beauty in the outer world, and in the human form; and the ardent love of truth — the desire to understand the world, to know the causes of things. Good things both, and leading to good; neither without a bearing on conduct; for the broad line of division between the æsthetic and the ethical is to a large extent artificial and abstract. The feeling for nature, so conspicuous in Greek poetry, as in the descriptive epithets of Homer, and in many a felicitous allusion in the tragic poets, has a higher sanction, even in the words of Him who said, 'Solomon in all his glory was not arrayed like one of these.' An open eye and ear for the sights and sounds of nature is one of man's most precious endowments. It yields a pure, exquisite delight which never palls; it qualifies for appreciating the immortal productions of poetic and artistic genius, if it do not make all poets and artists; it brings the soul near to the Divine Source of all beauty and goodness. How unforgetable the song of the lark on a dewy summer morning! As you listen your first thought is: It is the happy bird's gladsome song of praise; your second: Let it be my own! How unforgetable even a realistic description of some natural scene read long years ago in a book! I recall one from a lyric strain in the *Rhesus* of Euripides. The chorus consists of a band of Trojan soldiers doing sentinel duty by night. It is drawing towards dawn, and they are retiring to their tents to sleep. But their ear is quick to catch the welcome sounds of daybreak: the nightingale singing on the banks of the Simois, the sheep bleating on the top of Mount Ida, the simple music of the shepherd's pipe. Καὶ μὴν ἀίω· it begins: 'Hark! I hear.' There is little in it; yet if you read it once in sympathetic mood, it will haunt you while you live; for the poet felt a thrill when he wrote it.[1]

It is not an accident that the gifted men who had this tremulous sensitiveness to the charms of the physical world were also the men who proclaimed to their countrymen with unwearying emphasis the solemn doc-

[1] *Rhesus*, verses 542–552.

trine of *Nemesis*. The *moral* order of the world revealed itself to them almost as clearly as the *œsthetic* order, and they preached both alike with equal earnestness and persuasiveness. We see here how artificial is the cleavage between art and conduct. Æschylus, Sophocles, and Euripides are poetic artists, doubtless, but they are also preachers of righteousness, not unworthy to be named along with the Hebrew prophets. They, too, were artists. Nothing more truly poetic, more rich in imagination, more felicitous in expression, more indicative of an open eye for the sublime and the beautiful, than many of their oracles. But they were preachers above all, using their poetic gifts for the more impressive delivery of their message. In their case poetry and prophecy were intimately interblended. So in the case of the Greek tragedians, so in the case of all first-class poets. The æsthetic sense and the moral sense appear as kindred, and art helps conduct.

And what of philosophy? It too at its best is allied to the good. It is not a mere idle play of intellect, a vain hunting after solutions of insoluble problems in the mere wantonness of an undisciplined reason. It is the fruit of a serious desire to penetrate the mystery of the universe and to find God. The desire is instinctive, irrepressible, human. It revealed its presence in man's soul at a very early stage. *Animism* was the philosophy of primitive man, and, as even Mr. Herbert Spencer acknowledges in his lately published concluding volume on the *Principles of Sociology*, there was 'a germ of truth' in that crude philosophy. There is a germ of truth in all the philosophies. There is profit even in their failures. The desire to know the ultimate truth is always good. It is characteristic and worthy of man as a spiritual being. The effort it originates brings into play man's highest powers — his reason, his imagination, his religious nature. All true philosophers are poets, theologians, and philosophers all in one. This is pre-eminently true of Plato, the greatest, loftiest, and most inspiring of Greek philosophers. Not in vain did he live and write those inimitable dialogues on knowledge, righteousness, temperance, love, law, immortality, etc. They are a κτῆμα εἰς ἀεί. They vindicate once for all the need and use of philosophy, and they *set the pattern;* which is the *second* service claimed for Greek genius in all its manifestations.

The Greek set the pattern not only in philosophy, but in other matters, very specially in the sphere of art. And this, one would say, was a service of permanent value. Not so, however, thinks M. Renan, if we may take in earnest what he says in those charming but whimsical pieces entitled *Dialogues Philosophiques.* 'High art,' he makes one of his interlocutors say: 'high art will disappear. The time will come when art will be a thing of the past, a creation produced once for all, which men will continue to admire, while conscious that they have nothing more to do with it. The sculpture, the architecture, and the poetry of the Greeks are already in that position. These marvels are in our day absolute impossibilities. Admirable imitations of them may be produced, but they are mere imitations, without *raison d'être*, and without life. . . . The reign of sculpture terminated when people ceased to go half naked, and beauty of form became a secondary thing; the epic disappeared with the age of individual heroism.'[1] This is a depressing prospect for those who live in the advanced epochs of the world's history. It raises a wide question: this, viz., Is it possible for us who live so late in the day to be anything but imitators and echoes in any department of thought or action? Has not everything been said that can be said in religion, philosophy, poetry; about God, the world, and man; have not all the possibilities of art, in painting, poetry, sculpture, music, been long ago exhausted? If the fact be so, why, we are ready to exclaim, did the best come so soon? Why not reserve the contributions of the ancients in religion, art, philosophy, and politics for a far distant future, that it might remain for long ages possible to be original, and that men might not too soon be crushed by despair of excelling? To all this let two things be said in reply. First, It was well that the perfect came soon, because human progress is promoted by the influence of ideals; second, The proper function of ideals is not to crush but to inspire. They *may* crush, but that is the abuse of them. As long as they are used as an outward law, in a servile spirit, the result must be soulless mediocrity. But let them become inward laws of the spirit, working by inspiration and aspiration; then room is left for originality and life, and the products have real value, even though they fall short of the excellence of the model. So it is still possible to be something better than spiritless imitators and echoes in religion, in poetry, in painting, in music,

[1] *Dialogues Philosophiques: Probabilités*, p. 83.

in philosophy, and to do better in all lines of activity than if we had no models to inspire us. No need to swear slavishly by any master in philosophy, however great; no need to load our verses with stock phrases culled from the poets of the past; no need to repeat mechanically worn-out formulæ concerning God. To escape the last-named doom two things only are requisite: an eye to see for yourself, and the power to say simply and sincerely what you see.

2. In passing from the Greeks to the Romans, one is conscious of a certain feeling of aversion. In all that relates to temper, spirit, endowment, the two peoples are widely different; surprisingly so when it is considered that they were not only near neighbours, but belonged to the same family of nations and spoke kindred languages. The transition we make is from sunny geniality, intellectual brightness, and intense individuality, to a character marked by a total lack of brilliancy, prosaic, monotonous, intellectually commonplace. But such has been the character of many worthy persons who have done good service to the world, and we cannot afford to cherish dislike to the instruments of Providence on merely sentimental grounds. Esau was a much more interesting and likeable man than Jacob, nevertheless it was Jacob that gained the blessing. Wellington was an object of intense dislike to the poet Heine, yet it was to the prosaic 'Iron Duke' that England owed her victory over Heine's idol, the brilliant Napoleon. Doubts as to the possibilities of such a people as the Romans having a vocation to promote the ends of a beneficent providential order must rest on

more substantial grounds. But such it does not appear, on first sight, difficult to discover.

We have looked at certain historic dawns, and found them very bright and full of promise. The dawn of Rome was not auspicious. It was shrouded in the dense clouds of a legend which, if it possess any historic value, discloses the unwelcome secret that the primitive Alban Rome was a robber-city, a place of refuge for outlaws and runaways and adventurers from beyond seas, objects of suspicion and fear to their neighbours, and unable to get wives except by theft. And the subsequent career of this strange people may not unnaturally seem worthy of such a beginning: centuries of constant fighting; first with neighbouring tribes — Latins, Volscians, Samnites, Etruscans, — ending with the conquest of Italy; then with outside nations bordering on the Mediterranean, and with the barbarians of Northern Europe; the process of conquest ceasing only when there were no more peoples to subdue. The result was a huge empire built up by brute force, as unlike, one would say, as possible to the benign kingdom of the *human*, which it is the supposed aim of Providence to bring in.

Turning from the external history of Rome to cast a hasty glance on its internal social condition, we easily find here also features that may well appear to justify doubt. The very religion of this people is, like itself, prosaic. The religion of Greece is the religion of beauty, the religion of Rome is the religion of *utility*. The Romans value their gods solely for the benefits they can procure from them for the State or for private individuals. In Greece divination was free, every man might practise the art who had a mind or a talent that way, and his oracles were taken for what they were worth. In Rome divination was under State control. Care was taken that no prophecies should be uttered in the name of the gods contrary to the public interest, and laws were passed against private diviners, Chaldeans, astrologers, mathematicians, as dangerous to the State. And provided the will of the gods was known, and that it was favourable, it did not matter to the utilitarian Romans whether the revelation came through a man or through a beast. If they had a preference, it was for the latter medium. They would rather hear the Deity speak through an ox than through a man. We seem in all this to be on the low level of primitive man rather than, as we should expect, in the case of an elect people, on the march towards the religion of the spirit. Gross utilitarianism in religion is the mark either of a crude and undeveloped, or of a degenerate, condition. 'After all these things do the Gentiles seek.' The prayers of the Vedic Indians, mostly for material good, illustrate the statement, and alongside of them may be placed as equally illustrative, the religious rites of their late-born kinsmen, the Romans.

In family life, as in religion, Roman custom seems a survival from primitive humanity rather than the way of a people destined to make a new departure in the direction of an elevated or advanced social ideal. I refer here to the absolute power of the father, *patria potestas*, manifestly a relic of the patriarchal state of society. Concerning this, Sir Henry Maine in his work on *Ancient Law* thus writes: 'So far as regards the person, the parent, when our information commences, has over his children the *jus vitae necisque*, the power of life and death, and *a fortiori* of uncontrolled corporal chastisement; he can modify their personal condition at pleasure; he can give a wife to his son; he can give his daughter in marriage; he can divorce his children of either sex; he can transfer them to another family by adoption; and he can sell them.'[1] He further states that it was not till late in the Imperial period that these powers were reduced within narrow limits, and that they remained substantially unrestricted till the whole civilised world was brought within their sphere.[2] The conservatism herein revealed seems more in keeping with the spirit of a stereotyped custom-ridden Oriental race, like the Chinese, than with that of a Western European people destined to exercise a vital influence upon modern civilisation. The particular custom referred to is thoroughly Eastern in character. It is irresponsible despotism within the family sphere, analogous to that of an Eastern monarch within the larger sphere of an empire. And the one form of despotism was apt to lead to the other. Abject obedience to fathers was a training for a not less abject obedience to the State.

This survival of family despotism, besides disqualifying, to all appearance, the Romans from themselves promoting social evolution, tended further to neutralise a benefit coming to the world from another quarter.

[1] *Ancient Law*, p. 138.
[2] *Ibid*, p. 142.

Christ, as we all know, gave to God the name 'Father.' In so doing, He made, in a very simple way, a most important contribution to theology, the full significance of which has not yet been realised. Who can tell how much that may be due to the Roman *patria potestas?* The world living under Roman rule, and familiar with that custom, could hardly think it much of a Gospel that God was to be regarded as a Father. If they accepted the conception, with its established associations, so much the worse for them. Practically it would mean thinking of God as an irresponsible Despot who might do as He pleased with His children. True, some fathers might be benevolent despots, dealing wisely, justly, and even benignantly, with their children; and it was always possible for those that had known such to take them as human models of the Divine Father. Still the fact remained that, in the eye of the law, fatherhood was an irresponsible relation, giving absolute power over person and property. And as the power over property was usually exercised without scruple to the full extent, men living under this system would have difficulty in thinking of God as a Being whose nature and delight it was to give good gifts. They would be more ready to think of Him as One whose inclination and habit it was to appropriate everything to Himself.

In view of all these considerations, one is tempted to ask, What good could come to the world through Rome? The answer must be, that in spite of all appearances to the contrary, good did come from that quarter. And the good that came was kindred to the evil.

Rome's faults were the faults of qualities that made her a benefactor. She had boundless ambition, and a stern will that demanded absolute obedience from all over whom successful ambition gave her jurisdiction. But the obedience exacted was not servile subjection to despotic caprice, but intelligent compliance with general laws impartially enforced. Her authority was the authority of reason inspired by the love of justice. In the best days of Rome, the reins of government were in the hands, not of kings or emperors, but of a senate, composed of a body of men trained to judicial habits of mind by grave responsibility, and by having to deal with internal problems of vital interest to the republic, created by the conflicting claims of classes: patricians and plebeians, rich and poor. The very name for the body politic, *Res publica*, brings out the difference between Eastern despotism and Roman sovereignty. Not the irresponsible will of an autocratic individual, but the *public interest* was the august power before which all had to bow. Yet this impersonal abstraction spoke with an authority greater than that of any Oriental potentate. To its claims all others must yield, even those of the *Patria Potestas*. A son, as general, might command a father, or as magistrate try him for offences. All accepted this subordination of private to public authority as reasonable and right. And the result was a pervading spirit of self-surrender to the commonwealth, than which nothing more complete or whole-hearted can be conceived. It speaks well for the justice and wisdom of Roman rule that it could inspire such a spirit of prompt, unhesitating obedience among citizens. It is true that patriotism is a common virtue in all countries, even in those which are but indifferently governed; but Roman history abounds in instances of pure, disinterested devotion, exceptional in degree and touching the sublime. Readiness to serve the public interest at all hazards was the commanding passion of the Roman.

That a people characterised by this heroic virtue should be victorious in war is almost a matter of course. And it is equally a matter of course that its victory should be a benefit not merely to itself but to the conquered. Apart from the rights and wrongs of particular contests, taking a broad providential view of Rome's conquering career, it may be affirmed that she brought substantial benefits to all the peoples subject to her sway, uniting them in one great political body, under a rule the same for all, and comparatively just and equitable, and in many cases introducing elements of civilisation previously unknown. The last-named benefits he conferred especially on the Northern barbarians out of whom the modern European nations have sprung. The service rendered was effective because Rome moved slowly towards universal empire, and because, wherever she gained a footing, she retained her position with tenacity. Her career was as unlike as possible to that of Alexander of Macedon, who with his victorious army overran the world in a few years, leaving in many places no permanent trace behind him. Roman slowness compares unfavourably, from the dramatic point of view, with Greek rapidity and brilliancy. But the slow movement was sure. The Roman Empire was built up, stone by stone, not inflated. The Roman power came to stay, and its stay was long enough to give time for the laws, the social customs, the language of the conqueror taking permanent root among the conquered peoples. The influence of the Romans lives still, among ourselves, and it is for our advantage that they were long enough in our land to leave behind them as a legacy, the ruins of Roman military walls, and of Roman baths.

3. We have now to speak briefly of Israel and her service to humanity. The difficulty here is not, as in the case of Rome, to see that Israel had a place and function under a beneficent providential order, but rather to form an adequate conception of the largeness of that place and the importance of that function. The service rendered was in the sphere of *religion*. The Semitic genius had no talent for philosophy or art, and little capacity for sympathetic appreciation of such talent in other peoples. Neither was it in the line of Hebrew endowment or opportunity to do much for the world in the way of legislation and government. Israel's own national law was in many respects excellent, but it was in some points too peculiar to become a law for mankind. Her attempts at establishing wide empire were not successful. Her strength and wisdom were to sit still and dwell alone. But in religion she was peerless. Her God was her glory; One, and worthy to be the sole Divine Ruler in heaven and on earth, in the majesty of His righteousness and the condescension of His grace. Her distinctive contribution to the religious education of

mankind was her doctrine of ethical Monotheism. And, just because the Hebrew conception of God was ethical, this contribution had a vital bearing on the moral, not less than on the religious education of the world. It established an indissoluble connection between religion and morality. In Israel, as among all peoples, in all ages, the tendency to divorce these was active, but it found no countenance from the best interpreters of Hebrew faith. The prophets unweariedly denounced religious zeal severed from right conduct. 'In vain,' said they to their countrymen, 'do ye offer sacrifice while ye neglect justice and mercy.' The tone of the whole sacred literature of Israel on this subject is emphatic, and clear beyond the possibility of misunderstanding, except on the part of such as do not want to understand.

Israel communicated her message through Moses and the prophets, but above all through Jesus Christ. I can here speak only of the final weightiest word, spoken by One who was greater than Moses and all the prophets. This is not the place for a full statement of the faith of the Church concerning Jesus and His teaching. The least that can be said of Himself is that in Him was realised the moral and religious ideal of man, a perennial object of admiration and source of inspiration for all who bear His name. For the catholic faith He is not merely the great Master in morals and religion, but a Divine Redeemer; one in whom the Eternal Spirit dwelt in pleromatic fulness, as the spirit of love, and who in His death became the power of God in sacrifice. This faith is consonant with the general view of man's place in the universe, and of God's relation to man set forth at an earlier stage. It enforces the lesson taught by ordinary providence, that God cares for man, and exemplifies the Divine care in an august manner, and in a unique degree. But we can speak here only of that which brings Christ into comparison with other religious teachers, and gives Him a place in the general scheme of providence for the good of mankind. In this connection a prominent position is due to his epoch-making thoughts concerning God and man and their relations. He called God Father, indicating, not by abstract definition, but by discriminating use of the title, what He meant thereby; viz., that God is a holy, loving, gracious Being who does good to all, just and unjust alike, pities the most depraved, and regards with intense approval the heroic behaviour of the morally noble, and with equally intense contempt the self-complacency of counterfeit sanctity. He taught by word, and still more by His bearing towards the fallen, that man at the worst has value for God, is indeed a son of God, if only a prodigal son; and that as such he ought to be respected by others; and also that as such he ought to respect himself, and seriously endeavour to realise and fulfil his moral obligations. This doctrine of man has immense *religious* value as opening a door of hope even for those who, to a charity less than Christ's, may appear beyond redemption. It has also great *ethical* value as insisting upon that which is common to all men as more important than anything that divides men into classes and castes. It has *social* value as a virtual protest against all institutions which dehumanise sections of society, such as slavery, or marriage laws and customs which reduce wives to the category of property to be disposed of at will by husbands. Christ's doctrine of man says in effect, if not in so many words, All men ought to be free, and women have equal rights with men; the *human* is the supreme category, and the human, when it comes to its kingdom, knows no insurmountable distinctions of bond and free, male and female.

This is manifestly the message of a *universal* religion which has burst the bonds of Jewish particularism, and which cannot rest till it has subdued the world. In presence of this inspiring faith, all other religions lose their *raison d'être*, and any good that is in them can be only relative and temporary. All peoples, nations, and languages should serve the 'Son of Man' and his beneficent aim. Greece and Rome did unwittingly recognise their obligations. The one provided a universal language, and the other a universal government to facilitate the diffusion of Christianity. But it is an easier thing to render external aid to a new religion, than to imbibe and propagate its spirit, when that spirit is far in advance of the time. Greece and Rome did the one thing, they failed to do the other. The spirit of Christianity is the spirit of full unrestricted fellowship between man and God, of filial trust and glad devoted service. That spirit the ancient world neither shared nor understood. Above all the Roman world was disqualified for understanding it. It might be predicted that if it accepted Christianity, it would turn what was, to begin with, the religion of the spirit into a *law*, or an institution, to be submitted to in the way in which its conquered subjects submitted to its own iron rule. This is what actually happened. The Roman world adopted Christianity, and Christianity became *Roman*. The religion of faith and filial freedom became a religion of legalism, with its law of belief and its law of ritual; the former framed in categories supplied by Greek philosophy, the latter reviving an antiquated Leviticalism with its accompaniments of priesthood and sacrifice.

For the old world this neo-legalism was natural, one might say inevitable. Christ inaugurated a new era, but the peoples to whom His gospel first came belonged in spirit to an old era, and they could hardly be expected to understand and appreciate fully the genius of the new time. But what of the peoples of Northern Europe to whom the future belonged, and out of whom has sprung the modern world? Were they likely to comprehend at once the mind of the Lord Jesus and of St. Paul; or was it necessary that to them also Christianity should first come as law, before it came in the fulness of the blessing of the Gospel? As a matter of fact, it did come to them also as law, and on reflection we see that it could hardly fail to do so. The Germanic races, with all their promising qualities, could not enter into the glorious liberty of Christian sonship all at once. Preparation was needed for that, as, in the case of the Jews, preparation was needed for the advent of Christ. According to St. Paul, indeed, the world entered on its spiritual majority when Christ came. That was without doubt the objective significance of the new era. But objective significance is one thing, subjective realisation is another. A great part of the world over which Christianity was destined to spread, was as unprepared for it as were the people of Israel in the centuries before Christ was born. Therefore it had to become afterhand a legal discipline analogous to that to which the Jews had been subjected beforehand. The cycle — promise, law, promise fulfilled — had to repeat itself. And as the period of legal discipline in the pre-Christian era had lasted long, some fifteen hundred years, it should not surprise us if it turned out that the analogous period in the history of Christianity was likewise of long duration. That it was we know. It covered a thousand years, that long dreary space of time which we are accustomed to call the *Middle Ages*. That millennium was the winter night which followed the historic day of the ancient world, and preceded the bright dawn of the modern world.

A beneficent Providence was at work in those dark ages, with all their rudeness, as it has been at work in all periods preceding historic dawns. The best proof of the statement is the brightness of the dawn which eventually came. But even in the night there were signs of the Divine Presence as, *e.g.* the *Crusades*, which shone like an *Aurora Borealis* in the spiritual sky. These movements, in which all Europe took part, revealed, at least at first, till crusading became a trade, a sincere enthusiasm for a cause at least conventionally holy. One may say indeed: How much better had that enthusiasm been expended in discovering the true nature of the Christian faith, instead of in rescuing the Holy Sepulchre from the profane hands of Saracens! But the time for that higher work had not yet come, and it was well, meanwhile, that the Christian peoples were capable of generous devotion to any cause in which the honour of the Christian name was supposed to be involved. Zeal at least was there if not according to knowledge, revealing vast stores of spiritual energy to be brought into play when the time of enlightenment arrived.

The time of enlightenment came in the sixteenth century of the Christian era, bringing reformation in the sphere of religion, significantly heralded by the Revival of Learning, the flourishing of the Fine Arts, and the enlargement of man's ideas as to the extent of the world by the discovery of America. No one who has any real faith in a beneficent providential order can fail to recognise the immense significance of this new time. Hegel did full justice to its importance when he compared the three heralding events to the morning dawn which, after protracted storms, announces the advent of a bright day, and the Reformation itself to the all-illumining sun.[1] The latter comparison will not commend itself to every one. The Christian world was divided into two by the reforming movement, the larger portion maintaining solidarity with the past; and there are still not a few, even in Protestant communities, whose sympathies are with the

[1] *Philosophy of History*, Bohn's translation, pp. 428, 429.

pre-Reformation type of Christian faith and life. Such division of opinion on so vital a matter, in past and present times, is greatly to be deplored, but it ought not to create a prejudice against the Reformers. It must be remembered that a similar cleavage took place at the beginning of the Christian era. The majority of the Jews rejected Christ. The legal discipline had shut their eyes and hardened their hearts, instead of preparing them to give Jesus a welcome. It is ever the way at times of change. Many do not know when the old order has lasted long enough, and, grown hoary and decadent, ought to vanish away. That is the tragic side of progress.

We live in the new time, in the historic day auspiciously ushered in by the dawn of the sixteenth century. Where are we, whither do we tend, how long is the impulse communicated at that crisis to last? These are questions that readily suggest themselves, but which it is not easy to answer. One thing is certain: the rate of progress, in all that relates to the higher interests of humanity, is slow. Fifteen hundred years from Moses to Christ; sixteen hundred years from the beginning of the Christian era to the Reformation; above three hundred years from the Reformation till now. Centuries may elapse before a crisis equally momentous occurs. Within that time how much there may be to do! There is the battle to be fought out between competing, incompatible conceptions of Christianity. The social applications of Christ's doctrine of God and man have to be worked out. War has to be made amenable to the Christian conscience. Philosophy may make fresh attempts to find out the true theory of the universe. Science may go on its triumphant path, making new discoveries that may be turned to account for the benefit of mankind. The world is not worn out. We are not doomed henceforth to a dull, monotonous existence. The wisdom, power, and grace of the Almighty are not exhausted. Providence does not need to repeat itself, or to live on a past reputation. It can and will do new great things. Years of the right hand of the Most High are still before us. And it is our part to be fellow-workers with God, not passively trusting to His immediate action, or to the evolutionary forces at work in society. Some seem to imagine that these forces will do everything for us in a spontaneous way, and that our part will be simply to look on. As Mr. Huxley has reminded us, the fact is not so. We must exert ourselves, play the man, be heroes in the strife, dismissing the dream that 'humanity is to be automatically conveyed to the gates of universal peace.'[1] Let us serve ourselves heir to the rich inheritance bequeathed by Greece, Rome, and Israel, and make it our aim to add to the treasure, or at least to estimate duly its value.

[1] *Vide* Kelly, *Evolution and Effort*, p. 98, where this dream is ascribed to Mr. Spencer.

LECTURE IX

PROVIDENCE IN THE INDIVIDUAL LIFE

THE reality of a providential order ought to be more easily verifiable in the lives of individuals than in the corporate life of nations. The subject of study is much less complex, and the range of time is greatly restricted. From a few years of a nation's life there is little to be learned. One providential day there may be equal to a thousand common years. It is only when the long history of a people lies before our eye, a completed drama, that we can read its lessons: perceive a vocation, recognise a service rendered, detect evil tendencies which in due season meet with appropriate retribution. In the life of a man we have to do with a short, manageable story of threescore years and ten, whose moral import ought to lie on the surface. It is true indeed that the very brevity of the period may appear a drawback. If Providence move with slow, leisurely step, how, it may be asked, can its action be observed within such narrow time limits? Might not one as well expect to observe an appreciable advance in a glacier within the compass of an hour? But in the physical world there are two kinds of motion: quick motion in the molecule, slower motion in the mass. There may be something analogous in the moral world.

Whatever may be the fact as to relative verifiableness, we may *believe* even when we cannot see. Faith in the presence of the providential order in individual life is reasonable. It is a natural inference from our doctrine of the value of man for God. It is also a corollary from the omnipresence of the providential order, by all means to be insisted on. For we are not to think of the providential order and the physical order as dividing the universe between them, the one here at certain critical points in the world's history, the other there where things run in accustomed grooves. They are different aspects of the same universe. All is mechanism, and all is purpose. The Rabbis said, 'There is not a thing in the world, not even a tiny blade of grass, over which there is not an angel set.' In their theory of the universe, angelic agency occupied the same place as physical causation in ours. But there is no need to displace physical causation to make room for Providence. Leaving to the former its full sphere and function, we can still accept the consolatory doctrine of Christ: 'A sparrow shall not fall on the ground without your Father.'[1]

Sometimes it is very easy to see the providential order in individual life, as in the case of great historical characters like Moses, Paul, Luther, Alexander, Cæsar. Without being suspected of religious fanaticism, one might say of such men that God *made* them, furnishing them with endowments suited for a definite task, and providing in their experience the needful training, and in their environment the fit opportunity.

[1] Matthew x. 29.

In their history, providential action exhibits itself in an accelerated form which is complementary to the more usual slow movement. For the full law of providential movement is: slow for a long period, then sudden and catastrophic at the last. The sojourn of Israel in Egypt continues through generations of bitter bondage, during which Providence seems to be wholly indifferent, like a man standing aloof, and looking on with folded arms, while some tragedy is being enacted. But at length the crisis comes. The grain which slowly grew and ripened has reached its harvest time; the husbandman, listless before, is now astir, getting together his reapers, and sending them with their sickles into the wheat-field. Moses comes at the critical moment, God's chief reaper in that harvest day of judgment for Egypt and of deliverance for Israel. He comes suddenly with great gifts and marvellous experiences, a kind of providential miracle. But, even in his case, slow secular action in a long period of preparation has been at work. Who can tell how far back the process of *making* Moses began, and what various influences of heredity and environment co-operated to produce the result? The marvel is that he at last came just when he was needed, and his work was ready for him.

The lives of common men are too obscure to find a place in the pages of history, and we are tempted to think that they are also too minute objects for the eye of Providence to rest on. Yet the gracious care of the Divine Father may be there also, unknown to the world, possibly even to the subjects of the experiences in which providential action reveals itself. Ignorance of the fact, on either hand, does not cancel the fact. This remark is specially apposite in reference to the ignorance of bystanders. The outside world is not the final court of appeal in regard to the question, Does the life of any ordinary man possess providential significance? Still less in regard to the question, What is the precise nature of that significance? Speaking broadly, Providence is of private interpretation. The vision is for him whom it concerns. The humblest artisan may have good reason to believe that in his little life the saying has been verified, 'Trust in the Lord and do good; so shalt thou dwell in the land and thou shalt be fed,'[1] though neighbours, even if well inclined, may fail to see the grounds for such a faith. The devout artisan may find it necessary to keep his faith to himself, in order to escape ridicule. 'How could the life of so mean a person verify the reality of a moral order? How could any modest man in lowly state dare to cherish so presumptuous a thought?'

Outside judgment as to the *quality* of providential significance is still more precarious than as to the fact. What the world sees is the external event, and no man can tell what that means till he knows the man to whom it has happened. In the providential order, events are relative to moral ends, and are to be interpreted in their bearing on these. The interpretation is a delicate problem in which not merely the outside world but even the subjects of the experiences to be interpreted may easily err. The perplexing nature of

[1] Psalm xxxvii. 3.

the question is instructively exemplified in Hebrew literature. About the time of the prophet Jeremiah, the providential significance of individual experience became the subject of reflective thought. Till then attention had been preoccupied with the traces of Divine purpose in the corporate life of the nation, the experience of the individual being left out of account, except in so far as it participated in the fortunes of the entire people. But from that time forth it began to be seen that individual experience raised new questions, or lent new emphasis to old ones. The prophet Jeremiah was a puzzle to himself. He had but one aim in life, that God's will might be done, and yet he was a sorrow-laden man. Whence this glaring contradiction between character and lot? Unable to unriddle the mystery, in his hours of depression the prophet cursed his birth, and gloomily asked, Wherefore came I forth out of the womb to see labour and sorrow, that my days should be consumed with shame?[1] In the book of Job, supposed with some probability to belong to the period of the Babylonish exile, the problem thus set is taken up and discussed, in a dramatic form, the literary product presenting a combination of poetic genius with moral intensity that has never been surpassed or equalled. But while the effort awakens our admiration and even our amazement, it does not satisfy us. The problem remains unsolved, the last word has not been spoken. Yet one great step in advance has been taken. The writer, whoever he may have been, sees clearly that the old, simple, traditional theory, that

[1] Jeremiah xx. 18.

the good man prospers and the bad man suffers, is not true. That theory, advocated by Eliphaz, is completely demolished by the hero of the work, not merely by his triumphant argument, but by his very existence as a good man undergoing sore adversity. Whether Job was a historical personage or not does not matter. The creation of such a character as a basis for discussion implies that such cases were known to exist. And the value of the book which bears Job's name lies, not in its solutions, but in its broad, emphatic assertion that an experience like his is *possible* in the life of a good man; or in other words, in its protest against cut-and-dried, superficial, premature theorising as to the cause and meaning of suffering in human life, and by implication as to the cause and meaning of prosperity.

The Eliphaz theory, from an *a priori* point of view, is very plausible. Looking from the outside, what more natural than to regard prosperity as the smile of Providence on a good life, and adversity as the frown of Providence on a bad life? Yet, viewed in the light of experience, no judgment could be more superficial, and, it may be added, more heartless and cruel. It is the easiest thing in the world to put cases in which this comfortable theory will not work. In the first place, there is that large region of human experience in which both good and evil come to men in common, irrespective of character. The boons of sunshine and shower are bestowed on evil and good alike. When a Nineveh is destroyed, destruction overtakes not merely the adult population, for the most part, presumably, ripe for judgment, but 'sixscore thousand persons that cannot discern between their right hand and their left hand; and also much cattle.'[1] Then take success in business. Is every millionaire a good man: just, humane, able to say with Job, 'I delivered the poor that cried, the fatherless also, that had none to help him. The blessing of him that was ready to perish came upon me, and I caused the widow's heart to sing for joy. I put on righteousness and it clothed me, my justice was as a robe and a diadem'?[2] Is it uniformly or usually the case that every man who is strictly upright in business, scorning all tricks of trade, gets on? Is not such a man too apt to be pushed to the wall by unscrupulous traders who, by cunning devices and plausible lies, impose on a public desiring, doubtless, to get an honest article, but still more bent on getting all things cheap? How many people would sincerely sympathise with the unprosperous upright trader, and abstain from pronouncing him a simpleton and an incapable? Yet his one fault and misfortune is that he has a conscience too sensitive to accommodate itself easily to commercial morality. And in that very conscientiousness lies the best evidence that this man's life, failure though it may appear, possesses providential significance; for the moral order of the world cares more for the making of *character* than for the making of *money*. It would help our faith in that order if there were a good many more 'failures' proceeding from the same cause. 'Is the purpose of the Maker of this world to increase the number of noble lives, or to fill the world with mere comfort?

[1] Jonah iv. 11.
[2] Job xxix. 12-14.

Is it His aim to produce a condition of material life or a temper of the soul?'[1] Or, again, look at Jeremiah. At a dire political crisis he says to his countrymen, 'Resist not the Chaldean; better to submit at once, it is the least of two evils.' They call him a traitor and threaten his life. Is he really a traitor? Is it not rather a case of extremes meeting: the noble man mistaken for an ignoble man, the true friend of his country treated as one in league with its enemies?

Accepting the underlying assumption of the Eliphaz theory, viz., that there is a connection between suffering and sin, the precise nature of the connection remains to be determined. The suffering, *e.g.* may seem to be, to a certain extent may really be, punitive, and yet in a deeper sense it may be salutary. Consider the prodigal: he is, it is true, only a character in a parable, but it is a character frequently exemplified in actual life. He has been a waster, he is now a beggared, starved, ragged wretch. His present state, you say, is the direct effect and penalty of past folly, and as such is an exemplification of the judicial aspect of Divine Providence. This is true, and this is all that can be seen from the outside, and all that hard-natured men would expect or care to see. Yet how much more is possible? What if the acute stage of misery reached should prove the turning-point in the prodigal's career, the point at which the thoughtless man turns thoughtful, comes to himself, in the expressive phrase of the parable? In that case, the

[1] *The Life of William Denny*, p. 355. From a lecture by Mr. Denny on *Success*.

truest formula for that man's whole career may be: A benignant Providence leading him by a very long, roundabout way to goodness and bliss; through folly to wisdom, through misery to joy. To how many cases this formula may apply, including not merely a motley collection of brands plucked from the burning, of whom history takes no note, but not a few of the illustrious ones, like Saul of Tarsus, Augustine, and Bunyan! And what reflections radiant with hope the formula suggests in reference to the whole history of our sin and sorrow-laden world! That history, not a mere depressing, monotonous spectacle of men sinning and God punishing sin; the Power making for righteousness engaged in the futile work of judgment, destroying the race with a deluge, and at the end obliged to confess that it was all to no purpose![1] That history, rather, a grand redemptive process, in which even sin is compelled to serve the aim of a beneficent Providence, so that just where sin breaks out most lawlessly and abounds most disastrously, there ultimate superabounding in grace and goodness and sanctity may be looked for! It may seem to prudent moralists a dangerous thesis, but it is the thesis of Jesus Christ and of the apostle Paul. 'The last shall be first,' said Jesus; 'Where sin abounded, grace did much more abound,' said Paul.

Another case still is conceivable. The sin supposed to be punished may lie outside the person suffering. A man may suffer, not because he is unrighteous, but because others are unrighteous. Not to speak of the

[1] Genesis viii. 21.

highest instance under this category, there have been innumerable instances of this type in the history of the world. Suffering for righteousness' sake is almost as common a phenomenon as suffering for sin's sake. The two phenomena are bracketed together in the sombre teaching of Ecclesiastes as equally familiar and equally deplorable. 'Be not righteous over-much; neither make thyself over-wise; why shouldest thou destroy thyself? Be not over-much wicked; neither be thou foolish; why shouldest thou die before thy time?'[1] Poor advice, but important testimony to the effect that there are those who suffer because they are righteous, as well as those who perish through folly. There are, indeed, and they are those who have redeemed the life of mankind from vulgar mediocrity, and thrown on the page of history the divine light of heroism and moral sublimity.

It is in the experience of the so-called 'righteous over-much,' when properly understood, that the providential order of the world is seen to receive its most conspicuous verification. But, misunderstood by onlookers, it may readily lead either to cruelly unjust judgments on the subjects thereof, or to an eclipse of faith in a providential order. Misunderstanding on the part of the subjects of the experience is very possible, and may be detrimental. It brings an alternative temptation either to self-distrust or to distrust in God. The tried one has to choose between two unwelcome conclusions: either, I am not in singleness of heart devoted to the good; or, God is not good, does not care

[1] Ecclesiastes vii. 16, 17.

for the right. Safety lies in bold rejection of both alternatives, and in holding fast at once faith in personal integrity and faith in God. On the hypothesis that, under a real moral order, lot ought to be the unfailing, universally recognisable index of character, these two faiths present a hard antinomy, but it is in its power to surmount such antinomies that faith shows its heroic quality. The Job-like man can say at once, 'Till I die I will not remove mine integrity from me,'[1] and, 'I know that my Vindicator liveth.'[2] With his back to the wall, he says to friend and foe among his fellow-men, I am not going to give the lie to my good conscience to please you, or to verify shallow theories; and towards the Power above he assumes the attitude of one who *trusts* and *waits*.

Trusting and waiting occupy a large place in the experience of the men who are generously interested in the progress of good in this world. They cannot but believe that the Divine Being is on the same side, and they commonly have to wait a weary while for practical evidence of the fact, the pace of Providence being slow. This is no rare or exceptional situation. It is the regular experience of those who are identified with the noblest causes in the incipient stage. At that stage such causes are purest in the motives of their promoters, and the characters of their adherents. But just when they are most divine in moral quality, they are least divine so far as apparent providential backing is concerned. The forces of custom, prejudice, worldly interest, are arrayed against them, and the Power over all

[1] Job xxvii. 5.   [2] *Ibid.*, xix. 25.

seems merely to look on, if He even do so much; and they are constrained to cry, Why standest thou afar off?[1] O Lord how long?[2]

Such outcries are *prayers*,—prayers of faith struggling with unbelief. It is in connection with such crises in the individual life that the nature, the need, and the use of prayer are most clearly seen. To pray is a natural impulse acted on instinctively in time of need by men of all religions. In the crude religions of primitive or pagan men, prayer has comparatively little moral significance, because the things desired are for the most part material goods. It rises to its true dignity on the lips of a man whose supreme desire is for all that is comprehended under the title, 'The Kingdom of God.' Whatever views may be entertained by particular persons as to the objective validity or efficacy of prayer, the matter of the petition, 'Thy Kingdom come,' must command the respect of all. And when the coming is intensely desired, and, in the form contemplated, long delayed, any one can further understand how natural, nay, how inevitable, it is to put the longing of the soul into the shape of a prayer. The heart unburdens itself in this way. As when deep thoughts have been stirring in our minds we eagerly communicate them to a bosom friend, so with equal eagerness and no less legitimacy we utter our moral and spiritual aspirations in the ear of God. We cannot help doing so if we believe in God at all. It is but speaking to the great *Atman*, the other Self. To many, I own, this urgency and inevitableness will ap-

[1] Psalm x. 1. [2] *Ibid.*, vi. 3.

pear a mystery. There are not a few whose lives are not pitched sufficiently high to supply material for prayers of the noblest type, or to make intelligible an intensity of longing comparable to that of a parched land in a famine-stricken country, for refreshing rain.[1] Such pray also, but too often in compliance mainly with pious custom, and in a spirit of routine, forcing themselves, rather than inwardly constrained, to assume the attitude of suppliants. But our present concern is not to sit in judgment on the prayers of any man, but rather to suggest that, if the legitimacy or value of prayer is to be discussed, it should be in connection with prayer at its best, prayer for the highest moral and spiritual ends, for the furtherance of Divine interests, expressing in struggling, inadequate language desires of unutterable vehemence.

But do even such prayers prevail? Science and philosophy, by the mouth of some representatives, may pronounce them without effect, except perchance in the form of reflex influence, soothing the heart's pain and reanimating languid hope. The grounds on which this verdict rests may appear so conclusive as to justify the inference that prayer is possible and allowable only for the weak and the ignorant, impossible in any real sincere sense, for those who know how rigidly all events are concatenated by the iron chains of physical law. Perhaps the truth is that here, as so often elsewhere, extremes meet, and that prayer is not only for children but for the wisest; for those, that is, who sink *below* the perplexities of reason, and also for those who

[1] Psalm cxliii. 6.

rise *above* them, treating them as unanswerable and at the same time as not needing answer, unhesitatingly and habitually asserting the claims of the moral order as against monopoly on the part of the physical order. For Kant, God was an imperious postulate of the practical reason, though He had been previously pronounced inaccessible to pure, theoretic reason. Even so for the devout wise man, prayer may be an imperious postulate of the spiritual nature, though science may seem to have supplied a triumphant demonstration of its futility. He may think it best to leave the demonstration on one side, and go on his way, saying in effect, 'For a believer in God, the only consistent course is to pray without ceasing, and to pray with full assurance to be heard.' This position is certainly unassailable. It is idle for a man who really believes in God to waste his time over scientific puzzles concerning the utility of prayer. The previous question, Is there a God? is the point on which all depends. 'Between freedom and fate,' it has been truly said, 'between a personal God and blind chance, between faith in prayer and trust to luck, we must choose. It is only the short-sighted and superficial mind that can find a resting-place between these two opinions.'[1]

This, however, is an appeal to theory, which, while legitimate, cannot take the place of an argument from experience. It would give satisfaction to devout hearts if it could be shown that the fervent prayer of a righteous man indeed availeth much. For some it would suffice to point to the case of Elijah praying, not in

[1] Hyde, *Outlines of Social Theology*, p. 123.

vain, for rain after a three years' famine, and to similar remarkable instances of fulfilment recorded in history. But there are others whom such cases would not satisfy, because they savour of the miraculous, and because the alleged fulfilments lie outside the moral sphere. They would prefer evidence of prayer answered within the moral sphere and by the action of the immanent laws of the moral world. Is such evidence forthcoming? I believe it is. There is nothing more certain than that fervent desire for the coming of the Divine Kingdom, under some definite form, is followed sooner or later by its advent. The fact is so both in the individual and in the community. He who supremely desires to be good becomes good. Such desires issue eventually in the ripe fruit of the Spirit: 'Love, joy, peace, long-suffering, gentleness, goodness, faith, meekness, temperance.' Fulfilment comes likewise in the community. Elijahs do not live in vain or alone. They propagate their kind. Their prayer, and that of which it is the index, a consuming passion for the right and the rational and the humane, tend to bring about fulfilment. Moral enthusiasm is infectious. Tribulation increases its infective power, deepening sympathy in friends, conquering enmity in foes. As natural fire kindles dry fuel, so the Divine passion for righteousness, even in a single man, sets prepared hearts burning all around. These are sure laws of the moral world, through which God works as the Hearer of prayer.

As the devout wise man may disregard the cloud of speculative difficulties that has been raised around the subject of prayer, so he may treat as of secondary importance the distinction sometimes taken between two spheres — the material and the spiritual — in reference to the legitimacy of petitionary prayer. The man we have in view is concerned above all about the spiritual, the kingdom of God and its sovereign interests; only in a very subordinate way for the lower interests represented by food and raiment. Yet he need not, ordinarily he does not, trouble himself with scrupulous endeavours to confine his prayers strictly within the spiritual sphere. The theory which dictates such endeavours may appear an ingenious compromise,[1] but in practical life it will turn out to be an unworkable pedantry. The two spheres cannot be kept apart, they *will* run together. Then, be the spheres two or twenty, they are parts or aspects of the one universe of God, the pliable instrument of His sovereign will. Therefore the prayers of the cultured saint, like the prayers of children, are simple, spontaneous, realistic, unembarrassed by subtle distinctions between natural and spiritual, foreordination and freedom, physical law and miracle. His first petition is, 'Hallowed be Thy name,' his second, 'Thy Kingdom come,' his third, 'Thy will be done': all meaning the same thing, iteration revealing intensity of desire; but his fourth may be a prayer for daily bread, or for some other form of temporal good, though he full well knows what a vast network of physical law is involved in the answering of it.

The answer to prayer by which the Divine interest is conclusively demonstrated may be long deferred; it

[1] For this theory *vide* Miss Cobbe's *Broken Lights*.

may not come till faith and hope have almost died out of the hearts, even of the elect. But it is not in the far-off event alone that traces of the providential order are to be found. These may be discovered in the mere existence of men cherishing desires to which the far-off event is the Divine response. The rising up, in any generation, of a band of men endowed with clear spiritual intuition, fresh inspiration, moral enthusiasm, is the best possible evidence to that generation that God has not forsaken the world. God is in these men; they are His instruments, by whom He means to achieve a work fraught with blessing to humanity. The hardships they undergo, so far from being evidence that He is indifferent, are really shared by Him. When they suffer, He suffers in them. The sorrows they endure are tragic enough; they have been described as 'the tragedy of the brute chance, to which everything spiritual seems to be subject amongst us, the tragedy of the diabolic irrationality of so many among the foes of whatever is significant.'[1] There is comfort in the thought that the tragedy exists for God as well as for men, and that we may conceive of Him as saying, ' O ye who despair, I grieve with you. Yes, it is I who grieve in you. Your sorrow is mine. No pang of your finitude but is mine too. I suffer it all, for all things are mine; I bear it, and yet I triumph.'[2]

The real trial of faith in the providential order does not lie in delayed fulfilment of devout aspirations, or in the hardships which befall moral pioneers, but in the

[1] Royce, *The Spirit of Modern Philosophy*, p. 465.
[2] *Ibid.*, p. 470.

degeneracy which overtakes good causes when at length they have won for themselves not merely reluctant toleration but friendly recognition. That which was divine in the primitive epoch of frustration, then becomes undivine, vulgarised, secularised. So it happened in the case of Christianity, so it happens more or less in the case of all great movements. What are we to make of this? Is God to be found only among the persecuted, the battling, buffeted minority, the men who are 'made as the filth of the earth and the offscouring of all things'? There especially, emphatically, but not there alone. God is also in the secularised community, as salt is in a mass of flesh, as an antidote to corruption, or as leaven hid in a lump of dough. For the salting and leavening processes ample time is allowed, possibly a millennium. If the result be failure, the salt losing its savour, the mass becoming utterly corrupt, a fresh departure is made. New prophets arise, heralds of a new era, mouthpieces of the Eternal Spirit of Goodness, with a message of hope for future generations. So the world goes on, alternating between two providential phases, one in which the Beneficent Presence reveals itself conspicuously in the chosen few, followed by another in which it is latent in the many.

In the foregoing paragraphs I have had occasion to touch on the important subject of prayer. I must now allude, however briefly, to another topic, if possible still more momentous, *the future life*. Our theme is the providential order in this present world, but it seems most natural that, in connection with those with whom that order is most intimately connected, the soldiers of righteousness, we should ask, Is Divine Providence done with them here, or does it follow them, to beneficent intent, beyond the tomb? Do the righteous survive, and in a life of pure bliss enjoy the reward of their heroic conduct in this mortal state? It is in connection with this question that the faith in immortality seems to reach the highest degree of probability, viewed in the light of natural reason. If any are to live on, surely it will be earth's noblest ones, those whose one concern in this world is to promote the higher interests of humanity! One could imagine them surviving death while other men perished, as unworthy of the life eternal. If even they cease to exist when the last breath is exhaled, then the life beyond must be indeed an idle dream. And if that be the fate appointed them, how hard, one naturally reflects, their lot! Their life here, a constant fight with evil, with little to sustain courage and patience save perchance just the hope of heaven's rest by and by; and it turns out to be a delusion. Had not one of their number, and speaking as it were in their name, good right to say, 'If in this life only we have hope, we are of all men most miserable'?[1] And what is to be said of the Providence that lets them drop out of existence in this way, using them as its instruments for a while, appointing to them arduous tasks, and suffering them to undergo many harsh experiences, then throwing them aside when their powers of work and endurance are exhausted? Can such a Providence be said to be paternal? Can it even be believed to be real? Does not the whole idea of Providence, in the case

[1] 1 Corinthians xv. 19.

supposed, fall to pieces in our hands? And, finally, in that case, why waste one's threescore years and ten in fruitless, unrecognised, unrecompensed heroisms? Heroism does not pay: it has no proper place in the social order: it is not even sane; it is simply the morbid excrescence of a scrupulous conscience. Let us lower our tone, and be happy, acting on the maxim: *dum vivimus vivamus.*

I have stated the case strongly, as it might present itself to one having no clue to guide him save the groping surmises of his own reason. To some it will appear an overstatement, to others it will seem to keep within the limits of strict truth; for the thoughts of men in our time, on this solemn theme, are diverse. Traditional faith in the future life has to a large extent lost its hold, and earnest minds are thrown on their own resources, and compelled to think out the question *de novo;* and it is neither surprising nor to be regretted that all inquirers do not arrive at identical conclusions. To some it seems obvious that not only religion but morality hangs on the answer to the question, Is there a life beyond? Thus a recent American writer remarks, 'If into that sleep no dreams can come, then I, for one, am ready to justify suicide, and to declare that the greatest fools are those who deny themselves any pleasures that will not in this life give them pain.'[1] Others again, while sincerely believing in the life to come, adopt a more moderate tone. Thus another very thoughtful American author, in a work recently published, expresses himself in these terms, 'Immortality

[1] Bradford, *Heredity and Christian Problems*, p. 238.

is not necessary as a foundation for religion. There have been and are to-day profoundly religious spirits of whose faith this larger hope forms no certain part. Even if this little life be all, the life of love is better than the life of selfishness; the life of service is nobler than the life of sensual pleasure; God is a more worthy object even for our short-lived devotion than appetite and passion.'[1] In this statement most thoughtful men will acquiesce. They cannot well do anything else in view of the fact that in the religion of ancient Israel the hope of immortality had only a very subordinate place, if any place at all, among the motives determining conduct. Their hope was to see the goodness of God in the land of the living,[2] *i.e.* in this present life, and it was in the same sphere that they sought for traces of the moral order in general. The very core of prophetic teaching was this, that there is a providential order in this present world, and in this present life of individual men, and of communities. And however far beyond the prophets Christians may have advanced on the subject of the life to come, they ought to hold fast the prophetic creed. It will not do, because of our faith in an eternal recompense, to be indifferent to what happens in this world, and to regard human life on earth, even in the case of the good, as a chaotic scene in which few traces of a providential order can be discerned. This dwarfing and eclipsing of time by eternity is not conducive to the interests either of religion or of morality. If there be no moral order here, what reason have we for believing

[1] De Witt Hyde, *Outlines of Social Theology*, p. 258.
[2] Psalm xxvii. 13.

in a moral order anywhere? If the two worlds are divorced from each other as wholly dissimilar in character — God in evidence there, not visible here — is that not likely to end in a disastrous separation between the secular and the religious aspects of life — the one becoming an atheistic, inhuman, unprincipled struggle to make the most of this world, the other a ghostly, artificial contrivance for making the most of the next? Let these be fundamentals in our creed: that the right at all hazards and in all departments must be done, that God is evermore and in all worlds on the side of right, and that if there be another life in store for man, it will be but the natural sequel to the present life, wherein men shall reap what they have here sown.

These remarks do not tend, as they are not intended, to encourage underestimating views as to the value of faith in a life hereafter. On the contrary, they recommend a habit of thought and a way of life whose direct tendency is to strengthen that faith. They certainly give no countenance to the idea that we are under no obligation to live well, and that we need not even take the first step in right conduct till we have been assured of the life beyond. But they teach in effect that the best way to reach such assurance is to pitch life on the highest level possible. Live nobly, and it will begin to appear to you credible that you will live for ever. In the words of an author already quoted, 'While immortality is not a demonstrable fact of science which we can hold up in advance as an inducement for beginning the religious life, it is a confident assurance which grows brighter and brighter with each new experience of the blessedness of love and each fresh revelation of the goodness of God.'[1]

It is only when the assurance in question rests on such grounds that it possesses ethical value. That the soul is by its inherent nature indefeasibly immortal, is, if true, which may reasonably be disputed,[2] simply a proposition belonging to the physical world. It amounts to this, that the thinking principle continues after death, presumably remaining the same as before. Primitive man as represented by anthropologists believed as much. In his crude creed the ghost of a dead man lives on, and continues the pursuits of the man before he died. The theory, even if true, would possess little more significance than the messages from the dead reported and believed in by modern spiritualism. It is when it is made to rest on moral and religious grounds that faith in immortality becomes ethically important. It means something when you say, Let those be immortal who are 'worthy to obtain that world.'[3] It means still more when you say, Let man be immortal because of the worth which man has for God, as evinced by the place assigned to him in the universe, and the care bestowed upon him in providence. That implies that immortality is not merely the prerogative of the dis-

---

[1] De Witt Hyde, *Outlines of Social Theology*, p. 259.

[2] Mr. Gladstone discusses the question of 'natural immortality' in his *Studies Subsidiary to the Works of Bishop Butler*. His position is that the tenet has no right to the place which it holds in the religious mind of our generation, and that it is not a doctrine of religion, but only a matter of philosophical speculation, on which we are neither bound nor able to come to any certain conclusion. — *Vide* p. 256.

[3] Luke xx. 35.

tinguished few, but the common destiny of mankind. It is a vast thought, and raises momentous questions which must here remain unanswered. On the whole subject 'we see through a glass, darkly.' In absence of a sure, authoritative word of God, we must, with Socrates and his companions, sail through life on the frail raft of the most probable opinion. Even when we have got this raft, it is difficult to trust without misgiving to its guidance. In the quaint words of one of the interlocutors in the *Phaedo*, we 'are haunted with a fear that when the soul leaves the body, the wind may really blow her away and scatter her, especially if a man should happen to die in stormy weather and not when the sky is calm.'[1] The construction of our raft out of materials supplied by natural theology is an affair of much dubitating reflection. For one engaged in a study of the providential order, the question is, What inferences or surmises naturally arise out of the general position: man a chief end for God? The answer may be tentatively stated in the form of presumptions as follows:—

1. There is a life beyond the tomb.
2. This life, however conditioned, is for all men.
3. It will be a blessed life for as many as possible.
4. Human freedom introduces uncertainty: eternal miscarriage is possible.
5. Yet, on the other hand, if human freedom were the determining factor, the result might be total failure, universal bankruptcy in regard to eternal life.

[1] Jowett, *The Dialogues of Plato*, vol. i. p. 453.

6. A power of God is needed to insure eternal bliss for any, a power which, with adequate good will, ought, we are apt to think, to insure the same boom for all.

7. Yet that power, however strong, must not be so applied as to cancel freedom and the moral nature of man.

8. Between the two theses last enunciated we are landed in an antinomy which seems insurmountable by reason.

9. Heaven is for *man*, not for all sentient creatures, as Theodore Parker extravagantly taught. God cares for beasts, even for plants; yet the flowers of the field which He clothes with beauty are to-morrow cast, as common grass, into the oven.

LECTURE X

PROVIDENTIAL METHODS: ELECTION

WE now enter on the study of the methods by which Providence seeks to accomplish its beneficent aims for the good of mankind. We take up first the method of *election*. Occasional allusions in previous lectures have prepared us for recognising the procedure denoted by the term as among the providential ways of God, and we have now to consider at some length its nature, rationale, conditions, and results.

The general aim of election is service to mankind in some particular sphere within the wide range of human interests. It is a method whereby Providence uses the one — one man or one people — to bless the many. The purposed benefit does not centre in and terminate with the elect, but passes out beyond them in ever-widening spheres of benignant influence. Privilege, prerogative, may be involved in the method, but whatever element of this kind there may be is secondary in comparison with the universal service contemplated. If the method in its actual working generate in any instance a spirit of monopoly, it is an accident and an abuse tending to frustrate rather than promote the designs of the providential order.

Special service or function implies special fitness: endowment, capacity corresponding to the appointed task. That signifies much. Many things go to the making of an elect man or people: heredity, environment, experience. It is not a matter of arbitrary choice: laying hold of any chance man or people, and forthwith destining him or it to a certain vocation. Race is involved, and when you have got the race, there is further needed discipline, opportunity, suitable location. Take the case of Israel, with which we have been accustomed very specially, if not exclusively, to associate the idea of election. The basal fact connected with Israel's election is the origination of a Semitic type of mankind, with a peculiar temperament and a peculiar proclivity or genius for religion. Then on this basis of racial resemblance there had to be built up a superstructure of specific difference to insure that Israel should make a new religious departure, and not follow the ways of pagan Semitic peoples. That meant a peculiar history from first to last: Egyptian bondage, settlement in a land favourable to isolation, the raising up from time to time of remarkable men capable of communicating a powerful new impulse to their people: Moses, Elijah, Isaiah, and the like.

The fundamental fact involved in election, racial peculiarity, must for our purpose be accepted simply as a *datum*. We see that the providential order needed races with definite mental and spiritual endowments, but how they were produced we are not obliged to inquire, and we do not profess to know. It is a hard problem even for scientific experts. Some have thought that racial differences, such as those which exist between white, black, yellow, and red men, run back to primitive origin, and presuppose distinct first parents. Against this is not only the Hebrew tradition of the common descent of all men from one primal pair, but the bias of science in favour of unity as opposed to plurality of origin. On the other hand, accepting the unity of origin, and corresponding original homogeneity in physical and mental features, the difficulty is to conceive by what means such wide differentiation as now exists could possibly be brought about. The difficulty appears all the greater when it is considered that the great race distinctions, as we know them, were established at a very early period, and that history makes us acquainted with no later variations comparable to them in extent and importance. The 'race-making force,' to use the apt phrase of Mr. Bagehot, must have acted with great intensity in the prehistoric period, and as it were exhausted itself, giving place to the feebler 'nation-making force,' which has been in operation within the historical period producing specific varieties. In this respect there seems to be an analogy between the origin of race and the origin of language. In both cases forces appear to have been at work producing extraordinary results without parallel in later times; yielding in the department of language such widely disparate phenomena as the Sanskrit and Hebrew tongues, and in the department of race two families of mankind so broadly discriminated as the Aryans and the Semites. The forces in either instance may fall under the general category of evolution, and may even be simply exemplifications of the theory of natural selection acting under exceptional conditions.[1] It may be a kind of duty we owe to modern science to believe that this is so, even in absence of proof; but it will certainly be a case of trusting where we do not see. The origin of race, like the origin of language, is a mystery; a subject of speculation rather than of exact knowledge. In making this remark, I have no intention to suggest the hypothesis of preternatural causality. It is not necessary to postulate such causality in order to invest race with providential significance. The physical order and the moral order are not two mutually exclusive spheres; they interpenetrate each other.

The method of election has an intelligible *rationale*. It is simply this, that all important human interests demand for their furtherance emphatic representation. With reference to the bearing of this principle on the case of Israel, Mr. M. Arnold has truly observed, that 'unless a sense or endowment of human nature, however in itself real and beneficent, has some signal representative among mankind, it tends to be pressed upon by other senses and endowments, to suffer from its own want of energy, and to be more and more pushed out of sight.'[2] It follows from this that if the world is to be duly impressed with the supreme importance of righteousness, and with the value of a conception of

[1] On this *vide* Wallace's *Contributions to the Theory of Natural Selection*, chap. ix. where the theory is applied to the question of race. *Vide* also Bagehot's *Physics and Politics*, p. 108, and Westermarck's *History of Human Marriage*, p. 272.

[2] *Literature and Dogma*, p. 55.

God in which the divine and the ethical are intimately connected, there must be at least one people possessed with the passion for righteousness and cherishing a kindred idea of God, and able by its intensity and persistency to stamp its convictions indelibly on mankind. The adoption of the method is no more arbitrary, or without reason, than is the application of it to a particular man or people as the agent of Providence. There must be a particular instrument for a particular service, if the service is to be efficiently rendered. And this demand of the service is in harmony with evolutionary law, which ever tends to increasing specialisation. Generic types of life come low down in the scale; the higher we rise the more specialised the type, the more pronounced the individuality. But individuality means limitation: strength here, weakness there, enhanced fitness for certain functions, diminished fitness for others.

It is a corollary from this that more elect peoples than one are needed to do the work of Providence. One people can no more perform all the functions necessary than all men or peoples can be made equally expert in any one function. A certain people may by race and training be supremely qualified for giving to the world the true religion, but it is not at all to be expected that the same people should be able to give the world lessons in science, philosophy, art, or government. If Providence attach importance to these things, it will have to prepare other races for becoming in connection with them the instructors and benefactors of mankind. If other races are found to possess the needful fitness and liking for the task, then they also must be numbered among the elect. For, although we have been accustomed to apply the term specially to the people of Israel, and to associate it with the subject of religion, there is no reason in the nature of things why its use should be thus restricted. *Signal fitness for an important special function constitutes election.* If it be thought that past usage should be respected, and that the term in question should be consecrated to the expression of religious ideas, good and well; only let it be remembered that the essential truth involved is not confined to religion, but pervades the whole providential order of the world. When that fact is duly recognised, it will not be deemed profane to employ, at least provisionally, so expressive and suggestive a word to invest the fact with appropriate importance.

So far from the epithet 'elect' being exclusively applicable to one people, it may appear a reasonable position that all peoples are elect, that is to say, possess some special aptitude for some particular service whereof mankind is to get the benefit. In the abstract, that thesis may have something to say for itself, but I do not think it would serve any practical purpose to contend for it. Such a sweeping generalisation would only tend to obscure the significance of the principle as exemplified on a less ambitious scale. It is much more important to see clearly the great services rendered by Israel, Greece, and Rome, under the providential order, than to set ourselves to the somewhat hard task of discovering the function assigned by that order to China and other nations that might be named, all in order to justify the thesis that election is absolutely universal. For aught we know, China's time may be coming, and the future may bring the day, predicted in a recent forecast, when the globe will be 'girdled with a continuous zone of the black and yellow races, no longer too weak for aggression or under tutelage, but independent, or practically so, in government, monopolising the trade of their own regions, and circumscribing the industry of the European,'[1] having fleets in European seas, and taking part on equal terms in European politics. That would be a great change, but whether such a state of matters would entitle the Chinese to the dignified appellation of an elect people is another question. The very vastness of that nation suggests a doubt. Providence has hitherto shown a preference for small nations as its instruments: Israel, Greece, Rome (small in its beginnings), the inhabitants of the British Isles. Is that an accident, or is there something in the nature of things that connects special gifts and service with limited numbers and dimensions? Great epoch-making men are scarce. Must greatness in the intellectual and moral sphere always be forthcoming only on a reduced scale? Is it a law of the providential order that all movements on the higher levels must begin obscurely, and slowly advance to world-wide influence and renown? Such a law, if verified, would invest the elective method with impressive moral significance. A little stone growing to a great mountain, a tiny seed becoming a great tree, is a stirring spectacle.

[1] Pearson, *National Life and Character*, p. 89.

Providence not only seems to prefer small peoples as its instruments, but even within these it works mainly through chosen *men*. The elective method exhibits its highest potency in the individual. In no case do all the members of any community, in any appreciable measure, inherit its gifts or participate in its service. 'They are not all Israel which are of Israel.'[1] The genius and vocation of a people become incarnated in a choice few. A nation that has no great men has no great destiny. A nation that has a great destiny will never want great men. Even Hartmann remarks that the right time has never wanted the right man, and that the cry sometimes raised that the men needed for pressing tasks are not forthcoming simply means that these supposed pressing tasks have no place in the plan of history.[2] From a pessimistic philosopher this is as welcome as it is unexpected. Sombre forecasts of the future include in their depressing picture the disappearance from the earth of great characters— no great poets, no great saints, no men endowed with irrepressible individuality and power of initiative; a monotonous *régime* of mediocrity, 'when the lower races will predominate in the world, when the higher races will lose their noblest elements, when we shall ask nothing from the day but to live, nor from the future but that we may not deteriorate.'[3] Let us hope that this is the ill-founded surmise of a gifted thinker, whose mind has been unduly influenced by a colonial type of

[1] Romans ix. 6.
[2] *Philosophie des Unbewussten*, p. 328.
[3] Pearson, *National Life and Character*, p. 363.

sentiment. For the prospect set before us is dismal enough. When the higher races have lost their noblest elements, whether as diffused in the community or as concentrated in the individual, life will not be worth living. The very idea is a renunciation of faith in Providence. That faith we are not prepared to renounce on evidence far from overwhelming. Therefore we will continue to expect the appearance, at the appointed hour, of elect men, with great minds, great souls, great faith, hope, and devotion; men of forceful individuality, predestined, mightily impelled, under a Divine necessity, to expend their stored-up energy in a manner that shall redeem their time from oppressive commonplace, and give humanity a new impetus onwards in its way towards its appointed goal.

Such elect men always belong to an elect people. The two, the elect man and the elect people, are relative to each other, belong to each other, and each is to the other the instrument of usefulness. The mutual relation and its importance are not recognised with equal clearness on both sides. Sometimes an elect people does not know its elect men when it sees them, does not appreciate their value, does not understand what they are there for. Puzzled by their personality, and provoked by their unwonted line of action, it may even think that the best thing to do with them is to disown, banish, or destroy them. But the elect man generally understands and values his relation to his people. While something more and higher than a patriot, he is in the best sense patriotic. He regards himself as the servant of his people. 'I am not sent but unto the lost sheep of the house of Israel.'[1] Every elect man has a similar sense of national vocation, and acts accordingly. His life-work may ultimately turn out to concern the whole world and all time, but he works above all, and consciously, for his own race and his own generation. He is intensely endowed with racial peculiarities, and, however wide his sympathies, he is content to live and die, and be remembered, as one of his own beloved people. And this is no disqualification for permanent universal influence. Particularism and universalism are not mutually exclusive. The best way to serve the universal interest is to be thoroughly the particular man you were destined to be by individual and racial endowment.

Particularism has its place and value in the character of elect peoples, not less than in that of elect men. It is good that an elect race should for a time dwell alone, and become intensely conscious of its own apartness, and define itself in hard antithesis over against the rest of the world: Jew against Gentile, Greeks against barbarians. Such self-consciousness easily runs into vicious excess which may prove disastrous to a chosen people; nevertheless in its own place and time it serves the purpose of the providential order. It secures the isolation necessary to give fixity to racial type, without which a people cannot be a chosen people, or have anything distinctive or valuable to give to mankind. The good of the whole is ever the ultimate aim, but for that very reason the parts must for a season be detached from the whole. Premature mixture yields a bastard

[1] Matthew xv. 24.

universalism which means degeneracy rather than progress. Israel cannot keep too much aloof from her Canaanitish neighbours in social and religious custom, if she is to give to the world an idea of God which shall be her glory, and the world's permanent gain. Genial relations with her environment will mean participation in the revolting practices of Pagan Semitic worship — sacred prostitution and human sacrifice. Puritanic exclusiveness with reference to such a neighbourhood is her only chance of an honourable destiny as the providential bearer of the purest faith. To become the best she must bitterly hate the worst, till she has become strong enough to exchange a policy of isolation for a policy of free intercourse, without risk of contamination. This doctrine of temporary separation in order to eventual fellowship may be summed up in these words of Mr. Bagehot: 'In early times Providence set apart the nations, and it is not till the frame of their morals is set by long ages of transmitted discipline, that enlargement can be borne. The ages of isolation had their use, for they trained men for ages when they were not to be isolated.' [1]

The effective performance of its allotted function by an elect race thus appears to depend on two main conditions — original peculiarity and careful conservation of the distinctive feature. These two conditions in the providential order correspond to variation and heredity in the physical order. In both spheres upward progressive evolution is rendered possible by the combination of counterbalancing forces. In the physical sphere no

[1] *Physics and Politics*, p. 40.

progress would be possible if either variation or heredity acted alone. Heredity alone would mean absolute likeness of offspring to parent, whereby animal life, *e.g.* would be kept for ever at its lowest stage. Variation alone would mean endless change without significance; an infinite number of freaks of nature of brief duration, and leading nowhere. Combine the two and you get change and order, movement and repose in equipoise, resulting in the steady ascent of life from lower stages to higher. In the moral sphere the conditions of progress are analogous. There is needed first a people able to give to humanity an onward, upward impulse in a certain direction, in virtue of a useful, intellectual, or moral variation, constituting its distinctive racial endowment. But there is needed also the fixing of this useful variety in an abiding type, that its appearance in history may not be like that of a comet, but rather like that of a star, steadily shining in the firmament. The elect race must have permanent and emphatic distinctiveness. It must last long enough to become known to the world, and when it comes to the knowledge of men it must possess characteristics which arrest attention, invite study, provoke admiration, or it may be antagonism; it matters not greatly which, in the first place, for the one thing needful is that it be seen and felt to be there, a stubborn fact that must be reckoned with, that can by no means be ignored as a nullity. That secured, the service it was destined to render humanity cannot be frustrated. The servant may perish, but the service will be performed. An elect race may perish by the faults of its own high qualities, but the boon which is the ripe fruit of these high qualities will not fail to be reaped. Israel may pass away, or become a wanderer among the nations, but not before giving to the world the oracles of its prophets, and the incomparable teaching of its Christ. Greece may vanish before the invincible power of Rome, but the victim of brute force will bequeath to the conqueror as a dying legacy its own inimitable culture. Rome may undergo a tragic 'Decline and Fall,' but in doing so it will communicate to the barbarians before whom it succumbs its legislative wisdom and its spirit of obedience. The Germanic nations, one or more of them, may lose their place of pre-eminence, but the world will inherit from them the spirit of liberty, and the conception of freedom as, not the prerogative of one or of a few, but the birthright of man as man. By these various contributions of elect peoples the world will be permanently enriched. 'One soweth and another reapeth. I sent you to reap that whereon ye bestowed no labour: other men laboured, and ye are entered into their labours.'[1]

When elect peoples perish, it is not to be supposed that the fact is sufficiently accounted for by the remark that the providential order, having got its use of them, heartlessly throws them aside. This may be the superficial aspect of the matter, but the real causes lie deeper. Such peoples perish by their own fault. The apostle Paul was very careful to assert this principle in reference to Israel. He saw the bulk of his countrymen failing to understand that the future belonged to Christianity, and by that failure doomed, as he believed, to

[1] John iv. 37, 38.

national disaster. He asked himself what this meant, and in especial whether it meant that God had cast away his people? His answer was twofold: it did not mean absolute and final casting away; but even if it did, the doom had been deserved, and simply illustrated the retributive action of the moral order of the world. This view, applied comprehensively, must command general assent, though we may be inclined to insist less exclusively on moral causes, and to trace in disaster not only fault but misfortune. With an exception to be hereafter named, all elect peoples and persons have characteristic defects, not to say vices. One of these is *onesidedness*, shown by attaching undue importance to that which it is the vocation of a people to hoist into prominence, to the neglect of other things. This defect is involved in the very idea of election. An elect people just means a people so endowed and trained as to have an intensified affinity and predilection for one particular good of humanity. Peoples or persons that take an equal all-round interest in all things may be very worthy of respect, but they can, as a rule, lay no claim to the epithet 'elect.' The elect man, be he philosopher, poet, prophet, artist, warrior, or saint, commonly cares more for this than for that, cares very much for one thing, very little for most things. His motto is, One thing I desire, think of, aim at, strive to do;[1] in St. Paul's laconic phrase: ἐν δέ.[2] He cannot help himself; he is predestined that way, impelled, driven on by spiritual forces in his soul lying deeper than his will. He may shrink from his destiny, try to evade

[1] Psalm xxvii. 4. [2] Philippians iii. 13.

it, as if with instinctive foreboding of the sorrows of an elect soul, but he must fail; his very misery, while he makes the futile attempt, will constrain him to yield, for the word of the Lord, the behest of destiny, will be in his heart as a burning fire shut up in his bones,[1] and to surrender will be the least of two evils. And surrender will mean *blessedness:* existence fulfilled, mysterious yearnings and obscure impulses satisfied; probably not *happiness*, for the predestined man, the man of genius, suffers both from his *intensities* and from his *apathies;* from excess of susceptibility in one direction, and from defect of susceptibility in other directions. His ideal torments him, and he finds no escape from the torment in recreative interests and occupations. Hence the specially gifted, of all sorts and in all spheres, are apt to be men of sorrow and acquainted with grief, and the saying of the Greek poet is verified: The sons of the gods are seldom happy.[2]

Onesidedness is a manifest characteristic of the elect peoples best known to history. The best of Israel's sons had a passion for righteousness, but they cared little for the æsthetic, though they were by no means insensible to the sublime and the beautiful in nature. The Greeks had a passion for art and philosophy, but the love of righteousness, though conspicuous in a few, was not in the ascendant. The Romans were devoted to the State, but they possessed neither brightness of intellect nor tenderness of conscience.

Each of these peoples did good service to the world by that in which it was strong, each suffered through

[1] Jeremiah xx. 9. [2] Euripides, *Ion.*

lack of that in which it was weak. Onesidedness is always a source of danger. One form of onesidedness may be more serious than another. Thus the defect ascribed to the Greeks, lack of a due sense of the importance of conduct, may be much more serious in its nature and consequences than that ascribed to the Hebrews, indifference to art. And it is not unnatural to ascribe to the comparative seriousness of the Greek defect the brevity of its brilliant career. This moralistic explanation of Greek failure, adopted by some moderns, seems to find support in the following fragment from a lost play of Euripides: 'I must blame my countrymen in this that they bestow crowns for no cause. For when an enemy is at our gates, of what use is he that can wrestle with skill, or run like a hound, or hurl a quoit to a distance, or break with a blow the jaw of an antagonist. Will a quoit or a kick drive an enemy away? . . . The men that deserve honour are such as by wisdom and integrity direct the counsels of our country, that forewarn against peril, and intermediate between contending factions. These men are the glory of our own land, and a blessing to the great commonwealth of all lands.'[1] Those who think the theory suggested by these lines too easy, and hardly fair to the Greeks, may prefer the solution offered by Mr. Freeman, who accounts for the brevity of their career by the form which political organisation assumed among them. The gist of that distinguished historian's explanation is as follows: The State for the Greek meant a single city, as distinct from a nation, or country in our

[1] From *Autolycus*, translated in D'Arcy W. Thomson's *Sales Attici*.

sense. This conception of one's own city as the political whole is highly stimulating to the individual citizens. But the civic life is too brilliant to last; 'the high-strung enthusiasm to which it owes its being, and without which it cannot be kept up at the same level, is not likely to last for many generations.' The system has this further drawback: the citizens of any particular city care supremely only for their own city, and are indifferent or even hostile to the fortunes of other cities. The inevitable result is, that for lack of union, all alike become the prey of any strong power, like Macedon, whose ambition prompts it to attack them.[1] The theory possesses intrinsic probability, but it does not eliminate moral causes. The Greek preference for the city as the political whole, and the comparative insensibility to the claims of race, language, and religion, had their roots in the moral spirit of the people: in an excessive love of liberty, and an unbridled subjectivity from which ruin, at no distant date, was only too likely to follow.

Even the onesided passion for religion and righteousness is not without its dangers. For lack of some counterbalancing interest helping to preserve a sense of proportion, it is apt to degenerate into a blind fanaticism. This was what befell the Jews. After the captivity, which cured them of the old indifference to their privileges and vocation as an elect people, their God-given law became to them a Fetich, and their religion proved their ruin. They became inaccessible to new ideas and incapable of adapting themselves to unwelcome situations. They held on desperately to

[1] *Comparative Politics*, pp. 93, 94.

an ancient faith when it had become worn out, and they cherished the dream of a Messianic kingdom of a political type when stern facts made it impossible. The result was a collision with Rome, which demolished their temple, and put an end to their national existence.

The subjectivity of the Greeks, and the fanaticism of the Jews, were the defects of their qualities. Elect peoples and persons are, further, liable to faults connected with their *vocation*. They may fail to realise their vocation, or they may realise it simply as a *privilege*. How often does it happen in individual history that men turn aside from the path into which their endowments would lead them, sometimes with disastrous effects to character, always with loss to the service which it was in them to render! The young man in the Gospel who made the grand refusal is the type of this class. He had nobleness enough to be dissatisfied with Pharisaism and to perceive the supreme value of the ethical in religion. Had he followed the behests of what was best in him, at the bidding of Jesus, he might have become an apostle of the Christian faith, a substitute for Judas, a companion to St. Paul. Tragic mistakes like his excite compassion as well as disapproval; for to find the true path to the highest use of life, and therefore to blessedness, is not easy. Decisions of vital consequence have to be taken in the dark, in the inexperience of youth, when men do not know the meaning of the impulses which are stirring in their souls. Yet fatal, final mistakes are never due to ignorance alone; always in part, and even chiefly, to lack of singleness of mind.

To the upright light ariseth in the darkness. God guides the blind, who are willing to be led by the hand of Providence, to their appointed destination. And it may be said that all truly elect spirits are willing; or even that they must go in the divinely appointed road whether they will or no. The men that fatally err are they who, so to speak, are not sufficiently *predestined*, compelled by forces deeper than their wills, to choose a high calling that shall not be pleasant or profitable or creditable to themselves, but serviceable to mankind.

What is true of many individuals may also be true of peoples. For a time they may fail to understand their providential reason of existence. This appears to have been for long the case with Israel. The conception of Israel as an elect people seems to have originated with the great prophets. It may have flashed across the minds of earlier prophets and seers like Samuel, but it was through the influence of Amos, Hosea, Isaiah, and their successors that the great thought took its place in the religious consciousness of the nation. Then the inner circle of devout spirits, if not the great mass of the people, began to realise that it was the vocation of Israel to be a peculiar treasure unto the God of the whole earth by becoming a kingdom of priests and an holy nation.[1] The state of exile in Babylon tended to deepen and diffuse this lofty sense of responsibility, and to prepare expatriated Israelites for receiving the solemn message of the unknown prophet of the captivity, which summoned them to

[1] Exodus xix. 15, 16.

become the missionaries of the true religion to the Gentile world. The exiles on their return to their own land brought with them this sense of a high calling, and the reforming work of Ezra and Nehemiah had for its aim to fit their fellow-countrymen for discharging the duties incumbent on an elect race. From that time forth Israel never forgot that she was a 'peculiar people.'

Such self-consciousness of providential distinction exposes to new dangers. The sense of a peculiar vocation may be perverted into food for a pride which, while very conscious of privilege, neglects duty. This is the besetting sin of all privileged classes. They turn into a monopoly of favour what Providence meant to be an opportunity of universal service. It is a grievous offence against the moral order of the world and the interests of mankind. Ultimately the offenders themselves are the greatest sufferers. An elect race, an *élite* section of society, that has got into the way of thinking only of its superiority, is a savourless salt whose inevitable doom is to be trodden under foot of men. God makes no man, nation, or order, great or distinguished, that he or it may have the inhuman satisfaction of despising, not to speak of insulting, the little and the obscure; and nothing more powerfully witnesses to the reality of a providential order than the thoroughness with which such crimes against humanity are punished. Under the righteous reign of a Divine Father, jealous for the well-being of the world, and specially mindful of the classes liable to be trampled on, it is the doom of the proud one to have a millstone hanged about his neck and to be drowned in the deepest depth of the sea.[1] No people ever was more guilty of the sin than Israel, and no people ever endured in harsher form the appropriate penalty. Both facts are explained by the circumstance that her vocation lay within the sphere of religion. Religious pride is of all kinds of pride the most odious, and a religious war is one in which there can be no compromise. The alternatives are conquest or ruin.

Few men, and perhaps no peoples, have kept entirely free from the sins and defects of the elect. There is one who stands alone in this respect, the elect man *par excellence* in all human history. Jesus Christ was not characterised even by onesidedness, not to speak of graver faults. He was a Hebrew, a Greek, and a Roman all in one; a Hebrew in His genius for religion and His passion for righteousness, a Greek in His sensitiveness to the beauty of the world, and a Roman in the sternness of the discipline to which He subjected the men through whom He hoped to influence the future. The puritanic limitations to which the Hebrew temperament is liable, are not traceable in those exquisite parables through which the Greek side of Christ's rich nature found expression. Objectionable characters, such as the selfish neighbour, the unjust judge, the unrighteous steward, are occasionally selected to be the hero of the story, and the motives of action in the natural sphere from which the parable is drawn are sometimes such as cannot find recognition in the spiritual sphere; as when the giver of a great feast desires

[1] Matthew xviii. 6.

his house to be filled with outcasts, not out of love to them but to exclude those who had saucily declined to come at the first. There are indications even in the Gospels that the primitive church had some difficulty in sympathising with this genial freedom from scrupulosity which characterised the Master.[1]

The Roman sternness of Jesus, in relation to the Twelve, betrayed the spirit of One who meant to found a kingdom not less extensive than the Roman Empire, and, if possible, more lasting. An important result, if not the full realisation of this purpose, was the *Christian Church* to which are transferred in the New Testament the predicates applied to Israel in the Old Testament: 'a chosen generation, a royal priesthood, an holy nation, a peculiar people.'[2] The community of those who believe in Jesus is for St. Paul the true Israel of God.[3] The designation does not awaken any expectation to find in the new society all the higher goods of humanity, but only the highest — the true, perfect, final religion, the satisfying, sanctifying, saving, rest-bringing knowledge of God. The manysidedness of Christ, as attested in the records of His life, might indeed suggest that it was His personal aim, and that it was also the natural tendency of His life-work, to create a society not only universal in its membership, but comprehensive in the benefits it offered; bringing to all men not only salvation from sin, but moreover all that tends to make life

[1] *Vide* Luke xvi. 10-13, which some commentators regard as words of Jesus not spoken in connection with the parable inserted here by the Evangelist as a corrective to possible abuse of its teaching.

[2] 1 Peter ii. 9.

[3] Galatians vi. 16.

full and complete. On this view the 'City of God,' would be Israel, Greece, and Rome all in one. The evolution of Christianity actually brought about a state of things presenting a certain approximation to this ideal in a church with a theology expressed in terms of Greek philosophy, finding in Biblical scenes and in the lives of saints materials for Christian art, providing in its ecclesiastical rule a substitute for the Roman Empire, and, over and above these benefits, undertaking by its cultus to perform the supreme function of saving men's souls. But this endeavour after comprehensiveness really meant to a great extent the secularisation of Christianity.[1] It is possible to render more effective service by a less ambitious programme. Organised Christianity, instead of striving to combine Church and State, and to become a purveyor of every form of benefit, would serve humanity best by making it its one business to reproduce faithfully in teaching and life the spirit of Christ; in Biblical language, 'to show forth the excellencies of Him who called' men 'out of darkness into His marvellous light.'[2] That is the *raison d'être* of the Christian election. That is why a church, as distinct from a nation or an ordinary society, exists. How far the Church has ever succeeded in rendering this supreme service is a matter for grave consideration. Churches are as liable to the defects and vices of the elect as are nations or individual historic characters, and they enjoy no protection from the penalties. We must always contemplate as a possibility that any given ecclesiastical society may become a savourless salt and be treated

[1] On this *vide* Harnack's *History of Dogma*. [2] 1 Peter ii. 9.

with contemptuous neglect. Such a result would not necessarily be a disaster. It might mean the setting free of the spirit of Christ for a new career of wide, unfettered blessing, influencing the whole of human life, and inspiring men for every form of noble activity, without seeking to bring them under any strict rule. That may be what is before us in the centuries to come. Be that as it may, of one thing we may be sure: Jesus Christ is not going to be forgotten. Elect peoples and holy commonwealths may pass away, but the service for whose sake they existed will abide. The 'gifts,' if not the elections, of God are without repentance.[1] The teaching of Jesus, more than all the contributions of all other elect men, is a possession of humanity for ever. And if under the providential order there be, as I doubt not, good in store for the world in the years to come, one large part of the good will be a better understanding of, and a more loyal compliance with, the mind of the Master, and a serious endeavour to apply that mind to the complicated social life of the community.

[1] Romans xi. 29.

LECTURE XI

PROVIDENTIAL METHODS: SOLIDARITY

THE meaning of the term 'Solidarity' can be best understood by placing it in antithesis to the term 'individuality.' We are individuals, each one of us a moral personality, having his own responsibility and bearing his own burden. But we are not exclusively and absolutely individual, completely isolated from and independent of each other, each man wholly uninfluenced by, and exercising no influence upon, his fellow-men. We are connected with each other, dependent on each other, mutually influenced and influencing, receiving and communicating good and evil, forming together a social organism in which all parts act and react on each other, and are each to the other at once cause and effect. No man liveth by himself or to himself. No man's experience is confined to himself; no man's character is entirely of his own making. We are in both respects largely what others have made us, and others are in both respects to some extent what we have made them.

Solidarity is an all-pervasive fact. It is the universal law of the moral world, exercising sway at once over individuals, communities, and the whole human species. Its power is revealed in individual idiosyncrasy, in racial peculiarity, in broad, common features which combine all races in the unity of one human family. One generation goeth and another cometh, but the generation that cometh is dependent on the one that goeth for being, for a common nature, *men* from *men;* and for characteristic qualities — children like their fathers not merely in so far as they are men not beasts, but in features, temperament, talents, even to a certain extent in virtue and in vice.

With regard to the ethical significance of this great universal law of the moral world, our first observation must be that we have no reason to regret its existence. Broadly viewed it seems fitted to serve the ends of a beneficent providential order. On the face of it, it is a good law, such as we might expect to prevail in a universe under the dominion of a good God. It is good that we are not absolutely independent and alone. Whatever evils may arise out of solidarity as one of the methods on which Providence works, on the whole, humanity will fare better with these than it would in a world in which unqualified individualism, if such a thing were possible, was the supreme law. In such a world we should escape the ills, physical and moral, which in the actual world men have it in their power to inflict on others. But with the ill we should likewise lose the good, which solidarity enables men to receive from and to communicate to each other. And with the power to give and receive would pass away the *will*. Love would die out, brotherhood would cease, society would be dissolved, family life, with its sweet, wholesome play of affection, would be unknown; the human world would consist of a countless multitude of isolated egoists:

brought into being otherwise than by birth; not less intellectual, possibly more, than the men of the actual world, but cold as icicles, loveless, caring only for themselves, with not so much as an occasional thought, wish, or effort for the benefit of other men. A *just* world that might be in the sense that no man would suffer from, or be responsible for, other men's misdeeds. But who cares for justice divorced from love? Who would not prefer a world in which love had free scope to work its beneficent will and do good to many, possibly at the cost of pain to itself, possibly also at the risk of conferring on bad men an equal power to do evil, to a world in which love had no place, but which afforded perfect protection from wrong?

But to our first observation we must add a second: that solidarity is not an unmixed good. It involves tremendous possibilities of evil. It is a two-edged sword cutting two ways, giving to the bad their opportunity of inflicting injury, as well as to the good of conferring blessing. How far the injury may go through the one channel of heredity is exemplified in the dark story of the 'Jukes' family in America, as related by Mr. Dugdale, which presents a melancholy record of vice, crime, pauperism, and disease, as the salient characteristics of the numerous descendants of one man born in the middle of the eighteenth century, described as a hunter and fisher, a hard drinker, jolly and companionable, and averse to steady toil. What a power of mischief lies in a single human being! In the course of a century the one becomes a thousand, embracing hundreds of worthless characters, each an active source of evil, and costing the state, collectively, a vast outlay in connection with maintenance, imprisonment, etc. 'Over a million and a quarter dollars of loss in seventy-five years, caused by a single family, 1200 strong, without reckoning the cash paid for whiskey, or taking into account the entailment of pauperism and crime of the survivors in succeeding generations, and the incurable disease, idiocy and insanity, growing out of this debauchery, and reaching further than we can calculate.'[1]

Such a dismal story readily creates the impression that heredity is a onesided power which works for evil far more than for good. And this impression may appear to be abundantly justified by the theological doctrine of the 'total depravity' of man caused by the transgression of the original parent of the human race. That doctrine, worked into the blood of Christendom, may in part be responsible for a tendency, which certainly prevails, to emphasise the dark side of hereditary influence, and to think of it as a power which secures the transmission only of morbid corporeal conditions and of vicious propensities. Max Nordau suggests this as the explanation of the sinister part played by heredity in Ibsen's dramas. He represents the poet as the child of a religious race whose creed he has to a great extent discarded, but as retaining three theological ideas which dominate his imagination — original sin, confession, and self-sacrifice; and as applying heredity only in the sense of inheriting evil qualities, not a single instance of the opposite occurring in his writings.[2] Whether this criticism of Ibsen be just, I am not in a

[1] 'The Jukes,' pp. 14, 15, 70.   [2] *Degeneracy*, p. 358.

position to say, but I feel certain that a pessimistic view of heredity is to be deprecated, and to be carefully guarded against by all who desire to retain earnest faith in a beneficent providential order. It is not necessary to that faith that heredity should be conceived of as a power working solely on the side of good. It is not reasonable to expect that we should reap all the beneficent effects of solidarity, under all its phases, without any of the incidental drawbacks, any more than it is reasonable to demand for man at once the gift of freedom and protection from its abuse. But it is necessary to faith that heredity should not be regarded as a malign power whose sole effect is to blight the promise of moral life, to blast hopes of progress, and to fill the world with sin and misery. If it *were* — it is not lightly to be affirmed that it *is* — the legitimate tendency of the dogma of original sin to foster such a view, it would be necessary in the interests of Theism to subject it to careful revision, to prevent one item in the developed creed of Christendom from being the destruction of a more radical and fundamental belief, this, viz., that *God is good*.[1]

These preliminary observations have for their aim to obviate a prejudice which may exist in some minds against regarding solidarity in any form as one of the

[1] In the *Westminster Catechism*, the sinfulness of the state into which man fell includes, *inter alia*, 'the guilt of Adam's first sin,' and 'the corruption of his whole nature, commonly called original sin.' The former is a theological conception, but the latter falls within the scope of the natural law of heredity. The question thus arises, Could total depravity be the effect by way of heredity of one sin or of all the sins of the first man?

methods employed by Providence for the accomplishment of its benignant purposes. In proceeding now to deal with the topic in a more formal way, I remark that solidarity presents itself for consideration under two main forms —*family* solidarity, for which the alternative name is heredity, and *social* solidarity manifesting itself very specially, though not exclusively, in the dominion of custom. To these two forms has been added a third — *personal* solidarity, by which is meant an identity with our past selves which is due to habit, and revealing itself in the permanence of character. This type, though in its own place important, may here be disregarded.[1]

1. *Heredity.* — We are not here directly concerned with the disputes among scientists as to the physical causes of heredity, or as to the question whether acquired characteristics are transmissible from parent to child. At first sight, indeed, this might appear to be a very vital question for our purpose, as on the answer given to it it might seem to depend whether through a change for the better in the moral condition of one generation it would be possible to effect improvement in the following. But Weismann's theory, which makes heredity depend on germ-cells continuous in being, and to a great extent in quality, from generation to generation, and that supported by Herbert Spencer, which regards acquired characteristics as freely transmissible, though far apart in their initial formulation, approach each other in their ultimate adjustment. Weismann admits that germ-cells are not so fixed in their nature

[1] On this *vide* Marion, *De la Solidarité Morale.*

as to be inaccessible to influence from their environment. Ultimately the difference seems to reduce itself to a question of the directness or indirectness of the influence of environment through parentage on offspring.[1]

Our interest in heredity is not scientific but ethical. We wish to know, not the natural laws or conditions of its working, but to what effect it works within the moral sphere, whether for good as well as for evil, for good not less than for evil. Students of the subject on scientific principles have been able to trace the influence of heredity in all other spheres physiological and psychological: in bodily features, in instincts, in peculiarities of the senses, in memory, in artistic talents, in intellectual endowments, in morbid corporeal and moral tendencies. Does its action stop there, or does it pass over into the region of the good, and become a propagandist of virtue?

Now, in the first place, *a priori* presumptions are in favour of an affirmative answer to this question. The mere fact that the law obtains in all the spheres of human life above enumerated, renders it probable that it obtains also in the remaining sphere to which our question refers. Why should there be in the Bach family, through many generations, a well-ascertained hereditary tendency to eminence in musical talent, and no hereditary tendency anywhere discoverable to moral excellence? Why should vicious propensities to gambling, avarice, theft, homicide, be inheritable, while for opposite virtues each man must

[1] On this *vide* Bradford, *Heredity and Christian Problems*, chap. ii.

entirely rely upon himself? Look again at the matter from the point of view of evolution. Heredity and variation, acting together, brought the universe of being from the lowest form of life up to man. Why should the same forces, acting in the human sphere, not have a *tendency* at least to carry men onwards in a course of moral development? There may be good reason why the course of that development should not be so smooth and regular as we might desire, but there ought to be some indications that the drift and strain of things is in the direction of moral improvement.

Such being the *a priori* presumptions, how stands the fact? Are the traces we desiderate forthcoming? Now it must be acknowledged that even those who bring to the inquiry the utmost good-will to arrive at an affirmative conclusion have some difficulty in doing so. It is much easier to find striking examples of heredity in the line of evil than in the line of good. Why? That is a question to which it is not easy to give a completely satisfactory answer, but a partial solution may be found in a study of the connection between physiological and moral conditions, in Pauline language, between flesh and spirit. This is a subject which deserves more careful consideration than it has received from theologians in connection with the Christian doctrine of *sanctification*, and it has also very important bearings on the matter now in hand. How does it come to pass that a saintly father may have a profligate, worthless son? Shall we say that the saintliness is a make-believe, and that the father is a hypocrite? By no means. But the saint may once have been a great sinner himself, like Augustine, or his goodness may be a moral conquest in a fierce fight with innate evil proclivities which have never been allowed to break forth into actual transgression. In that case his holy habit is an acquired characteristic which does not pass over from sire to son. It may, like all other acquired characteristics, have a tendency to transmit itself, but it is not able to prevail against the stronger force of evil bias still inherent in the flesh. The law of the flesh wars against the law of the mind, and by its superior power determines the channel along which heredity runs. Of course it is always possible that bad proclivity in a son may not be an inheritance from his father, but from a remote ancestor, a case of reversional heredity, or *atavism*.

However numerous may be the instances in which heredity acts as a sinister influence, blasting fair hopes of a godly seed, there is no reason to doubt that in many cases it has also acted as a power predisposing to goodness. But it is still more important to remark that even when it is adverse to goodness heredity is not to be regarded as an irresistible force or an inescapable doom. Two positions here must be strenuously maintained: 'Original sin' by itself, apart from personal transgression, cannot carry eternal consequences, and evil bias in our nature is a foe to be fought with, not a fate to be succumbed to. The former of these two positions can speak for itself; on the latter a few explanatory remarks may be useful. I repeat, then, that a bad 'natural inheritance,' though a serious thing, does not necessarily settle beforehand a man's moral career. There are elements of good as well as of evil in many men who seem predestined to vice and crime; and the former may ultimately prevail, springing up like an artesian well from depths beneath unto everlasting life. There is a latent will-power in man which, duly roused, may fight successfully against heredity, preventing it from being a source of moral mischief in our own life, or through us in the lives of others. A man is not doomed to be a drunkard because he has alcoholism in his blood; he can abstain though he cannot safely touch. If he dreads the malign influence of the virus on offspring, he can remain a celibate. Dr. Bradford reports the case of a lady, beautiful and much sought after, who to a female friend gave this as her reason for shunning marriage: 'My grandfather was intemperate; my father died intemperate; I have a brother who is a drunkard; the love of liquor is in the blood, and I will never be a party to perpetuating this terrible tendency.'[1] There is nothing more to be deprecated in the interest of morality than a fatalistic resignation to heredity as a tyrant whose will it is futile to oppose. Much to be desired is the diffusion throughout society of the hopeful creed of Jesus that the last may become first, the greatest sinner the greatest saint, heredity, evil desire, and bad habit notwithstanding. How this comes about, whether by the reserve power for good latent in the human soul being brought into play, or by the almighty grace of God, as theologians would prefer to say, is a

[1] *Heredity and Christian Problems*, p. 110.

secondary question; the main point is that the thing is possible, and not so rare an occurrence as some may imagine. Cherish this humane creed, and let it inspire you to fight manfully against an evil natural inheritance and all the woes it may entail.

Environment, not less than the energy of resolute will, may be successfully brought to bear on heredity to counteract and even to modify its evil tendency. The power of environment for good and for evil is admittedly great. Take, for instance, the effect of climate. 'Certain virtues,' remarks Marion, 'are easy in certain regions, very difficult in others. . . . For example, temperance is almost a matter of course for the inhabitants of hot countries, next to impossible for Northern peoples; while, on the other hand, the energy of the latter stands in marked contrast to the languor of the former. Laziness is far from being a dominant vice on a poor soil, and under an ungenial sky.'[1] The statement, if strongly worded, has substantial truth. Now climate is not in our power. We must take our climate as it is, or leave our native land and go where temperance, health, and possibly other blessings can be had on easier terms. But in many cases environment, with due determination, can be altered so as to give the culture of virtue even for inheritors of evil bias a better chance. This is the direction in which effort is counselled by those who have made the moral amelioration of criminals, paupers, etc., the subject of careful, prolonged study. Mr. Dugdale, author of 'The Jukes' already referred to,

[1] *De la Solidarité Morale*, p. 81.

offers the following 'tentative generalisations on heredity and environment': —

1. Where the organisation is structurally modified, as in idiocy and insanity, or organically weak, as in many diseases, the heredity is the preponderating factor in determining the career; but it is, even then, capable of marked modification for better or worse by the character of the environment.

2. Where the conduct depends on the knowledge of moral obligation (excluding insanity and idiocy), the environment has more influence than the heredity, because the development of the moral attributes is mainly a post-natal, and not an ante-natal, formation of cerebral cells.

3. The tendency of heredity is to produce an environment which perpetuates that heredity: thus the licentious parent makes an example which greatly aids in fixing habits of debauchery in the child. The correction is change of environment.

4. Environment tends to produce habits which may become hereditary, especially so in pauperism and licentiousness, if it should be sufficiently constant to produce modification of cerebral tissue.[1]

These conclusions of an experienced investigator may be accepted as proof that environment is certainly one of the forces to be taken into account in all schemes of social amelioration. It is one of three forces on which the character of human life depends. These are heredity, environment, and personal effort. A distinguished scientist, who is a philanthropist as well, has likened

[1] 'The Jukes,' p. 65.

them to three Fates or Norns, and speaks of them as sisters, thoroughly intelligible only as a Trinity. 'There would,' remarks the author to whom I refer, ' there would be more progress and less invidious comparison of ameliorative schemes, if we realised more vividly that the Fates are three. Though it is not easy to appreciate the three sides of a prism at once, of what value is liberty on an ash-heap, or equality in a hell, or fraternity among an overpopulated community of weaklings? Organism, function, and environment must evolve together.'[1]

How far this joint evolution may be carried, and with what beneficent result, is a question to which no lover of man can be indifferent, but to which conflicting answers may be expected. Some forecasts are very optimistic. Herbert Spencer anticipates that the social evolution of the future will be chiefly in the direction of morality, increased power of self-regulation, acquisition of sentiments responding to the requirements of the social state before which the crimes, excesses, diseases, improvidences, dishonesties, and cruelties that now so greatly diminish the duration of life will disappear. He also expects pressure of population with its accompanying evils to disappear, leaving a state of things requiring from each individual no more than a normal and pleasurable activity.[2] This looks like a heaven on earth, sin abolished and misery at an end. Another writer, contemplating the subject from the view-point of the Christian faith, hopes for a time

[1] J. Arthur Thomson, *The Study of Animal Life*, p. 306.
[2] Vide *Principles of Biology*, vol. ii. chap. xiii.

when salvation shall mean not merely pardon, or the sanctification of the *soul*, but the sanctification also of the *flesh* down to its lowest roots, 'such a clarification of the fountains of being as will make us the parents of those whose tendencies shall be upward.'[1] This is a large demand. To say that it is utterly unreasonable and groundless might be to betray too much sympathy with the Greek or Manichæan idea of the flesh as something inherently and incurably evil. Mitigation of evil bias in man's corporeal nature must on general grounds be admitted to be possible, and higher or lower estimates of the extent to which it can be carried involve no question of principle. But when the writer in question hints that 'the transmissibility of the spiritual life which is in Jesus Christ'[2] is among the possibilities of the future, he allows his enthusiasm of humanity, perhaps inadvertently, to run into a wrong channel. Spiritual life, moral life in general, cannot be transmitted, as a mere natural inheritance, like a sound physical constitution. It must be each man's own achievement. All that can be transmitted is a set of corporeal and mental conditions predisposing to, facilitating, the culture of morality and Christian piety.

2. *Social* solidarity is a wide theme, with many aspects, and covering a great variety of phenomena in human history. Solidarity in this form exerts its power over the individual in many ways: through family life and early education, through laws and customs, through the spirit of an age, through religious rites and beliefs.

[1] Bradford, *Heredity and Christian Problems*, p. 221.
[2] *Ibid.*, p. 222.

Its power is so great, that on a broad view it might appear as if the individual could have no thought, mind, will, conscience, or faith of his own, but must be entirely the creature of his social environment; just what the corporate life of his time and country have made him. Men become amenable to the sway of this dominating influence through various psychological channels, very specially through the instinct of imitation. As naturally as our ear catches the accent of the province in which we are born, our mind catches the tone of thought and sentiment of the social circle to which we belong. Our spirit not less than our speech bewrayeth us. Social solidarity dominates the soul as heredity dominates the body. We are born into society, bearing the image of our parents, there to be born again out of the womb of corporate humanity, as it exists under certain conditions in a given time and place, with the features of our social parentage almost as well defined as those of our natural face. The two forms of solidarity play into each other's hands. This is especially the case where, as in India, the social divisions known as castes prevail. The origin of caste may be traced to various causes, such as conquest, or diversity of race or of religion, but its main root seems to be birth. Birth determines a man's caste, and nothing that can happen in after life can avail to change it. In India, birth has from of old been conceived as determining not only caste but character. In the Laws of Manu it is laid down that a woman, even when of a lower caste, always bears a son possessing the same qualities as his father; that a man of a low caste will always reveal himself by his occupations even when he tries to hide himself; and that a baseborn man resembles in character his father or his mother, or both, and cannot possibly conceal his real nature.[1]

The institution of caste, as it has prevailed from time immemorial in India, exhibits solidarity, in its two interrelated forms, as a curse rather than as a blessing; a malign power destroying brotherhood, arresting the progress of humanity, and defying rather than serving the ends of a beneficent providential order. It puts individual men in a social prison from which there is no escape till death, if even then. It withers up personality and reduces the social unit to a nullity. It predestines not only to lot but to character, proclaiming nobility of soul an impossibility for the base-born, and doing its best to fulfil its own malign prophecy. Nothing can be more utterly cruel and inhuman, nothing more thoroughly deserves to be overthrown, and every lover of his kind must wish well to efforts directed towards this end in the name of a religion whose mottoes are: God the common Father in heaven, and every man, be he Brahman or Pariah, prince or peasant, a potential son of God. It will, let us hope, eventually pass away, though it may take centuries, as other forms of overdone solidarity characteristic of barbaric stages of society have disappeared, *e.g.* corporate responsibility for offences committed by individual members of a family or tribe. That the many, connected by ties of blood, should perish for the sin of one, once seemed just and

[1] *The Laws of Manu* (*The Sacred Books of the East*), chap. x. §§ 6, 40, 59.

right, and the indiscriminate manner in which innocent and guilty are often involved in a common calamity, such as a visitation of plague or famine, might well appear, to those so minded, a Divine sanction of their ruthless way of thinking. As against this rude, primitive type of justice, what a great emancipating word was that of the Hebrew prophet, 'The soul that sinneth, *it* (not other souls) shall die.'[1]

Some emancipating word or act, some 'law breaker' or custom-changer, some counteracting power that can lift the crushing weight of a too dense solidarity off its victim is always needed that oppressed humanity may rise to its feet and move on. Social solidarity unqualified, like absolutely perfect heredity, tends to perpetual stagnation, and a complementary influence, analogous to that of variation in animal life, is necessary to prevent it from acting as a fatal obstructive to progress. The counterbalancing force need not assume a personal form, in the shape of the energetic will of an epoch-making man brought to bear on the situation. It may arise out of an inevitable change in the circumstances of society for which no individual man is responsible. Thus, *e.g.* has been explained the gradual disappearance of one of the most characteristic institutions of ancient civilisation, *slavery*, to our modern, Christian way of thinking as irreconcilable as caste with the true interests of humanity. We have been accustomed to trace the decline of this state of compulsory inferiority, so far as Europe is concerned, to the leavening influence of the humane teaching of

[1] Ezekiel xviii. 4.

Jesus. That this is true, as a partial explanation, no one disputes, but we are reminded that other less elevated causes co-operated to bring about the result. Slavery, it is pointed out, stands and falls with a warlike condition of society. 'While all the native males in each society were devoted to war, there was great need for the labour of prisoners to supplement that of women. The institution became, under such conditions, a necessity.' On the other hand, as wars decrease, captives become fewer and free labour is required, and when slave labour and free labour come into competition, slave labour, as less economical through lack of energy, interest, and intelligence, must steadily decrease.[1] So be it; even on this view we see the truth of the statement that the conservative principle of solidarity requires to be balanced by the progressive principle of variation in order to serve the ends of a beneficent Providence.

Care must be taken to put just the necessary amount of emphasis on this statement. It must on no account be taken as implying that solidarity is a thing of questionable value, and that all the virtue lies in the power that tends to break it up. The real truth is that both together are as necessary to the well-being of society as are the centripetal and centrifugal forces to the stability of the planetary system. Without social coherence, a community of men could not maintain its existence in this world of which struggle is so prominent a feature. It was a necessity of life in early times when tribal wars were incessant. 'Shoulder to shoulder'

[1] Herbert Spencer, *Principles of Sociology*, vol. iii. p. 470.

was the motto then for every people that meant to live and thrive. Everything that tended to cement union — law, custom, rite — was on that account valuable. Every people that gained for itself a place in the page of history possessed well-defined solidarity in these respects, for the simple reason that incoherent social aggregates had perished in the prehistoric stage. The solidly coherent races alone survived. And one can understand why the survivors should attach vital importance to the minutest symbol of the coherence to which they owed their persistence, were it only an apparently meaningless, absurd, or revolting religious ceremony. Woe to him who attempted to innovate!

And yet the time comes to every people when the alternatives are: change or political death, or stagnation which is death in another form. It has been said that the difficulty for a community is not that of 'getting a fixed law, but getting out of a fixed law.'[1] It may be so, but getting out of a fixed law becomes as necessary at a certain stage as it was at an earlier period to have the fixed law. Law-breakers are as much needed as lawgivers. Happy is the people which has among its political or religious institutions some provision for abrogating or modifying at the proper time existing law and custom. Nations that do not know how to adapt themselves somehow to an altered environment are doomed to slow decline. Religions that have finality for their watchword become fossilised. The Germanic races have had a great career because, from the time they first appeared on the stage

[1] Bagehot, *Physics and Politics*, p. 53.

of history, they had a provision in their political system for change and progress in the practice of submitting all great matters for free discussion to the assembled nation.[1] The Hebrew religion was saved from being strangled through priestly routine and Rabbinical tradition by the noble succession of prophets who always spoke the true word of God for the time, and kept men's minds in contact with reality. The crowning service was rendered by Christ, the great Law-breaker, who indeed came not to destroy but to fulfil, but who nevertheless destroyed by fulfilling.[2]

It lies in the nature of the case that where solidarity exists in a high degree progress must be slow. In all closely coherent communities there is apt to be an intense dislike and dread of change, tending to secure for existing customs age-long endurance; and, when the community is large, the momentum of the body to be moved renders it all the more difficult to set it and keep it in motion. Even in the industrial sphere of life peoples which have not emerged out of the lower stages of civilisation are extremely conservative, clinging to rude implements and methods of work from generation to generation, even when they know that better are in use elsewhere. In Western parts of the world this aversion to change in connection with industry has been completely overcome, with the result that greater progress has been made within the present century than

[1] Bagehot, *Physics and Politics*, p. 66. The whole chapter on *the use of conflict* is instructive.

[2] Matthew v. 17. *Vide* Hinton, *The Law-breaker*, for suggestive thoughts on Christ's function as an innovator in morality and religion.

that achieved within the whole previous history of mankind.[1] But in the higher spheres of life, above all in that of religion, the conservative spirit still rules with almost undiminished authority. In this region imagination and conscience come into play, giving to the fear of change fanatical intensity, and enforcing strict submission to established beliefs and rites by the awful sanctions of the eternal world. Nowhere, therefore, is advance in thought or conduct so difficult and so tardy. It is well when a single important step can be taken in a century; the replacement of a crude theological theory by a better may even require a millennium.

To men of original minds and reforming temper this snail's pace may well appear dismal and depressing. Yet it should help them in the exercise of patience to reflect that slow secular movement is the law of the universe. How infinitely leisurely the movement of life from *protozoa* up to man under the combined influence of the complementary laws of heredity and variation! What wonder if, under the continued action of these same laws, the advance of man from lower to higher degrees of civilisation be even at the best a matter of wearisome, insensible progression, varied only at rare and distant intervals by accelerated, catastrophic movement! Instead of complaining of the slowness, a wise man will rather be thankful that there is movement at all, in the part of the world in which his lot is cast, and that we are not all doomed to the deathlike immobility of Asiatic peoples. Another aid to patience is the consideration that the rate of movement must be slow when

[1] *Vide* Spencer, *Principles of Sociology*, vol. iii. p. 333.

what is aimed at is the advance of the *whole*. Rapid progress is conceivable when only the individual is concerned. There are occasional large variations in animal life; 'sports' they are called. 'Sports' are possible in the moral world. A man may arise now and then who passes at a bound from a lower to a greatly higher ideal of life, to loftier thoughts of God, and man, and duty, and destiny. If by prophetic utterance of his new conceptions he succeed in gaining currency for them, in even an imperfect measure, in the thought of any considerable portion of mankind, he has not lived in vain. But if the fact turn out to be that he alone has advanced far before his time and left all other men just where they were, what has been gained? In vain does a railway engine start off at lightning speed, and reach its destination in an incredibly short time, if it leave the train behind it. What boots it that the propeller rising out of the water revolves furiously if the ship make no headway? The supposed original man has simply seen a vision which no other man has seen, and at last left the world as dark as it was before. It were better not to see quite so clearly and to be able to communicate the little light one has to others. The distinction might be less but the charity would be more. The law of love dictates a slackened pace. Take the train along with you.

The world's best men have been content to move slowly, when by so doing they were able to carry their fellow-men along with them. They have respected the great law of solidarity and accommodated their pace to its requirements. The Hebrew legislator did not attempt to abolish blood feuds and private vengeance. He appointed cities of refuge, as a mitigation of the existing evil, which there was some chance of getting generally recognised. He did not question the husband's unlimited right of divorce; he simply prescribed that a bill of divorce be given in proof that the husband had voluntarily renounced all future claims upon the love and service of her whom he had put away. Far short of the ideal, doubtless, both these pieces of legislation, but they were at least improvements, and they had some chance of being *effective*. The whole community might in this way move on, one little step at a time, from primitive barbarism towards Christian humanity. And when the great Idealist came, He recognised the wisdom of Moses. He did not say that Moses did wrong in legislating for the hard heart. He simply claimed for Himself the right to set forth the perfect ideal, and He did so, not as an ordinary legislator, but as a religious teacher. And by setting forth the ideal, in that capacity, He rendered a supreme service to mankind, in full accord with the principle of solidarity. He did not turn the ideal into a statute law enforceable by penalties. He simply held it up in view of the world that it might work through inspiration and admiration, and gradually change the hard heart of the old barbarous time into the soft, tender, humane heart of a new, better era. He was content that the ideal should work as a leaven, taking plenty of time to the process of leavening the whole lump. It has not leavened the whole lump yet. There is plenty of the hard heart still. Christ's ideal is still an ideal hovering above reality. But it is well that it is there, above us but in view; much better than if we did not know what the best is. That ideal is the light of the moral world. And if ever Christ's ideal of life become the actual law of society, and the hard heart on the great scale make way for the soft one, though the process should take ten thousand years, it will be found to have been worth waiting for. In a Christianised humanity, coming after no matter how many future ages, the delay of Providence would find ample justification.

But what, meantime, are we to think of the moral condition of the individual hindered in his spiritual development, and kept in a state of minority, by a too masterful social environment that refuses to move as fast as single members of the social organism might desire? This doubtless is the dark side of the great providential law now under consideration. Yet even here consolatory reflections suggest themselves. First, as a matter of course, limitations of power imply corresponding limitations of responsibility. Between heredity and environment the individual will is closely hemmed in — resembling a little island surrounded by a great ocean. How can this tiny, apparently insignificant, force assert itself against the predestining almighty powers of natural inheritance and corporate social influence? Well, however the case may stand as to the possibility of asserting personal freedom, this general principle always holds good, Unto whomsoever little is given, of him shall little be required.

This axiom, however, goes but a short way towards allaying our solicitude. For we naturally ask, Why, should not more be given to every man? Why should it be true of any man that he has practically no power to hold his own against forces which tend to give a malign bias to his life-course, or at least to dwarf his moral growth? Now it is necessary here to be on our guard against exaggeration. It is possible to form too sombre an estimate of the enslaving influence of social solidarity. It does seem to threaten us with the extinction of our moral personality, but, in many more cases than we imagine, the threat probably remains unexecuted. The ocean in a storm seems bent on annihilating the little sea-girt isle it assails with its tremendous waves. But strange to say it does not succeed. The storm passes, and when the mist and the blinding spray have cleared away, the island is seen to be still in its place, unharmed by the war of the elements. So fares it often with personal moral life in the midst of an untoward environment. It may be, frequently it is, better than its surroundings. Brahmanical caste tends to foster inhuman pride, but the individual Brahman may be humble. Low caste tends to low life, but the individual Sudra may be noble. Slavery tends to debase, but one of the freest, purest, most lofty-minded men that ever lived, Epictetus, was a slave. Instances can easily be multiplied. Abraham, living in a neighbourhood where human sacrifice was practised, was tempted to slay his son; but he found out, how it matters not, that the will was better than the deed. A Hebrew husband might treat his wife as property, and put her away when he was tired of her. But a rude law, while giving him opportunity, did not compel him to be unjust or unkind, and doubtless those who used their legal rights to the full extent were the exceptions. Rabbinism was a thing of evil omen in the later religious life of Israel. But even during its malign sway the 'still in the land' might lead a life of simple faith in a gracious God, who desires not sacrifice but only a thankful lowly heart — witness the Psalter, regarded by Biblical scholars as a literary product of the 'night of legalism.'[1] Christian asceticism was a fatal misinterpretation of the teaching of Jesus, and it bore much evil fruit; yet how many a saintly, sweet-hearted soul has tenanted a monk's cell! In a word, barbaric laws and customs are doubtless a prison to the spirit, but a good life is possible even in a prison. John Bunyan wrote one of the heavenliest books ever penned, in a literal prison. In like manner elevated thoughts, humane affections, virtuous habits, have been cultivated by countless unknown men and women who have spent their lives in spiritual prisons built up by rude social moralities and ruder religions. Progress is not essential to the being, but only to the well-being, the robust health, of morality and religion.

There is one thing more to be said. Individual wills may contribute in some small degree towards changing evil custom, and so preparing for the coming of a better time. For this purpose it is not necessary to be men of great intellectual originality or commanding force of character, like the few outstanding historic personages who have been the decisive promoters of progress. The upward movement of the evolutionary process does not

[1] *Vide* on this my *Apologetics*, pp. 272-3, 279-80.

depend exclusively on the great variations called sports. Smaller variations may serve the purpose. Even so, in the social world a very moderate amount of moral individuality may originate a movement which, though itself insensible, may silently, slowly, yet surely, prepare for a great eventual crisis. There were reformers before the Reformation — poor men of Lyons and the like, who wrought no great immediate deliverance, yet without whose prelusive efforts even Luther's mighty energy might have been exerted in vain. It needs only that a few be a little in advance of their time, dissatisfied with things as they are, sighing for a springtide of new life, communicating their aspirations and propagating their discontent here and there, as social relations and duties give them opportunity. Such is the obscure, though not ignoble part assigned to the many: to keep themselves as far as may be unspotted from an evil world, and to pray that existing evil may one day be mended.

Two sets of phenomena alone seem to defy attempts at apologetic interpretation, those, viz., connected with the savage state, and those exhibited in a class to be found in all civilised societies, consisting of persons who come into the world with innate proclivities to crime. The savage and the criminal are the opprobrium of Providence and the despair of the optimistic Theist. The most charitable view to take of them is that they are the all but irresponsible victims of an evil heredity and an unkindly social environment. They have not had strength of intellect or will to hold their own against these forces, and have remained in the position of primitive man, or have lapsed to something even lower. How this should be possible under a benignant Providence it may not be easy to say. It may have been one of the risks involved in the evolutionary method of working, not to be eliminated with certainty except by supernatural interposition. There are various risks of miscarriage within the human sphere. One is that of never rising out of the rudimentary stage into the measure of intellectual and moral capacity which qualifies for civilisation. Another is that of lapsing from a high degree of intellectual and moral development to a much lower state : reversion to the barbarism of a ruder early time. Savage tribes and criminals exemplify the former; the inglorious career of peoples that have sunk into obscurity, after having played a distinguished part in history, may serve as an illustration of the latter. Both types of social miscarriage try, but neither ought to shake or destroy, faith in the providential order; not even that exhibited in the accounts of savage life, or in the revolting records of crime. These degenerate forms of humanity are, after all, the exception. They show by contrast how great is the advance in rationality and morality made by mankind as a whole, and strengthen rather than weaken our conviction that the great mass of our race is marching on under Divine guidance. And may this comforting assurance not justify hope even for such as are left behind? Those who have been baptized into the Christian spirit will not readily resign themselves to despair. They will work for the improvement of the savage races, not for their extermination, after the bad example of men called Christians, but in reality further away from the kingdom of heaven Jesus preached than the savages themselves. It may be that after all has been tried, these races will remain intractable, and that those who come after us may have to reconcile themselves to their ultimate effacement. But the efforts hitherto made towards the civilisation of these children of nature have not been sufficiently earnest and persistent to justify pessimistic conclusions.

The two forms of solidarity we have been considering, exemplify two antithetic types of dependence. In heredity we see the dependence of the many on the one, in social solidarity the dependence of the one on the many. Both may be conceived as attaining the widest possible universality. We may think of the whole human race as to a certain extent affected, for good or for evil, through heredity, by the first man; and we may, on the other hand, regard the whole human race as an environment exercising a real, if not always an appreciable, influence on the individual. Something resembling the former of these generalisations may be found in the Adam-Christ section of St. Paul's Epistle to the Romans, wherein the whole religious history of mankind is epitomised in the influence of two representative persons, the one viewed as the source of all the evil, the other of all the good, in the lot of our race.[1] It is not certain that the writer had heredity in view as the medium through which the first man wrought with sinister effect on the destinies of his descendants, but heredity readily suggests itself as a means of throwing

[1] Romans v. 12-21.

some light on a theorem otherwise obscure. That a brief, pregnant paragraph on a vast theme should have created difficulties for interpreters is not surprising; and it is matter of course that perplexities have been increased by the assumption that the apostle's rapid impassioned statement is to be viewed as in all respects a final, complete deliverance on the subject. It is really fitted to stimulate rather than to silence thought. It shows us what a fascination central problems of humanity had for the apostle's mind, and encourages similar intellectual adventures. It shows us further in what interest such speculations should be carried on — even the strengthening of hopeful views as to the fortunes of humanity under the dominion of Christ; for such was the dominant motive in the mind of St. Paul. Beyond this it does not bind us, but rather invites us to attempts at fresh solutions in our modern scientific surroundings, always in the same religious spirit.

The Church, in the Pauline idea of it, exemplifies the other form of dependence. It is a new humanity created by Christ, conceivably co-extensive with the world; a social organism resembling the human body, in which each member performs its function for the benefit of the whole, and the life of the whole permeates all parts. The Church in a normal condition would exhibit social solidarity as a beneficent power, influencing each individual for his good, but not restraining or repressing his individuality. Had the Church approximately realised the ideal, she would have conferred a signal benefit on the world. How far she has failed can be learned from the records of ecclesiastical history. That history for our purpose may be divided into two great periods, in one of which the members of the Church were regarded as in a state of nonage, spiritual minors for whose eternal interests it was the business of Mother Church to care; while in the other the rights of the individual at length obtained recognition, and it was acknowledged that private persons might have, and ought to have, a moral judgment of their own. Neither in the one period nor in the other has the desirable ideal been realised. Catholicism has given us a dead mechanical compulsory unity. Protestantism is to a large extent the history of private judgment run wild, and of sectarian division *ad infinitum*. The healthy balance between the moral sway of the corporate body and the free, fearless play of the individual mind and conscience is among the *pia desideria* we cherish for the future. The religious community which shall realise that ideal will give to the world for the first time a unity which does not mean uniformity, a corporate influence which does not mean tyranny, a prophetic freedom which does not run to waste in separatism. The problem of harmonising solidarity with individualism is a difficult one, and there is no cause for complaint though we have to wait long for the solution. But it has been to an appreciable extent solved already in some countries in the political sphere; and the hope that it may one day be equally well solved in the ecclesiastical sphere is not Utopian.

LECTURE XII

PROVIDENTIAL METHODS: PROGRESS BY SACRIFICE

PERFECTION by suffering is a great moral law of individual life. Progress by sacrifice is a not less outstanding law of social life; progress of the many by the sacrifice of the few. Sacrifice is the cost of progress, and the instrument of redemption; not otherwise is real advance attainable. Some devoted one must give his life a 'ransom' when signal benefit is to be procured for the many.

This law, for long hidden or misinterpreted, is now receiving in increasing measure intelligent and emphatic recognition. It gives one a pleasant surprise to find Renan among the modern prophets who proclaim this doctrine. 'The world,' he writes, 'is in travail for something: *omnis creatura ingemiscit et parturit.* The great agent of the march of the world is pain.' ... 'There are always voluntary victims ready to serve the end of the universe.' And they devote themselves, we are assured, not in vain. 'O joy supreme for the virtuous man. The world hangs on him. He is one in a hundred thousand, but it is he who is the ransom of Sodom.'[1] Carlyle in his over-emphatic manner endorses the fact of sacrifice, but with less clear recogni-

[1] Vide *Dialogues Philosophiques,* pp. 23, 36, 40.

tion of the gain reaped from it under the providential order. In his famous Essay on Robert Burns these reflections occur: 'Homer and Socrates and the Christian Apostles belong to old days; but the world's Martyrology was not completed with these. Roger Bacon and Galileo languish in priestly dungeons; Tasso pines in the cell of a madhouse; Camoens dies begging on the streets of Lisbon. So neglected, so "persecuted they the prophets," not in Judea only, but in all places where men have been.'[1] The somewhat comfortless moral is, How unkind the world to its best men! A more cheering construction is put on the facts in a recent contribution to the new science of social theology. 'Vicarious suffering,' remarks President Hyde, 'is not an arbitrary contrivance by which Christ bought a formal pardon for the world. It is a universal law, of which the cross of Christ is the eternal symbol. It is the price some one must pay for every step of progress and every conquest over evil the world shall ever gain.'[2] The interest of this statement lies in the fact that by a professed theologian who, as I understand, accepts the catholic Christian faith, the principle of vicarious suffering is lifted out of the region of pure theology, to which it has by many been supposed exclusively to belong, and translated into the sphere of ordinary providence, recognisable there as a permanent, universal law of the moral order.

And who are the victims of this law? They are ever the noblest and the best of men; the sons of

[1] *Miscellaneous Essays*, p. 234.
[2] *Outlines of Social Theology*, p. 228.

God indeed, who, Euripides being witness, are destined to be unhappy; the just who, mistaken for unjust, are liable, as Plato understood, to be scourged, racked, bound, to have their eyes put out, to suffer every kind of evil, even crucifixion.[1] They are men who in any sphere of truth — scientific, moral, religious — in the words of Christ, 'Let their light shine,' and who in any sphere of action shape their conduct in accordance with their convictions. They are men of heroic temper, who love truth with passion and will speak it come what may; who hunger after righteousness, and will do it at all hazards. They are the original men, the discoverers of new truths, the inaugurators of better ways of thinking and acting, the pioneers of beneficent movements, the reformers of evil customs, the enthusiasts of humanity, whose ambition it is to leave the world in some way better than they found it. For all such is appointed a hard experience, presenting temptations to hide their light and suppress their convictions to escape trouble and sorrow. Their undying glory is that they yield not to the temptation, and the price they pay for eternal honour is life-long liability to misunderstanding, misrepresentation, vexatious frustration, crowned possibly by violent death.

The sacrifice of the noblest, the greatest mystery of history till it is explained, can easily be utilised by pessimistic philosophy to put a black face on human destiny. That philosophy may plausibly discover in

[1] *Vide* the *Republic,* Jowett's translation (vol. iii. p. 232) of *Plato's Dialogues.*

the facts sinister ironical nature-powers befooling generous souls by drawing them, through the best that is in them, into careers which, whatever good they may bring to the world, can bring nothing but evil to themselves. Renan agrees with the pessimists so far as the dupery is concerned, but he thinks Schopenhauer and the rest are wrong in assuming towards it a spirit of revolt. He sees clearly with Schopenhauer that there is a great Egoist who deceives us, but he resigns himself with a good grace to the inevitable; he accepts and submits to the ends of the Supreme Being. Just in this submission he thinks lies the essence of morality, while immorality, on the other hand, is revolt against a state of things of which one sees the dupery. It is necessary at once to see it and to submit to it.[1] This seems almost devout, but it is Parisian piety. It is easy to reconcile oneself to the deceit of the Eternal Powers when it is practised on other men whose hard lot you comfortably study in your library; it is not quite so easy when you are yourself one of the victims. We would like to know how one of the 'dupes' viewed the matter. Our wish is gratified by the recorded experience of a Hebrew prophet. To Jeremiah also God appeared a Deceiver: he felt as if he had been led on by Divine inspirations, unawares, into a career from which he would have recoiled had he known beforehand all that was coming. He made his complaint: 'O Lord, Thou hast deceived me'; he threatened to throw up his prophetic vocation, saying to

[1] *Dialogues Philosophiques*, p. 43.

himself, 'I will speak no more in His name'; but at last he submitted because he could not help himself, the misery of silence proving to be greater than the sorrows of speech.[1] Here is a piety, not of the melodramatic order, but of the true heroic type, as bold in its temporary doubt as are the utterances of the most audacious modern sceptic, yet true-hearted and grand in its ultimate submission. No need to tone down the complaint of deception; let it stand there in its unmitigated bluntness. The Divine Spirit, author of all noble impulses, judges men by the habitual bent of their will, not by the verbal escapes of their dark doubting moments.

To the worldly-wise the perplexities of a Jeremiah are unintelligible. That a man may easily get into trouble by letting his light shine they understand, but what hinders him from covering the light in obedience to the dictates of prudence, and the instinct of self-preservation? Why cannot he keep silent, or speak insincerely, and say, *e.g.* that the sun goes round the earth as long as other people say it, and ecclesiastical authorities deem it necessary, in the interests of the faith, that it should be said? Truly an idle question! For, as Renan has said, 'to preach to man not to devote himself is like preaching to a bird not to make its nest and not to nourish its young.'[2] Who would think of suggesting to one about to become a mother by all means to avoid birth pangs? The power of life is irresistible, the pangs must be endured, and the mother must find

[1] Jeremiah xx. 7-9. [2] *Dialogues*, p. 32.

her consolation in the joy that a man is born into the world. Let us hope that for those who are constrained by the prevailing power of conscience to speak unwelcome truth, an analogous consolation will never be wanting! Life is sweet to all, but for a good cause, a substantial addition to the well-being of the world, peradventure some, nay many, would dare to die.

But it is not given to all who devote themselves to know why they suffer. It was not given to Jeremiah, or perhaps to any of the Hebrew prophets. To one and all of them the sufferings of the righteous were a mystery. The key was not found till Christ came, though certain prophetic oracles contain remarkable anticipations of the truth. Then a change came over the spirit of men in regard to the tribulations of the good. Clear intelligence and triumphant buoyancy took the place of perplexity and depression. The cross made all the difference. The earthly career of Jesus was epoch-making, not merely in respect of the saving grace it brought to men, but also through the bright light it shed on the true theory of the providential order of the world at the point where light was most urgently needed.

In absence of the true theory it serves the purpose of a sedative to see that suffering is the normal lot of wisdom in advance of the time, and of righteousness rising high above moral mediocrity. There is comfort in the reflection that no strange, accidental, unprecedented experience has befallen us, that we are not alone in our misfortune, but bear it in common with a large influential company. 'Rejoice, for so persecuted they the prophets which were before you.'[1] To rejoice is possible even when one knows not why either he or the prophets should be persecuted. But to know the causes brings great additional sustaining power. Such knowledge is attainable by due study of society and of the ways of men. The law of social solidarity, considered in last lecture, of itself explains much. The heroic man is a pioneer; he is discontented with things as they are, desires to innovate, to change belief, to make new laws, to bring in new customs. To all this, solidarity opposes itself, through its blind, obstinate aversion to change, and the passive force of long-established habitude. Many causes co-operate to lend momentum to opposition: familiarity, convenience, interest, reverence. Old paths are so well known that we can walk in them mechanically, blindfolded, without thought, without effort. Then familiar ways of thinking, believing, and acting, fit so well into our tastes, prejudices, likes and dislikes, we cannot bear to have them disturbed. And when secular interest comes in, how powerfully it reinforces these arguments against change! 'This our craft is in danger.'[2] Was there ever a reform attempted in this world which did not endanger some craft, and imperil some vested interest for which the individuals concerned cared infinitely more than for all the grand ideas conceived by original thinkers, and the humane plans cherished by generous hearts? What are these airy notions and benevolent dreams compared to pounds, shillings, and pence? Let

[1] Matthew v. 12.   [2] Acts xix. 27.

no prophet, reformer, or pioneer reckon on indulgent consideration, or even on fair treatment, from that quarter; on anything short of truculent, bitter, unscrupulous hostility.

Reverence also has to be reckoned with. Even within the secular sphere old customs become invested with a certain sacredness. But it is within the sphere of religion that the feeling of reverence attains its highest measure of intensity as the opponent of change. Nowhere is the power of custom so strong. 'Cowardice in regard to the supernatural'[1] insures for religious traditions the maximum of permanence. Everything pertaining to religion — worship, creed, practice — tends to become an affair of routine, ceremonial, formula, mechanical habit. Fetters are forged for soul and body, for every faculty of our nature — for hand, tongue, mind, heart, conscience; and by such as are in bondage it is regarded as a point of piety and sanctity to wear with scrupulous care all these grievous fetters. Woe to the man who attempts the *rôle* of emancipator! The saints will rise in holy wrath against him, and think they do God service when they put him out of the synagogue or out of the world. And the hypocrites, who wear religion as a mask for greed or vice, will join them, and outvie them in zeal for the good old ways of their fathers.

The best-known object-lessons illustrative of the malign power of conventional reverence are supplied by

---

[1] Theophrastus defines δεισιδαιμονία as δειλία πρὸς τὸ δαιμόνιον. *Vide* Theophrastus, *Characteres*, 17; also Andrew Lang's *Myth, Ritual, and Religion*, vol. i. p. 260.

the fate of Socrates and the tragic story of Christ. When we consider the religious environment of our Lord, we are not surprised at the deadly animosities by which He was assailed, but we do wonder that the martyrdom of Socrates could have been possible in such a city as Athens. In a community rich in artists, poets, philosophers, statesmen, and all without exception lovers of political freedom, can they have been in earnest in this bad business; was it not all a fatal, unaccountable mistake? Was there not in the city enough of free thought, and sufficient appreciation of the advantage of having among them an earnest, original, stimulating ethical teacher, to enable them to estimate at its proper value the charge brought against Socrates that he did not believe in the gods of the State, and had other new divinities of his own? Apparently not. Superstitious veneration for the traditional religion seems to have prevailed even in freethinking, light-hearted Athens, not merely among the craftsmen, which one could understand, but among the poets and the rhetoricians who might have been expected to rise above popular prejudice. So difficult is it for even the cultured to escape from the spell of an ancient faith, even when among the articles of the creed are tales of the gods which one would now be ashamed even to repeat.

In passing from Greece to Palestine, we enter a wholly different world. A greater than Socrates is here, and also a vastly more superstitious community. Therefore we are not surprised at the cross; for what can happen to the purest and wisest but to be flung ignominiously out of the world by a people whose religion, as the corruption of the best, is the worst, and whose piety is too often a cloak for egoistic ambitions and mean jealousies? According to the Gospel narratives, Jesus knew from the beginning of His public career what was to befall Him, so far at least as the general fact was concerned. It is perfectly credible. He had studied, doubtless, the religion of the time before He left His retirement in Nazareth; the felicitous descriptions of Pharisaic ways contained in the records of His teaching are evidence of this fact. He learnt from that study how wide was the gulf between His thoughts and the thoughts of the Rabbis on all things divine, and also how very sure they were that their thoughts were the only orthodox and legitimate ones. It needed nothing more than ordinary sagacity to foresee what would happen when the new Prophet of Nazareth went forth to utter His convictions with unflinching courage, absolute sincerity, and at the same time with a grace and power that won for Him speedily the ear and the favour of the multitude. Suspicion, ill-will, and by and by murderous intentions on the part of the dominant faction were matters of course. The crucifixion of Jesus is perfectly intelligible in the light of natural causes at work in contemporary Jewish society. It is the case of a great religious Initiator sacrificed on the altar of social solidarity.

Nowhere in the world, perhaps, was the sacrifice of one playing the part of Jesus more inevitable than in Palestine, and that partly for a reason that was creditable to the Jews. As a people they were very much in earnest about morality and religion, and the moral and religious system that had been handed down to them by their fathers well deserved their high esteem. It was so good, it was difficult for them to comprehend how there could be anything better. Their one fatal lack was insight into the truth that however good a system may be it cannot be final; that the ideal of the past cannot remain the ideal for all time. Such insight is always rare, even among the wise, who, in consequence, are often the most formidable opponents of the few who see the defects of the existing state of things and desire to remedy them. 'The worst enemy of the better is the good.'[1] So it was in Athens, so in Judea; so it will be while the world lasts. The heaviest burden on the heart of those whom Providence calls to be the promoters of progress is the hard judgment and relentless opposition of men whom they cannot despise as indifferentists, hypocrites, or time-servers, but must honour as saints, albeit in bonds.

Sacrifice then, for the reasons indicated, is inevitable, in connection with all endeavours to promote social advancement, especially in that which relates to the higher interests of humanity. It is something to be aware of this fact, and to understand with some measure of clearness the grounds on which it rests. But mere inevitableness, even inevitableness explained, cannot be the last word. We cannot rest till we have got an answer to the question *cui bono*, What good comes out of the evil? The only answer that can give com-

[1] Hyde, *Outlines of Social Theology*, p. 43.

plete satisfaction is that the cause for which sacrifice is endured is advanced thereby. If, as has been stated, sacrifice be the cost of progress, the only thing that will reconcile us to the cost is the assurance that the price is not thrown away, that progress is the actual result. If on observation that turn out to be the case, we shall be reconciled to the method of sacrifice as an integral part of the providential order. If, further, it should be found possible not only to establish by induction a sequence between sacrifice and progress, but to discover forces brought into play by sacrifice which have a direct tendency to produce progress, we should have satisfaction to our intellects as well as to our hearts. The law of sacrifice would then be brought within the range of scientific theory.

This may appear an ambitious programme not likely to be soon worked out, and it may be needful, meanwhile, to fall back on considerations of a different order, which, though coming short of an ultimate solution, are fitted to yield a real support to faith. Such are those familiar to theologians drawn from a teleological view of the world. Two short sentences from the Hebrew Scriptures set before us the principle involved. 'I will not destroy it for ten's sake';[1] 'I will defend this city to save it — for Mine own sake, and for My servant David's sake.'[2] God will not destroy Sodom if so small a number as ten good men be found in it; He will rescue Jerusalem from its assailing foes, out of regard to the memory of Israel's hero-king. Salvation comes to the unworthy many for the sake of the worthy few.

[1] Genesis xviii. 32.   [2] Isaiah xxxvii. 35.

This may not be a final solution, but it is not a meaningless proposition. The idea it contains is of the same order as that which represents the creation of the lower world as taking place for the sake of man. Man, the crown of creation, the key to its meaning and to the nature of the Creator — such was the doctrine enunciated at the commencement of this course as the basis of our whole inquiry.[1] Man, endowed with rational and moral powers, redeeming the lower parts of creation from insignificance and making it worth while for God to have to do with it. This is the providential view of the creative process. It does not supersede the physical or mechanical view, but is simply a different way of contemplating the same thing. The universe is evolved according to ascertained or ascertainable natural laws. But all the time there is an ultimate Cause at work within the evolutionary process, who has an aim in view, and who directs the process so that that aim shall be realised. The aim is man, and all that goes before has its reason of existence in him, and its value through him. It is only an extension of this line of thought to say that the good among men redeem the race to which they belong, and give value in God's sight to the intrinsically valueless.

The view now under consideration receives further elucidation when it is looked at in connection with the law of solidarity. On reflection it is seen to offer compensation for the injury that law, on its dark side, inflicts. It is, as we have seen, through solidarity that the phenomena of sacrifice come into existence. The

[1] *Vide* Lecture III.

social mass stagnates, clings tenaciously to old ways however barbarous or bad, obstinately resists movement; whence comes suffering in some form to the man who urges it to move. He suffers because he belongs to a social organism, or closely knit brotherhood, in which the pulse of a common life beats. He cannot escape from the vital influence of the corporate body. It will either assert its power over his soul, controlling his thoughts and affections, or, if his spirit be free, it will act vindictively in the sphere of his outward lot. He must either be a comrade in full sympathy with his people, sharing their prejudices, errors, and vices, or he must be a victim suffering for their ignorance and sin. All this was plain to the prophetic vision of him who wrote that marvellous description of the 'Man of sorrows' in the book of Isaiah, which is not merely a prediction of what was to befall one unique Victim, but the proclamation of a great general law of the moral order, under the form of an individual experience.

That is one side of the picture. It is very dark, and needs another, brighter side to make the darkness tolerable. What can the bright side be but solidarity in another form? If there be a solidarity of the one with the many, which means for him sorrow, there ought to be, by way of compensation, a solidarity of the many with the one, which means for them blessing. That too the Hebrew seer comprehended when he said, 'By his knowledge shall my righteous servant justify many, for he shall bear their iniquities.' It may seem a profanity to quote these sacred words as applicable to more than one solitary experience. With reference to this, Horace Bushnell remarks, 'It belongs to the staple matter of our theologic teaching on this subject that, while we are to follow Christ, and copy Him, and aspire to be like Him, we are never to presume, and cannot without great irreverence imagine, that we are to have part with Him in His vicarious sacrifice. We cannot atone, it is said, or offer any satisfaction, for the sin of the world; we are too little, low, and deep in sin ourselves, and nothing but a being infinitely great and perfect, by an optional suffering that exceeds all terms of obligation on Himself can avail to smooth God's indignations, and so far even our debt, as to make forgiveness possible.'[1] While regarding this as a serious mistake, Bushnell readily admits that effects follow the vicarious sacrifice of Christ which cannot follow such sacrifice in any other case. All he contends for is that the principle of vicarious sacrifice is universal, and that wherever such sacrifice is endured, it counts in the moral order of the world as a price paid for *some* benefit. Unless this be accepted as true, I do not see how we are to do justice to such Scripture texts as those above quoted in reference to the saving of Sodom and Jerusalem, or how suffering for righteousness, as a broad fact of human history, is to be other than a dark, inexplicable mystery. It may, indeed, be thought that the explanation offered is little less mysterious than the thing to be explained. Blessing coming to the many through the merit or the sorrow of the few or the one — how can this be, how does it work itself out in the natural

[1] *The Vicarious Sacrifice*, pp. 66, 67, 68.

order? There are two questions here, not one only, and we may be able to answer the first in part, though baffled by the second. The author of Genesis was able to understand the providential position of man, as made in God's image, lord of creation, and the object of peculiar Divine complacency, though he did not know, as we know now, how he was connected with the lower orders of creation, having physiological affinity with, and summing up in himself, all inferior forms of animal life, each step in the onward process of creation contributing its quota to the making of him. Similar may be our situation in reference to the problem at present under consideration. In absence of insight into the relation in which it stands to the physical order, we may go a certain length in understanding its relation to the moral order. It is intelligible, for example, how when man first arrived on the scene, in a very rudimentary condition as regards the development of his mental and moral powers, as modern scientists believe, God might contemplate primitive humanity with complacency in the light of the ideal. It is equally intelligible that the Divine eye may view with favour the many samples of the human race who in themselves have little to win regard, for the sake of the few who approximately realise the human ideal. The few worthy thus represent for the mind of the Eternal the many unworthy: elect men and races the non-elect, wise men the foolish, saints sinners, martyrs for truth and righteousness the prejudiced ignorant mob who put them to death not knowing what they do.

What all this means in the order of natural causality,

neither theology nor science has as yet taken much pains to ascertain. But it may be taken for granted that if in the providential order the higher and better represent the lower and worse, there must be some tendency in the nature of things to cause streams of benefit to flow from the one class to the other. Some of the channels can even be indicated. I shall specify three, so offering a humble contribution to what may be called the scientific theory of the law of progress by sacrifice.

One of those channels, then, is that when grievous wrong has been done to the promoters of a new movement, a *reaction* can be counted on, with the result that many of those who with irrational violence resisted the movement repent of their deed. 'They shall look on me whom they have pierced, and they shall mourn.'[1] Passionate moods are unstable, and are apt to pass, sometimes suddenly, into the opposite extreme. Hatred turns into love, frantic hostility into generous, devoted discipleship; the quondam persecutor may even become a preacher of the faith which he once destroyed. The instance which suggests itself as an illustration here is that of the apostle Paul. His case shows what a gain it may be to the highest interests of humanity to win, at however great a cost, *a single man*. It may be said that St. Paul was the one man in the apostolic age who thoroughly understood the genius of Christianity as a universal religion, and that it was due to his almost unaided efforts that his grand conception of the new religion found practical embodiment in the creation of

[1] Zechariah xii. 10.

a Gentile Church. To gain him was to conquer the world.

St. Paul's subsequent history reminds us of a second channel through which what makes for progress attains an ever-widening diffusion; that, viz., of *controversy*. He represented a type of Christianity that was not in favour with the mass of Jewish Christians. In his religious experience extremes met. The fanatical zealot for the law went at a bound to the opposite pole of thought, and maintained the worthlessness of the law for salvation and the insignificance of Jewish rites. Few had any sympathy with his position, hardly one held it with enthusiasm. Hence arose an internal conflict between those who wished to reduce the novel element in Christianity to a minimum, and the one man whose watchwords were: Christ the great Innovator; Christ's religion itself new, and that which makes all things new. By a kind of poetic justice the persecutor became in turn the persecuted, not only at the hands of unbelieving Jews, but likewise at the hands of fellow-Christians in whom the old Jewish element was stronger than the new Christian element. This was one of the disasters of the Early Church, but, like many other tragic phases of human life, it was fraught with good as well as with evil. Religious controversy is certainly a source of many evils. It breeds much bitter, unholy feeling, creates temporary alienations, sometimes even permanent cleavage. There is not always compensation in the form of clearer light, firmer faith, richer spiritual life. The combatants sometimes retire from strife hardened into barren dogmatism, and driven by each other into polemical extremes, each thinking that the one safe course is to deny what the other affirms, and both alike becoming impoverished by the process. But controversy may be magnanimously conducted, and when it is, it conduces to better understanding and ultimate acceptance of great fruitful principles. Antagonism of thought promotes development passing from initial conflict through conciliatory efforts to final union of opposites. This process has been often repeated in the history of the world, and it is one of the ways whereby progress conditioned by pain is promoted, and the epoch-making man, emphatic in thought and resolute in action, communicates blessing to the many. He comes in the spirit of peace to create a war of misunderstanding issuing in the concord of a common faith.

The war of words expressive of conflicting opinions is not the only form of strife known to mankind. The pages of history are filled with tales of battles fought with more substantial weapons, inflicting physical wounds and death upon the combatants. It is a grave question, What view is to be taken of war in this literal sense, in relation to the providential order? The answer of some would be that war is an unmitigated evil, while others incline to an optimistic view which sees in war, however repulsive to modern feeling, a source of manifold good not otherwise attainable. With reference even to the rudest conflicts, those of barbarous peoples, exemplifying in the human sphere the struggle for existence issuing in the survival of the strongest, the optimist would defend his cheerful thesis. He would say, War makes nations, and in war the best nations conquer the worst, and so humanity is the gainer.[1] With reference to wars of conquest, like those of Rome, he would point to the benefit of good settled government brought to the conquered, and aimed at by a benignant Providence, whatever might be the motives of the conqueror. There are indeed some wars on which even the most optimistic interpreter of history would find it difficult to put a plausible construction, such as those of last century to maintain the balance of power, whereof Carlyle speaks in contemptuous terms, as not rising above the dignity of tavern brawls. For one who is not concerned to defend a drastic theory, and in whose view the moral interest is supreme, the only wars capable of inspiring enthusiasm are those waged in resistance to tyranny, in defence of liberty, in the cause of oppressed humanity, or at the bidding of conscience zealous for a faith dear to the heart. Even in connection with these it may be held that war is a barbarism, and that the only course compatible with the spirit of humanity, not to speak of the spirit of Christ, is patient endurance of wrong. That way certainly conducts to the highest, purest, most abiding kind of influence. It is he who is brought as a lamb to the slaughter that divides the spoil with the strong. The way of meek submission is the only one open to the promoter of a holy cause when he stands alone, one man against the world. It is in vain that he lays hold of a weapon of defence. But when one has grown into many, and the adherents of a movement bear no inconsiderable proportion to their foes,

[1] So Bagehot in *Physics and Politics*, pp. 77, 81.

the policy of resistance, if not the noblest conceivable, is the one which most readily suggests itself to brave, fearless, conscientious men. 'Why,' they ask themselves, 'should we submit to be crushed when, by a spirited effort, we can save not only ourselves and our families, but the cause which is dearer to us than life? Did not Christ, if He did not sanction this warlike mood, at least recognise its inevitableness, when He said, "I came not to send peace, but a sword"?'[1] Of wars waged in defence of sacred interests — for truth, freedom, justice — it can always be said that they have a noble end in view, and that they afford ample scope for the heroic element in human nature, the display of which, while the world lasts, will send a thrill of pleasure through every generous heart. What a poor thing the history of mankind would be without the heroisms and magnanimities, and the splendid acts of self-devotion called forth by such conflicts! Nor does the benefit end there. It is much that the temper of men is for the time raised above pleasure-seeking, money-making, and the dull monotonies of ordinary life to the heroic pitch. But besides doing this, these 'holy wars' secure permanent benefits for the world — toleration and even sympathetic recognition for new secular and sacred ideals, civil and religious liberty, abolition of barbarous social institutions like slavery, protection of life and property from the bloody cruelty and shameless rapacity of tyrants. Opportunist politicians may dislike and dread these wars and the enthusiasms they evoke, but to the great heart of a free people they are ever wel-

[1] Matthew x. 34.

come, and that they are is one of the grounds of hope for the steady onward progress of humanity. Wars of this highest type are entitled to be recognised, along with controversy and the reaction caused by the consciousness of wrong inflicted on the innocent, as a *third* channel through which benefit is conveyed from a central fountain of good influence to ever-widening circles. Happy they who have the privilege of taking part in them! They are happy even if they survive not the strife. Better die fighting for liberty than live the life of a slave. They are happy even if they know not fully what they do, what service they are rendering. They have a good conscience, they enjoy the light-heartedness of those who surrender themselves to the guidance of noble impulses. They are happier still if they understand what is going on, that they are sacrificing themselves not in vain, that their lives are the price whereby solid benefits are purchased for those who come after them.

We now see with some measure of clearness how the sacrifice of the noblest may be one of the methods employed by Providence for the working of its beneficent ends, and by what laws the beneficent purpose is fulfilled. It would crown the apology of Providence if we could conceive God, not merely as an onlooker, but as a participant in the vicarious suffering by which the world is redeemed and regenerated. This we may do under the doctrine of immanence. If God's relation to human experience be one of immanence, then He is more than a spectator of the self-sacrifice by which progress is promoted: He is in it, a fellow-sufferer. Still more clearly is this true if in Christ God be incarnate. That conception may labour under metaphysical difficulties, but on the ethical side it is worthy of all acceptation. It makes God a moral hero, a burden-bearer for His own children, a sharer in the sorrow and pain that come on the good through the moral evil that is in the world. The noble army of martyrs have the comfort of knowing that the Eternal Spirit is at their head. Christ is the visible human embodiment of His leadership — the Captain of the army of salvation — exposed not less than every individual soldier to wounds and death; not indeed the only sufferer in the warfare, but the chief sufferer. Who would not be content to fight and die under His flag?

Sacrifice, as it appears in the moral order of the world, the price of progress, presents, when duly considered, no stumbling-block to reason. It has an intelligible cause, it may be endured voluntarily and cheerfully, and it is fertile in beneficent results. How differently we feel towards human sacrifice as practised, for example, by Pagan Semitic peoples! The one is the moral antipodes of the other. The sacrifice demanded by the moral order awakens in us admiration; the sacrifice offered by rude peoples to equally rude deities, to appease their wrath, excites loathing and horror. A Father in heaven can be conceived as taking pleasure in the former, only a Moloch can find satisfaction in the latter. Yet there is a superficial resemblance between the two types of sacrifice which might easily engender misconception, and cause the higher type to be interpreted in terms of the lower, or to be taken as an excuse for the lower. It is not likely, indeed, that peoples who offer human victims to their gods are much influenced by observation of what takes place under the moral order. They are too rude to notice that the best men are often the victims of the worst. Those whom we might account the best — the men who try to change evil custom — if such were to appear in a rude primitive society, their fellow-countrymen would account the worst, and their sufferings they would regard as a just punishment for their offences, expiation for their own misdeeds, not for those of other men. Interpretation of the higher in the light of the lower, on the other hand, is by no means an imaginary evil. Opposite extremes in reality, they may meet in our thought, and become confused in character. We have already seen that the relation of the moral order to sacrifice has been conceived by some as that of a Deceiver leading generous souls through their noble instincts along a path which ends in disaster. It may now be added that it is possible to conceive of Providence as a Moloch demanding victims to appease his wrath — death, mere blood-shedding, His delight. This is the error of ancient theology as the other is the error of modern free thought. Both alike are false and pernicious. God is neither a Deceiver who makes dupes of good men, nor a Moloch who gluts their life-blood. He is a just, benign Father who seeks the good of mankind and uses sacrifice as one of His methods for promoting it, because it is efficient for the purpose. That the method involves pain and sorrow for those who are sacrificed is not in His eyes a fatal objection, because through sacrifice is given a golden opportunity to self-devoting love which transfigures pain, lends dignity to the most ignominious fate, and decks the rudest cross with flowers. Finally, the method is not an artificial invention — it is immanent in the natural order. While the world lasts the law of social solidarity will involve in trouble promoters of progress. All that Providence does is to turn the inevitable fact to benign uses.

The three methods of providential action we have been considering in this and the two preceding lectures are closely connected: they are indeed parts or aspects of one composite scheme. Solidarity is the fundamental fact, and might have been considered first. But our point of view was progress, and our aim, to see how the providential order works out good in ever advancing measure for mankind. Therefore we began with the propelling force, special endowment fitting for special service, and imposing the task of initiating new departures. Solidarity then fell to be considered as the law which insures that the result of such initiative, originating in the achievements of elect pioneers, shall be progress for the whole and not merely for the initiator. Solidarity demands election as its complement, and imposes sacrifice on the elect. It requires special endowment to rescue it from perpetual stagnation, and it treats cruelly the specially endowed, because it is unwilling to move.

These three laws in the human sphere answer to a kindred group in the lower sphere of animal life: heredity, variation, extinction of the unfit. Heredity is a form of solidarity; variation an election to an apparently capricious physiological distinction which qualifies for a distinguished career in connection with the ascent of life; the extinction of living creatures ill adapted to their environment is the sacrifice nature demands as the cost of the ascent. But in the two spheres there is a notable difference between the victims. In the lower sphere it is the least fit, intrinsically and in relation to environment, that perish; in the higher sphere it is the most fit, in reference to the ideal if not to the actual environment, that perish. The difference is due to the nature of the environment, which in the lower sphere is simply physical, while in the higher it is moral. In the lower sphere the environment works mechanically against the non-varying; in the higher sphere it works with conscious intention against the varying. But in both spheres the providential purpose is served. In the one, progress is promoted by the survival of the fittest, in the other by the perishing or tribulation of the fittest. In the latter case the fit may perish as individuals, but their influence remains. Their life embodies an 'eternal spirit' of self-sacrifice which does not die, but propagates itself in others; appealing to the heroic in human nature, and so securing an unfailing succession of men ready to lay their lives on the altar. So the grain of wheat dying bringeth forth much fruit of its kind. The moral world thrives through self-sacrifice. It cannot prosper without it. If heroism were to die out, the moral universe would go to ruin. Therefore, welcome anything that helps to foster heroism; even wars, even wars of the Crimean type in which valuable lives are thrown away in a cause not worth the cost. At the least they make it possible for men who have been going to waste to recover their self-respect and to say: —

'We have proved we have hearts in a cause, we are noble still.

. . . .

I have felt with my native land, I am one with my kind,
I embrace the purpose of God, and the doom assigned.'

And because this is true it is not likely that the time will ever come in this world when wars shall finally cease unto the ends of the earth. God's kingdom will surely come more and more. Moral progress, slow but sure, will be made; but it will be progress through conflict and sacrifice. This prospect will not satisfy extreme optimists. It may seem to contradict prophetic forecasts of the future which predict the advent of a happy time when, wearied of warfare, men shall beat their swords into ploughshares and their spears into pruning-hooks. It may even seem to imply denial of progress. For what, it may be asked, is progress, if not the fulfilment of the prophetic song of the angels through the wide prevalence of peace and good-will, putting an end to disputes, or bringing in more rational and humane ways of settling them? Progress, I reply, is advance of the whole towards realisation of the ideals cherished by the wisest, and that means general increase in knowledge, spiritual insight, regard for the good of others, with corresponding diminution of ignorance, superstition, and selfishness. But the advance need not be, is not likely to be, *at an equal pace*. There will ever be those who are eager to move forward, and those who incline to lag behind; a few whose motto is 'Onward,' a large multitude whose counter-watchword is 'Rest and be thankful.' Hence friction, strain, strife, war of words or of swords. To the world's end, when at any time the Christ-spirit finds new embodiment in the person of moral pioneers, those whose day-dream is of peace will be rudely reminded by events of the Master's word: 'I came not to send peace on earth but a sword.' This may not be the providential order some looked for, but it is the actual order. And with all drawbacks it is a good order. It does not give us a world in which all men are equally wise, true, generously devoted to noble ends. But it does give us a world in which there are always some for whom the true, the good, and the fair are the *summum bonum*, and who do their utmost to gain currency for their ideas and aims, with well-grounded faith that their labor is not in vain.

INDEX

A

Æschylus —
  conception of Zeus in *Prometheus*, 151.
  a preacher of righteousness, 212.
Africa —
  sub-historic condition, 198.
  future of, 201.
Agnosticism, ethical, prevalence of, 101.
Animal ethics, crudity of, 37.
Animism, philosophy of primitive man, 212.
Arabians, historic dawn of, 191, 192.
Arnold, Matthew —
  belief in moral order, 157.
  law of retribution in history, 167.
  rationale of election, 259.
Asceticism —
  Schopenhauer makes it our highest duty, 78.
  assumption underlying, 134.
  Schopenhauer's view of, 135.
Automaton, conscious —
  the theory, 51.
  Romanes on, 51.

B

Bagehot, W. —
  on origin of race, 258.
  use of national isolation, 266.
  difficulty of getting out of a fixed law, 298.
  on Germanic races, 298, 299.
Barratt, Alfred, on the teleological argument, 12.
Baxter, Richard, faith and doubt, 3.
Bradford, Amory H. —
  on the future life, 250.
Bradford, Amory H. —
  on theories of heredity, 285.
  on beneficent effects of heredity, 293.
Bradley, F. H., Deity non-moral, 87 (*note*).
Browning, R., purpose in evolution, 60.
Bunsen, on ancient Egyptians, 200.
Bushnell, Horace, on vicarious sacrifice, 325.
Butler, Bishop —
  moral government of God,
  moral order in society, 163.
  doubts as to certainty of moral order, 178.

C

Calderwood, Professor, origin of language, 32.
Carlyle, Thomas —
  hero-worship, 140.
  belief in moral order, 157.
  doctrine that 'might is right,' 168, 169.
  apparent exceptions to rule, 170.
  on Arabians, 192.
  on the world's martyrs, 312.
Carthage, its corruption its destruction, 199.
Caste —
  institution of, 295.
  evil of, 295.
Celsus —
  on the worth of man, 128.
  his theology epicurean, 131.
Chalmers, Dr. Thomas, beneficence everywhere, 113.

Chance, not incompatible with Providence, 65.
Chapman, C., on preorganic evolution, 46.
Church, the —
  its vocation, 277.
  may fail, 278.
  how it has failed, 309.
Cobbe, Miss, on prayer, 246.
Concepts, man's faculty for forming, 30.
Conduct —
  ruin of nations through lack of, 167.
  and culture, proportion between, 210.
Conscience —
  evolution of, 36.
  prejudice against theory of evolution, owing to frequent agnosticism of advocates, 40.
  testimony of, to moral order, 158, 159.
  theory of evolution, 160.
  Martineau's criticism of theory, 161.
  dogmatism as to theory unnecessary, 161.
Crusades, an *aurora borealis*, 227.
Cudworth —
  unconscious Deity familiar to Greek philosophers, 93.
  his theory compared with Hartmann's, 93.
Culture and conduct, proportion between, 210.

D

Death —
  belongs to normal order of life, 110.
  not an unmixed evil, 110.
Decalogue —
  necessary to every nation, 164.
  importance of observance by a nation of its decalogue, 174.
Deism —
  result of emphasising occasional preternatural action of God, 55.
Deism —
  underlying principle of, may survive, 55.
  result of this idea, 55.
Denny, William, on success, 237, 238.
Drummond, Henry —
  evolution of animal nature of man, 28.
  origin of love, 38.
Dugdale —
  on the "Jukes" family, 282.
  on heredity and environment, 291.

E

Ecclesiastes, book of, its moral teaching, 240.
Egypt, its history perplexing, 199.
Election —
  does not exempt from retribution, 169.
  rationale of, 259.
  essence of, 261.
  more than one elect people, 260.
  elect peoples small, 263.
  why elect peoples perish, 268.
Euripides —
  suffering of righteous, 116.
  Rhesus of, quoted, 211.
  preacher of righteousness, 212.
  on the sons of the gods, 270.
  on the Greek games, 271.
Evolution —
  man's relation to, 22, 23.
  view of Russel Wallace, 23.
  applies to animal nature of man: sources of proof, 27, 28.
  of intellect, 29.
  of conscience, 36.
  result of, general application of, 41.
  Romanes on result, 41.
  divine activity at outset, 46.
  C. Chapman on, 46.
  divine activity at origin of life, 47.
  divine activity at origin of *conscious* life, 49.
  the true idea, incessant activity of immanent Deity, 52.

Evolution—
> this view consistent with transcendence, 54.
> purpose guiding, 64.
> continuity of purpose in, 69.
> difference between physical and moral, 122.
> slowness of process, 123.
> this slowness an aid to faith, 124.
> in human sphere, 184.

F

Fiske, John—
> on teleological argument, 12.
> relation of man to lower animals, 22, 23.
> origin of family affection, 38.
> inference as to nature of God from process of creation, 66, 67.
> believes in progress, 119.
> but denies living beneficent providence, 120.
> immortality of soul, 138.

Flint, Dr.—
> on spread of pessimism, 81.
> on primitive man, 148.

Force, Schopenhauer conceives force = will ultimate principle in universe, 75.

Fraser, Professor—
> purpose in evolution, 64.
> a world wholly gone to badness, 168.

Freeman, E. A., reasons for brevity of Greece's career, 172, 271.

G

Gathas, the, oldest part of Zendavesta, 189.

Germans, historic dawn of, 196.

Gifford, Lord, leading features of his will, 1.

Gladstone, W. E., on natural immortality, 253.

God—
> true conception of relation to universe, 56.
> faith in, cannot be compelled by process of reasoning, 59.
> must be manlike, 66.

God—
> inference as to nature of, not dependent on category of casuality, 67; but on category of purpose, 67.
> man's relation to, as presented in the Hebrew books, 67.
> Greek conception of, in relation to man, 151.
> Hebrew conception of, in relation to man, 151.
> as moral governor, only one aspect of, 155.
> the preceding aspect exaggerated by eighteenth century apologists, 156.
> immanent in humanity, 183.

Gordon, G.—
> on primitive man, 146.
> God's care for the depraved, 154.

Greeks—
> post-historic condition, 203.
> dawn of, 206.
> vocation of, 206.
> theological estimate of vocation, 208, 209.
> services to humanity, 210.

H

Hardy, Thomas, his pessimism, 101.

Harnack, *History of Dogma* referred to, 278.

Hartmann, E. von—
> idea of God, 8, 18, 81.
> Sanskrit, appreciation of, 35.
> intellect of God unconscious, 82.
> teleology everywhere, 84.
> his pessimism, 85.
> Deity non-moral, 85.
> no intellect in creation, 87.
> consciousness of man redeeming feature of world, 88.
> illusions regarding happiness, 88, 89.
> criticism of theory, 91.
> comparison with Cudworth, 93.
> non-moral Deity damning sin of theory, 94, 95.
> inspiration, how far does it extend? 96.

Hartmann, E. von —
  denies living beneficent Providence, 120.
  on elect men, 263.
Hegel —
  rationality in history, 70.
  tolerance of age, 100.
  on the Reformation, 228.
Heine, dislike of Wellington, 215.
Herder —
  origin of family affection, 38.
  on the fate of Eastern nations, 171, 172.
  Divine immanence, 183.
  on ancient Egypt, 200.
  a balsam for every wound, 207.
Heredity discussed, 285.
Hero-worship, 140.
  advantages and disadvantages of, 140, 141.
Hinton, J. —
  on the use of pain, 118.
  the Law-breaker, 299.
Historic dawns, 187.
  of Vedic Indians, 187.
  Persians, 189.
  Beni Israel, 190.
  Arabians, 192.
  Germans, 196.
  significance of these dawns, 198.
Historic days, 205.
  of Greece, 206.
  of Romans, 215.
  of Israel, 222.
History —
  rationality in, 70.
  not a chaos, 186.
  providential order in, 186.
Huxley —
  evolution of animal nature of man, 27.
  impermanence of the universe, 137.
Hyde, W. de Witt —
  moral government of God, 156.
  on prayer, 244.
  on the future life, 251, 253.
  on vicarious suffering, 312.
  the good the enemy of the better, 321.

I

Immanency —
  of God necessary to faith, 142.
  divine immanence in humanity, 183.
  divine immanence in history, 184.
  in the sorrows of the good, 247.
Immortality —
  of man, 249.
  Bradford and Hyde on, 251.
  presumptions on, 253.
Indians, Vedic, historic dawn of, 187.
Intellect, evolution of, 29.
'Isolate,' use of term by L. Morgan, 32.
Israel —
  historic dawn of, 190.
  her service to humanity, 222.

J

Jeremiah —
  perplexities of, in reference to Providence, 235.
  misunderstood, 238.
  complains of God deceiving him, 314.
Jesus —
  His religious teaching, 224.
  not one-sided, 276.
  on Mosaic legislation, 302.
  death of, and its causes, 320.
Jews —
  post-historic condition, 203.
  possibility of regaining position, 203.
Job, book of, discusses problem of Providence in the individual life, 235.
Jones, Professor Henry, process essential to morality, 127.
Jowett, translation of Plato quoted, 254, 313.

K

Kant, E., progress by trial and error, 184.
Kelly —
  value of religion, 182.
  necessity of moral effort, 230.
Kennedy, J. H., Teleology in region of the beautiful, 13.

L

Language—
  use of, in forming abstract ideas, 31.
  origin of, 32.
  Max Müller on origin of, 33.
  Romanes on origin of, 34.
  Sanskrit, Hartmann's appreciation of, 35, 36.

Le Conte—
  monism not incompatible with theism, 43.
  uses of pain, 109, 110.
  immortality of the soul, 139.

Leopardi—
  suffering of righteous, 116.
  regards this as argument for pessimism, 116.
  insignificance of man, 137.

Life—
  worth of, 99.
  standard of judgment, 104.
  can only be truly judged from ethical standpoint, 104, 114.

M

M'Lennan on primitive promiscuity, 163.

Maine, Sir Henry, on the *patria potestas*, 217, 218.

Man—
  place in the universe reveals purpose, 15.
  relation of, to lower animals, 22.
  the great exception, 25.
  in view throughout world-making process, 57.
  exceptional in significance, 60.
  makes world-process rational, 63.
  relation to God as presented in Hebrew books, 68.
  essentials to respect for, 133.
  primitive, 144 *et seq*.
  perfect pristine state, theological conception underlying, 150.
  cynical underestimates of worth to be rejected, 152.
  must co-operate with God, 185.

Manu, laws of, on caste, 295.

Marion—
  on personal solidarity, 285.
  on the effect of climate, 290.

Martineau, Dr.—
  uses of pain, 109.
  on conscience, 159.
  on theory of evolution of conscience, 161.

Materialism, excludes rational and moral world-aim, 71.

Maurice, F. D., benefits of Mohammedanism, 193.

Middle Ages, a winter night, 227.

Mohammedanism—
  not an unmixed evil, 193.
  has no claim to finality, 195.

Monism—
  bearing on ethical evolution, 41.
  meaning of, 43.

Moore, Aubrey L.—
  on the theistic argument, 13.
  on Deism, 55.

Moral order of world—
  universality of belief in, 157.
  testimony to, 157-9.
  traces of, 159.
  in society, 162.
  recognition must be based on general view of history, 173.
  aversion to by some, 177.
  grounds for belief in, 178.
  has command of time, 180.

Morality—
  importance of, in national life, 172.
  and religion, connection, 181.

Morgan, Lloyd—
  origin of abstract ideas, 31.
  'isolate,' meaning of term, 32.

Morley, John, religious complacency, 103.

Müller, Max, origin of language, 33.

N

Nations, prehistoric, 186, 187.

Nordau, Max, on heredity in Ibsen's Dramas, 283.

O

Optimism, unqualified, an evil, 101.

Origen on Celsus' Ἀληθὴς Λόγος, 128.
Original sin, its nature and effect, 288.

P

Pain —
  Schopenhauer's theory of, 77.
  not an unmitigated evil, 109.
  service rendered to man by, 109.
  in association with love ceases to be an evil, 117, 118.
Parker, Theodore, a heaven for all sentient beings, 255.
Particularism —
  a characteristic of elect peoples, 265.
  compatible with universalism, 265.
Paul, St. —
  on Adam as source of sin of the race, 308.
  significance of his conversion, 327.
Pearson —
  on the future of China, 262.
  sombre forecast of future, 263.
Penalty, necessary to moral order, 165.
Perfection, pristine state of man, theological conception underlying, 150.
Persians, ancient, historic dawn, 189.
Personality, necessary to morality, 136.
Pessimism —
  Schopenhauer's, 76.
  criticism of Schopenhauer's theory, 80.
  Hartmann's, 85.
  criticism of Hartmann's theory, 91.
  not to be ignored, 97.
  to be regarded as a disease, 99.
  apparent justification for, 102.
  favourite theses of, 105.
  misconception of pleasure, 107, 108.
  denies progress, 119.
Pleasure —
  more than momentary relief from pain, 107.
  Pessimistic misconception of, 107, 108.

Porphyry, the worth of man, 130.
Post-historic nations, 203.
  possibility of regaining position, 203.
Prayer, legitimacy and value of, 242.
'Predominant,' use of term by L. Morgan, 31.
Prehistoric nations, 186, 187.
  Vedic Indians, 187.
  Persians, 189.
  Beni-Israel, 190.
  Arabians, 192.
  Germans, 196.
Pride, evil effects of, 175.
Process, essential to morality, 125.
Progress —
  vital question, 119.
  denied by pessimists, 119.
Providential Order —
  sense of phrase, 6.
  man's place in the universe, 15.
  as a retributive justice, 155.
  in individual life, 231.
  providential methods, 260.

R

'Recept,' meaning of term, 30.
Reformation, the, its significance, 229.
Renan —
  on high art, 213.
  on sacrificial lives, 311.
  on the great Egoist who deceives us, 314.
  on devoted men, 315.
Repentance, Schopenhauer's theory of, 107.
Retribution —
  necessary to moral order, 166.
  its action in universal history, 166.
  idea of, is different from pessimistic view, 168.
Reymond, Du Bois —
  on spontaneous generation, 49.
  origin of mental phenomena inexplicable, 50.
Richter, J. P., picture of universe without God, 97.
Righteousness —
  Carlylean view that might is right, 168.

Righteousness —
  apparent exception to rule, 170.
  problem complex, 171.
  has command of time, 180.
  connection between righteousness and religion, 181.
Romans, character of, 216, 217.
Romanes, G. T. —
  phases of religious belief, 3.
  on theistic argument, 13.
  'recept,' use of term, 29.
  advance to concept-forming faculty, 31.
  origin of language, 34.
  Monism, bearing on ethical evolution, 41.
  on 'conscious automaton' theory, 51.
  purpose in evolution, 58.
Royce, on the tribulations of the good, 247.

S

Sacrifice —
  in the providential order, 311.
  normal lot of wisdom, 316.
  causes of, 317.
  end served by, 322.
  teleological theory of, 322.
  laws by which self-sacrifice works benefit, 327.
  God a fellow-sufferer, 332.
  not a Deceiver, nor a Moloch, 334.
Sanskrit, phenomenal language, 35.
Schopenhauer —
  idea of God, 8, 75.
  his 'Wille,' 75.
  thinks world utterly bad, 76, 77.
  basis of all will is need, hence pain, 77.
  criticism of this theory, 79.
  theory of repentance, 107.
  asceticism, 135.
Seth, Professor, purpose involved in evolution, 57.
Slavery, causes of its decline, 296.
Smith, Bosworth, on Mohammedanism, 193, 194.
Society, moral order in, 162.
Socrates, death of, and its import, 319.

Solidarity, in the providential order, 281.
Sophocles —
  evils of pride, 175, 176.
  a preacher of righteousness, 230.
Spencer, Herbert —
  idea of God, 7.
  inference as to nature of God from process of creation, 67.
  believes in progress, 119.
  primitive conception of spirit, 150.
  a germ of truth in Animism, 212.
  Kelly's criticism of, 230.
  social evolution in the future, 292.
  on slavery, 297.
Spinoza —
  idea of God, 7, 18, 72.
  thinks world perfect, 73.
  moral distinctions have no reality for God, 73.
  an optimist, 74.
  no degree of value in universe, 132.
Spontaneous generation —
  generally discredited, 47.
  but may be merely 'difficult mechanical problem,' 49.
Strauss —
  world did not proceed from reason but has reason for its goal, 57, 72.
  belief in moral order of world, 158.
Sub-historic nations, Africa, 198.
Suffering —
  largely result of evil-doing, 114.
  justice of foregoing, 114.
  redemptive as well as penal, 115.
  of righteous, 115.
  not an accident, 116.

T

Tacitus, on Germans, 196.
Taylor, Isaac, providence and chance, relation of, 65.
Teleology —
  consistent with mechanism, 14.
  attitude of scientists to, 58.
  in Hartmann's system, 84.
Theism, alternatives if we abandon, 79.

Theistic arguments —
   the traditional, their value, 9.
   teleological, 11.
Theophrastus, on superstition, 318.
Thomson, D'Arcy W., *Sales Attici* quoted, 271.
Thomson, J. Arthur, the three Norns, 292.
Transcendency of God, not whole truth, 142.

U

'Unconscious, the' —
   Hartmann's Deity, 83.
   epithet not duly grounded, 92.
   idea an old one, 91, 92.
Ushas, 188.

V

Vedic Indians, historic dawn, 187.

W

Wallace, Russel —
   restricts evolution of man to physical organism, 23.
   denies evolution of intellect but admits continuity, 35.
   on origin of races of men, 259.
Westermarck —
   primitive marriage, 163.
   on origin of race, 259.
Westminster Catechism, on the fallen state, 284.
Whitman, Walt, God's care for the depraved, 154.
Will —
   Schopenhauer's idea of, 75, 76.
   identification of, with desire, bad psychology, 106.

www.ingramcontent.com/pod-product-compliance
Lightning Source LLC
Chambersburg PA
CBHW050429240426
43661CB00055B/2321